PRAISE FOR *THE CITIZEN'S SHARE*

"This provocative study exposes a long-lost history of successful profit-sharing within U.S. capitalism. Good b*-- the authors argue, holds the promise of a mc more democratically organized society. This i eminently plausible scenario." —Alice Kessler *Pursuit of Equity: Women, Men and the Quest for E Twentieth-Century America*

"A model of sober scholarly analysis and impassioned political advocacy. . . . Here is a book on economic policy that might make the Founding Fathers smile." —Jonathan I. Levy, author of *Freaks of Fortune: The Emerging World of Capitalism and Risk in America*

"An accessible, and informative, story of government and business support for worker ownership. . . . Spotlights an important area of American economic history." —*Library Journal*

"This book offers the compelling vision of a better, healthier American economy founded on the basic principles of employee ownership and profit sharing. The deep-rooted history of this American vision is elegantly interwoven with the results of modern rigorous research. *The Citizen's Share* is a wonderfully readable book with an important message that will provoke serious thought and discussion." —Martin L. Weitzman, Professor of Economics, Harvard University

"A few years ago, Blasi, Kruse, and Freeman caught people's attention with an intriguing thesis: that a company performs better when owned by its workers. In this book, the authors go a step further. They make the interesting and provocative claim that worker ownership also improves democracy. Readers may disagree with the conclusion, but they will want to understand the argument." —Eric S. Maskin, Nobel Laureate in Economics, Harvard University

"There is a depressing familiarity about much of the discussion on what to do about America's widening income inequality. Some remedies are uncontroversial but hard-to-achieve (such as improving education); others are the subject of furious argument (such as more progressive taxation). Debate is heated, but within a fairly narrow set of potential solutions. Once in a while, though, more creative proposals are added to the mix. . . . *The Citizen's Share* is one of those. The authors show, convincingly, that the logic of citizen capitalism has periodically motivated American politics and business since the Founding Fathers." —*The Economist*

"The American worker isn't doing so well. . . . Joseph Blasi, Douglas Kruse, and Richard Freeman offer a novel solution. . . . The impulse toward broadly extending property ownership is one that has a long history in America. . . . [E]xpanding employee ownership could be a solution to the problems of stagnating worker compensation and rising income inequality." —Christopher Matthews, *Time Magazine*

"Based on a series of national surveys, the authors reckon that some 47% of full-time workers have one or more forms of capital stake in the firm for which they work, whether from profit-sharing schemes (40%), stock ownership (21%) or stock options (10%). About a tenth of Fortune 500 companies, from Procter & Gamble to Goldman Sachs, have employee shareholdings of 5% or more. Almost a fifth of America's biggest private firms . . . have profit-sharing or share-ownership schemes. Some 10 million people work for companies with ESOPs." —Brad DeLong, University of California, Berkeley, and the Washington Center for Equitable Growth

"This important book demonstrates conclusively that employee ownership can be an effective business model, resulting in efficient outcomes." —Jonathan Michie, President, Kellogg College, University of Oxford

"Based on comprehensive data and painstaking historical research, *The Citizen's Share* provides a superb overview of employee ownership in the United States. At a moment when economic inequality has reached an apogee and trust in corporations a nadir, when the employment relationship has frayed in companies across the U.S., and American industry faces challenges from around the globe, the authors' message could not be more important." —Viviana A. Zelizer, author of *Economic Lives: How Culture Shapes the Economy*

"*The Citizen's Share* is a must-read for current and future business leaders as well as policymakers who believe all Americans are entitled to participate in a healthy and growing U.S. economy. This insightful tapestry of history, economics and psychology begins by telling the story that our country was founded with the right for all citizens to ownership and ends with 10 non-partisan policy recommendations that will ensure ownership is a right for all, not just the 1%." —Carine M. Schneider, Chairman of the Board, Global Equity Organization

"Rutgers management professors Joseph Blasi and Douglas Kruse and Harvard economics professor Richard Freeman wrote *The Citizen's Share*. . . . They argued that worker ownership had a long history in the American economy and a long history of bipartisan and cross-ideological support. . . . One proposal to implement [their] strategy would be to have state and federal governments link corporate tax rates to the extent of the companies' profit sharing: The more that's shared, the lower the rate." —Harold Meyerson, *The American Prospect*

"*The Citizens Share* demonstrates that employee ownership is as American as apple pie. Let's put it to use to improve our lives and strengthen our democracy. The authors do a superb job of showing the way to do so." —Thomas A. Kochan, Co-Director, MIT Institute for Work and Employment Research

"George Washington liked the basic idea, as did Thomas Jefferson. We should build on our rich national tradition of support for widespread asset ownership. Joseph Blasi, Richard Freeman and Douglas Kruse develop this proposition in a new book, *The Citizen's Share*, which lends historical perspective to their empirical research on shared capitalism." —Nancy Folbre, *Economix, The New York Times*

"Employee ownership—profit sharing, stock sharing and other employee-ownership plans—can increase your workers' productivity and innovation. Research shows that workers at companies with employee ownership plans work harder, are more creative and more loyal. That translates into better company performance. 'The impacts are larger when the programs are larger, as in many closely held ESOP companies and some model publicly traded companies,' say Rutgers professors Joseph Blasi and Douglas Kruse and Harvard economist Richard Freeman, in their new book *The Citizen's Share*." —Michael Kling, *Entrepreneur Magazine*

"One of the big frustrations about income inequality is that when corporate profits grow, they aren't shared equally—typical employees see very little from it, while the people at the top, and big investors, reap most of the rewards. . . . One solution? Give average workers direct ownership in the company and its profits. . . . [A] new book called *The Citizen's Share* advocates government tax incentives to encourage companies to introduce profit-sharing and stock-ownership programs for their employees, or expand the programs they already have. . . . The authors argue that increased ownership and share in profits may be the key to reviving the American middle class." —David Parkinson, *Economy Lab, Toronto Globe and Mail*

"Three professors would rather see income flowing into the hands of the many, and they've written a book to point the way. . . . 'The outstanding faults of the economic society in which we live are its failure to provide for full employment and its arbitrary and inequitable distribution of wealth and incomes.' Keynes wrote those words about England in 1936. To deal with the same faults, America needs more 'citizen's shares' in 2014." —Gerald E. Scorse, *Baltimore Chronicle and Sentinel*

THE CITIZEN'S SHARE

THE CITIZEN'S SHARE

REDUCING INEQUALITY

IN THE 21ST CENTURY

JOSEPH R. BLASI
RICHARD B. FREEMAN
DOUGLAS L. KRUSE
WITH A NEW PREFACE

Yale UNIVERSITY PRESS
NEW HAVEN & LONDON

Yale University Press books may be purchased in quantity for educational, business, or promotional use. For information, please e-mail sales.press@yale.edu (U.S. office) or sales@yaleup.co.uk (U.K. office).

Set in Meridien type by Westchester Book Group.
Printed in the United States of America.

Library of Congress Control Number 2014937820
ISBN 978-0-300-20933-4 (pbk.)

A catalogue record for this book is available from the British Library.

10 9 8 7 6 5 4 3 2 1

CONTENTS

PREFACE TO THE PAPERBACK EDITION

In September 2011, Occupy Wall Street, a motley group of demonstrators upset about the economic situation in the United States after the 2008 implosion of Wall Street and the Great Recession that followed, grabbed the attention of Americans and, indeed, the entire world with their protests about the unequal distribution of income in the United States. They complained that the wealthiest 1 percent had obtained so many of the benefits of modern economic growth that the remaining 99 percent of the population, whom they claimed to represent, were in difficult economic straits. The decline of the middle class has now begun to concern citizens across the political spectrum and throughout the world. Conservative political thinkers have noticed the problem of income inequality and argue that there is increasing anxiety about it in national opinion polls and that fewer and fewer citizens see the economy as a real meritocracy and more and more see it as something closer to a coin flip.[1] Extreme economic inequality, reduction in labor income, and the rapid spread of income to those who own capital, all now documented in the United States, are found worldwide and are hollowing out the middle class globally.

Given the financial disaster and the bailout of banks and bankers whose actions precipitated the disaster, the Occupy

Wall Street protests resonated with many people across the political spectrum. How could a small number of "too big to fail" banks and financial firms have gained enough economic power to cause the financial sector of the world's leading market economy to tank? How could these institutions emerge from the crisis, seemingly more powerful than before, when ordinary citizens are suffering from joblessness or sluggish or declining earnings and many other large businesses, and small ones, are also feeling the effects? Why has the recovery from the Great Recession been one of the weakest in economic history? The sense of unfairness is bipartisan, as we saw when conservatives in the U.S. House of Representatives initially opposed the Bush administration's proposal to bail out the financial institutions. The conservatives raised traditional concerns about concentrated economic power and established political elites. The same questions are increasingly being raised from Europe to China.

To be sure, the protesters offered no policy solutions to the problems that motivated their demonstrations, but they brought to the public a real economic issue that economists and other social scientists have been tracking for some time: the increased economic inequality that threatens the great middle class, traditionally the bulwark of the American economy. Progressives have now identified wealth inequality as their top political issue. Some conservative policy makers have called for a radical opportunity agenda to refocus government policy, regulatory and tax reform to expand entrepreneurship at all levels of the economy, and an optimistic plan for all citizens to unite in connecting personal responsibility to the opportunity for meaningful mobility.[2] How do we get there? *The Citizen's Share* offers a *nonpartisan* proposal to reduce economic inequality in the twenty-first century that we believe can have wide appeal across the political spectrum. It is based on long-held views of many of the Founders of the American republic about encouraging broad-based property ownership. This book tells the rich American-history story behind this idea, spanning almost two and a half centuries.

The protesters have largely disappeared from media attention, but economic inequality has gone on to become one of the pressing global issues in economic and political discourse. The facts are incontrovertible. Productivity increased in the United States from the 1970s through the 2010s while, for the first time in history, the real earnings of most workers stagnated, and the distribution of wages and salaries widened, first between the middle and low earners and later between the upper 1 percent and the upper 0.1 percent, on one side, and the rest of the workforce, on the other. The vast bulk of the benefits of modern economic progress have been going to the small number of people who own much of the country's capital stock or whose earnings and wealth are chiefly related to capital gains.

Fast-forward to the next twenty–thirty years. If the trend toward increased inequality continues, the United States, as well as the many other countries experiencing the same pattern of change, will no longer be a middle-class republic where the benefits of economic progress reach virtually all citizens. Its economy will instead more closely resemble that of a feudal society, where a small group of lords and ladies rule the economic world. Being human, the wealthy elite will use their wealth not only to protect their property but to lobby for regulations and rules that allow them to expand their wealth relative to the rest of the citizenry. In place of market capitalism we will have a crony capitalist society dominated by billionaires and, at some point, the first trillionaires. We say, if more citizens of all political orientations are capitalists, there will be more citizen support for capitalism.

Recognition that something is awry with the direction of advanced capitalism has spread from oddly dressed people with "we are the 99%" banners to the men and women in business suits who represent the mainstream global economic organizations that monitor the world's economy, to the middle-America members of the Tea Party who worry that the middle class is disappearing because of powerful political elites not answerable to the people, and to many middle-class citizens of all political stripes who are personally experiencing difficulties in today's economy. In 2014 the Organization for Economic Cooperation and Development—the club of countries with advanced economies that concern themselves with economic policies—declared, headline style: "Urgent action needed to tackle rising inequality and social divisions." The International Monetary Fund—the organization that seeks to defend the integrity of the global financial system and that many view as more interested in the well-being of banks than in the well-being of people—has raised similar concerns.[3]

A Google search for "economic inequality" finds millions of entries from politicians, policy analysts, business and labor leaders, and citizens with widely divergent perspectives and ideological persuasions. In a world in which the distribution of national income has shifted from labor to capital, in which ownership of financial assets and access to income from capital is highly concentrated, and in which a small number of high earners have pulled away from the rest of the society, a person does not have to be paranoid to be alarmed about the dangers that continual widening of income and wealth distribution poses for the well-being of the economy and society. Without a broad-based middle class, many citizens will not have the spending power to buy the services that modern society has to offer, which is another way economic growth could be stunted. A few capitalists cannot power a massive modern economy.

Can the United States and other countries arrest the trend toward greater inequality and restore the historic pattern—in which economic growth raises the income and the wealth of most workers while maintaining or strengthening the operation of market capitalism—or are we inexorably on the road to a new economic feudalism?

Analysts have offered a slew of policy ideas for trying to arrest or reverse the growth of inequality. These ideas cover a wide range: greater use of the tax system to redistribute income to middle- and lower-income citizens by adding, among other things, a global wealth tax, which many countries or a single region would have to adopt to be effective; higher minimum wages; expansion of higher education; changes in diverse regulations and social benefits to disproportionately benefit middle- and lower-income citizens. Some analysts have also called for improvements to market competition—for instance, by breaking up the large banks that dominate finance or by helping small and medium businesses better compete with the huge conglomerates, which place lobbyists in Washington and contribute to politicians in various parties. Judiciously set, some of these policies could possibly reduce inequality and improve the well-being of many citizens. Some may not really be politically feasible. But they do not address directly what we view as the critical element in modern inequality: the concentration of the ownership of business capital among a small wealthy elite. Why not address the source of the problem directly?

The Citizen's Share makes the case that the best way—and possibly the only way—to break the trend toward greater inequality

and to direct our society away from the road to economic feudalism is to increase the citizens' share of the business capital of
the country. The result would be a more efficient market capitalism that spreads rewards to the 99 percent.

The book has what may strike some readers as an odd structure for an analysis of current economic problems and potential
solutions. We give the history of the idea of citizen shares of capital from the founding of the United States to the current day,
interspersing it with what many readers would expect from a
book focused on the role of ownership in U.S. economic performance: evidence of how broad-based citizen ownership of the
capital structure through employee share ownership, profit sharing, and employee stock-ownership trusts combines with worker
participation to improve the operation of firms. We hope that the
American story will help the citizens of many other countries
look within their own traditions to find ideas about how citizen
participation in the economy can strengthen society.

Chapter 1 shows that the Founders of the American republic
were deeply troubled by high levels of inequality and saw inequality as linked to the very viability of a republic, its representative
institutions, and the well-being of its citizens. Their solution was
widespread property ownership with a focus on land, the major
capital asset of the time. Broad property ownership was their
economic-inequality policy of choice. Rather than have labor and
capital fighting each other, each citizen would have a share in land
ownership and have sufficient economic liberty to be truly politically independent. *The Citizen's Share* is about transforming that
vision into the modern world, where ownership of capital and
technology rather than land lies at the heart of the economy.

Chapter 2 gives examples of firms that operate by the basic
principle that workers have an ownership and profit-sharing

stake in their firm—proof that the ideas in the book are grounded in the experience of real companies throughout the entire economy, some with highly educated workers and some with less educated workers. Going beyond examples, Chapter 3 gives some numbers on the extent of citizens' shares nationally: employee share ownership, employee stock options, employee profit sharing, and employee gain sharing. The shares produce significant stakes for many workers, although we believe that the stakes can increase in amount as well as in depth.

Chapter 4 goes back to the long history of citizen shares and tells the stories about how U.S. business and political leaders moved from land-based shares to capital-based shares by designing approaches to profit sharing and employee share ownership in the nineteenth and twentieth centuries. The goal of having each person own a meaningful plot of land fit an agricultural society. It was gradually replaced by the goal of having workers participate in the rewards of capital ownership with shares. Chapter 5 demonstrates that firms that give their workers greater ownership and participation in economic decisions do better than others. It is based on detailed statistical studies by ourselves and many other researchers; the gory details can be found in our National Bureau of Economic Research (NBER) technical volume, *Shared Capitalism at Work,* and in scholarly journals and working papers. Thanks to the Internet and NBER policy, the chapters of the NBER book are downloadable from the NBER website (http:// papers.nber.org/books/krus08-1/). For readers with an interest in shares and their relevance to reducing economic inequality, *The Citizen's Share* presents all of those ideas in a less technical and more accessible form.

Chapter 6 wraps up by presenting our suggestions for far-reaching policies to invigorate broad-based shares through employee stock ownership and profit sharing and to fight inequality by spreading meaningful ownership and profit shares to more and more workers. To be sure, increasing the number of workers with ownership stakes in productive assets will not solve all economic problems, but we hope to establish beyond doubt that policies to accomplish employee ownership and profit sharing have to be a major part of any solution to economic inequality. The solution to economic inequality and many other economic problems lies not in a renewed battle between labor and capital but in increasing labor's share of capital, not in encouraging the redistribution of wealth but in providing incentives for business leaders to consider introducing shares in their company. Our discussion focuses on the United States, but the principles behind the ideas can easily be applied in many other countries.

The book's website, www.thecitizensshare.com, makes additional ideas and discussion available. We look forward to hearing reactions to our analysis and proposals and to hearing the ideas of readers about the issues addressed in *The Citizen's Share*. Together, we must all do everything we can to move our economy from the road to feudalism back to the road to a thriving middle class and a market economy that delivers for all citizens.

NOTES

1. These views are expressed in a piece by Arthur C. Brooks, "The Downside of Inciting Envy," *New York Times,* March 1, 2014. See also Brooks, "Introduction," in Kevin A. Hassett et al., *Inequality for All: How To Think about Income Inequality,* March 19, 2014, available at the American Enterprise Institute website, http://www.aei.org/papers/economics/opportunity-for-all-how-to-think-about-income-inequality/.

2. Brooks, "Downside of Inciting Envy."

3. For the OECD quotation, in a March 3, 2014, press release about the just-published *Society at a Glance 2014* report, see the OECD website,

http://www.oecd.org/newsroom/urgent-action-needed-to-tackle-rising
-inequality-and-social-divisions-says-oecd.htm. For the IMF statement
and media response see Ian Tally, "IMF Warns Inequality Is a Drag on
Growth," *Wall Street Journal,* March 3, 2014, http://online.wsj.com/news/
articles/SB10001424052702304185104579437193433238018.

THE CITIZEN'S SHARE

INTRODUCTION

In the first place, it is a point conceded, that America, under an efficient government, will be the most favorable country of any kind in the world for persons of industry and frugality, possessed of moderate capital, to inhabit. It is also believed that it will not be less advantageous to the happiness of the lowest class of people because of the equal distribution of property.

George Washington, letter to Richard Henderson, Mount Vernon, June 19, 1788[1]

In civilized communities, property, as well as personal rights, is an essential object of the laws, which encourage industry by securing the enjoyment of its fruits. . . . The United States have a precious advantage, also, in the actual distribution of property, particularly the landed property, and in the universal hope of acquiring property. This latter peculiarity is among the happiest contrasts in their situation to that of the old world, where no anticipated change in this respect can generally inspire a like sympathy with the rights of property.

James Madison, Constitutional Convention of 1787 in Philadelphia[2]

The Revolutionary War left the American cod industry in dire straits.[3] Cod was the fourth-most-valuable export of the American colonies and a mainstay of their economy. Fishermen caught cod off the coast of New England and to the north and brought them home to dry and export to Europe and the British West Indies. Demand for cod was strong in the Catholic countries of Europe, where religious people abstained from eating meat on Fridays. West Indian slave owners bought dried cod to feed slaves.[4]

During the Revolutionary War, Britain had sought to destroy the industry, whose seamen were the core of the colonial naval forces. John Adams called the cod ships "a nursery of seamen and a source of naval power."[5] The British navy attacked American ships and closed European markets to American fish in an effort to weaken the rebellious colonists both economically and militarily.

When George Washington assumed the presidency of the United States in 1789, the cod fishery had not yet recovered. Washington interrupted his first tour of the northern states to visit the fishing port of Marblehead, Massachusetts, where he heard about the problems of the fishery firsthand.[6] Later, Secretary of State Thomas Jefferson was asked to find a way to restore the industry to prosperity. He formed a committee that produced one of the first economic studies of a single industry ever made for the U.S. Congress, the *Report on the American Fisheries*, submitted to the Speaker of the House of Representatives on February 1, 1791.[7] Jefferson looked favorably on the cod fishery because it relied extensively on family businesses that required an investment of "small capital" and thus offered economic opportunity to average citizens. During the winter months, when agriculture did not demand much time, a seaman, his wife, and other family members, including the children, participated in drying and salting the fish. Cod fishermen did not own the sea as farmers owned their land, but the mode of production in the fishery sometimes resembled that of the typical family farm. Jefferson saw these families as small entrepreneurs engaged in "household manufacture."

The policy problem Congress faced was simple. In those days the government relied on tariffs—taxes on imports—to fund its operations. These tariffs raised the cost of the imports that cod fishers needed to operate the fishery, the taxes making the industry less competitive on the world market and thus making it harder to restart the industry. Jefferson's committee reported that many nations, including England and France, gave subsidies, called bounties, to outfit ships to build up their industry. While he opposed outright subsidies and bailouts of the industry, Jefferson favored removing the tariffs that fell on critical imports. After some debate, Congress enacted a law to pay a tax credit, based on the weight of vessels engaged in cod fishing, of $1.50 per ton up to thirty tons and $2.50 per ton over thirty tons, up to a maximum of $170 per ship for each year a cod ship went out to sea. Congress hoped that these allowances would lead the industry to rebuild itself.

But to whom should the allowances go?

Some wealthy shipowners knew who should get the tax credits: themselves. In 1790 they wrote Jefferson, saying the government must directly give the owners the entire tax credit.[8] The fishermen and their supporters in Congress objected to an allowance that went solely to the owners. They sought a profit-sharing arrangement in which each vessel's allowance would be split between the crew and the managers and financiers of each ship. Profit sharing had been common in the American fishing industry for over a century, where crews shared in the rewards of successful hauls. They were even called "sharesmen." Some fishermen even had ownership shares in the ship, which made them investors in the business as well as recipients of profit shares as workers. A 1790 letter from Joseph Anthony to Tenche Coxe, Alexander Hamilton's right-hand man at the Treasury Department, described the sharing system and declared it more efficient than straight wages because it induced the seamen to be "most attentive":

> Since then [before the Revolution] they have Extended the fishery much further, and of Course, their vessals fitted at much greater Expense. Formerly they Rig'd their Sloops Very Plain and Spareing. The Captain and the Crew Drew one half, and agreed among themselves in what Proportion to Divide the fare. Sometimes the Owners hire the men by the month, and give them about Common Seamans wages, which at that time was not more than Six Dollars a month throughout New England; at other times they would give them a fixed Sum for a Share, Success or Not, but they were generally found the most attentive, when their Dependence was on a Share of what they Caught.[9]

Coxe showed the letter to Thomas Jefferson, noting that "Mr. Anthony is a man of judgment and probity, and is now a partner of one of the principal [trading] houses in Philadelphia, who do half of the New England business of the port."[10] Jefferson put the letter in the committee's report. In the end, Senator George Cabot, from a well-known shipowning family, advanced the legislation that included the profit-sharing concept.[11]

This was the first time in American history that national leaders, the leaders of a major industry, and ordinary working people debated the shape of American business and how government should seek to encourage economic development. Would the Founders accede to the pressures from powerful shipowners and exporters to pay the tax credits to them, or would they support the long-standing traditional idea of broad-based profit sharing?

George Washington sometimes sympathized with the goal of broad-based distribution of property. He had used proportionate profit sharing of property seized in combat to reward soldiers after the battle of Trenton in the Revolutionary War.[12] As president he repeatedly requested that Congress grant land to the former officers and soldiers of the Revolutionary army so they could become independent property owners themselves.[13] In the issue of the cod fishery, he supported sharing any government allowance with the fishermen rather than giving it all to the shipowners. On February 16, 1792, Congress passed and Washington signed a new law mandating that three-eighths of this allowance would go to each vessel's owners and five-eighths would go to the crew. Allowances would be paid only if the shipowner had a written profit-sharing contract with all the sailors before the voyage, covering the entire catch. The shipowner could collect his allowance only if he could produce this agreement.[14]

The question of tax credits for rebuilding the American cod industry brought together two men who were often on opposite sides: Alexander Hamilton, the secretary of the treasury whose vision for the nation favored its financial leaders, and Thomas Jefferson, who championed independent farmers. After Congress passed the bill, Hamilton implemented the broad-based incentive payments to the shipowners through the offices that he supervised at the various ports. His *Report on Manufactures*, submitted to the Congress on December 5, 1791, several weeks before the cod law was signed, specifically endorsed these incentives on economic grounds. "This has been found to be one of the most efficacious means. . . . It is a species of encouragement more positive and direct than any other, and for that very reason, has a more immediate tendency to stimulate and uphold new enterprise, increasing the chances of profit, and diminishing the risks of loss in the first attempts." While Hamilton noted that "there is a degree of prejudice . . . from an appearance of giving away the public money without an immediate consideration, and from a supposition that they serve to enrich particular classes at the expense of the community," sharing the incentive between workers and shipowners avoided this problem.[15]

With periodic updates, the law stayed in force for many years.[16] On February 1, 1803, President Jefferson's secretary of the treasury, Albert Gallatin, reported to the Speaker of the House of Representatives about how the allowance had helped turn around the cod fishery.[17] Giving incentives to workers and owners encouraged the rebuilding of the fishing fleet, helped institutionalize the industry's traditional profit sharing on the entire catch of fish, stabilized the economies of the fishing communities and the export of fish, and developed the nursery of seamen for naval activities. The allowances continued well into the nineteenth century.

The federal government's requirement that the cod fishery tax credit be shared among all participants and that the traditional profit sharing on the entire catch remain a condition for this incentive is the first documented case in American history where the government made citizen shares a condition for receiving a tax break. While many in the executive and legislative branches of government were part of the wealthy elite, the leaders of the new Republic were not swayed by the cod fishery's owners and financiers, who no doubt had the eighteenth-century equivalent of K Street lobbyists pressing their cause. The Founders understood that the performance of the crews depended on shared rewards and that the well-being of the country depended on all citizens having a stake in the economy's performance. The government was willing to spend public money to help a depressed sector recover, as long as profit sharing was the general standard of the industry.

The case also shows something that is typical of the time: the desire to encourage citizens to do the economic work of the country themselves rather than have the state do it for them. Congress did not create a new tax to finance a state-owned company to rebuild the industry, or to pay welfare to the suffering fishermen. The fishermen did not vilify the owners and investors in ships but instead lobbied for a fair shake. Despite fundamental differences over how the economy should be structured, the Founders largely agreed that the nation required a strong and expanding middle class and a generally equitable and broad-based—although not equal—distribution of wealth in order to survive as a republic. In *Empire of Liberty: A History of the Early Republic, 1789–1815*, the historian Gordon S. Wood documents broad support for this notion among the general population:

Americans knew only too well that republics were very delicate polities that required a special kind of society—a society of equal and virtuous citizens. They believed that republics demanded far more morally from their citizens than monarchies demanded of their subjects, and that the social hierarchies that republics would permit had to be based solely on individual merit and talent. Since antiquity, theorists had assumed that a republican state required a general equality of property-holding among its citizens. Although most Americans in 1776 believed that not everyone in a republic had to have the same amount of property . . . all took for granted, that a society could not long remain republican if a tiny minority controlled most of the wealth and the bulk of the population remained dependent servants or poor landless laborers.[18]

Many of the Founders envisioned a nation of self-employed farmers, artisans, and mechanics. In discussions of labor and capital at that time, the term *capital* referred mostly to land, and to the income-generating crafts and small businesses that citizens owned and could use to support their families. They actually owned a share of the economic system. These provided what today is called capital income. As owners of their farms and businesses, many citizens derived additional income from owning the means of production and the services that they provided to customers. Few were simply wage laborers. In the cod fishery and many other fisheries, the seamen were entitled to a share of the profits, giving them a claim on capital income.

To be sure, America in the 1790s excluded many from free citizenry, especially women and blacks.[19] The great evil of slavery was still a central part of American economic life, as was the extensive exclusion of women from civil society. As noted, much of the U.S. cod catch went to the West Indies to feed slaves on sugarcane plantations, in a trade pattern that linked the cod fishermen to the slave plantations of the West Indies and the wage laborers of England.[20] As Alex Roland describes it, "New England foodstuffs fed Caribbean slaves, who produced sugar consumed by English workers, who manufactured goods purchased by New England farmers." The cod fisheries also sometimes relied for sailors on black men who were escaped slaves or freedmen; half of the free blacks in the country lived in northern seaports and did not enjoy the same privileges as white citizens.[21]

YESTERDAY AND TODAY

Today America faces daunting economic problems. The implosion of Wall Street and the Great Recession have left millions struggling to maintain their living standards. Even before the recession, the real wages of middle-class workers had stagnated for about three decades. The benefits of rising productivity went toward an increased share of income accruing to the wealthiest rather than toward pay increases for workers. Under President William Jefferson Clinton, the wealthiest 1 percent of families got 45 percent of the total income growth. During the George W. Bush presidency, the wealthiest 1 percent of families got 57 percent of the total income growth.[22] The financial implosion of 2008 reduced the wealth of upper-income families, but when the stock market recovered more rapidly than the job market or housing market, the best-off gained disproportionately again.

The job market, where the vast majority of citizens earn almost all their incomes, has seen a recovery that is anemic at best. Barring an economic miracle, the country is unlikely to regain full employment until almost 2020. The country seems further than ever from George Washington's ideal of a society that works for all "persons of industry and frugality, possessed of moderate capital . . . [including] the lowest class of people because of the equal distribution of property."

What can we do to rebuild an economy and a democracy that benefit all citizens?

A Citizen's Share provides one part of the answer. It argues that the way forward is to reform the structure of American business so that workers can supplement their wages with significant capital ownership stakes and meaningful capital income and profit shares. This will give them the potential for greater participation in decision making to increase the value of their firms and the opportunity for sharing the fruits of their performance.

This theme is invisible in current debates about the economy. Neither the Democrats nor the Republicans have given serious consideration to expanding the property ownership or profit sharing of citizens as part of their policies to improve the economy. Yet the public has grown increasingly critical of corporations and suspicious of the relationship between big government and the big corporate sector. In a March 2010 survey, the Pew Research Center asked: Are large corporations having a positive or negative effect on the way things are going in the country these days? Sixty-four percent said their effect was negative, compared to 25 percent who said it was positive. Sixty-nine percent viewed major financial institutions and banks negatively. By contrast, 71 percent of citizens had a positive view of small business, and 68 percent had a positive view of technology companies—which, as we shall see, share profits and stock ownership with their workers much more than companies in other sectors. A large proportion of Republicans, Democrats, and Independents even reacted negatively to the word *capitalism*, suggesting that James Madison was right in stressing the linkage between widespread property ownership and a "sympathy with the rights of property" on the part of the citizenry.[23] Given these critical attitudes, one might expect the political world to be abuzz with discussion of how the United States might reform its brand of capitalism to better meet the needs of its citizens.

Instead, the debates are concentrated on much narrower issues. Hopefully, this book will contribute to the broader discourse that the country needs to resolve our problems.

Serious consideration of increased broad-based profit sharing and employee stock ownership in the economy can change the way the country thinks about many of its problems. Widening the ownership of business capital offers a mechanism to share more of the benefits of economic performance and growth with average citizens by increasing their income and wealth. It offers a new way to address the concentration of both economic and political power that many citizens believe is distorting the country. It offers a new perspective on how to fight the links between the Washington politicians, K Street lobbyists, big corporations, and political donors that fuel many Tea Party members' opposition to government. It offers a new perspective on how to resolve the huge disparities in wealth and income that have troubled economists for many years and that Occupy Wall Street discussed. The Founders believed in small government, and many of them condemned control by powerful elites. To the extent that broader property ownership can make more citizens more independent, the idea may also offer the possibility of limiting the growth in the size of government and expanding individual liberty. The goal of broadening capital ownership and profit sharing offers a distinct approach to reforming the American model of market capitalism.

Given that this book is about a solution to today's economic problems, readers may wonder why we began this introduction with the story of cod fisherman and the ideas of George Washington, Thomas Jefferson, Alexander Hamilton, and their peers in the 1790s. Despite the vast differences between their time and ours, there is a close symbiosis between some of the ways our country dealt with problems in the past and how it does so today. The cod fishery history illustrates the tension between the democratic ideals of America as a land of "yeoman farmers"— persons with moderate capital stakes and sources of capital income—and an economic reality in which just a few persons with ownership and control of business property influence government to enrich themselves and foreclose opportunities for others. We will weave the history and current problems of the country together throughout this book because the challenge of balancing our democratic ideals and economic developments is a recurrent theme. There is much to be learned about what the Founders thought about these problems, how they struggled to resolve them, and how the "share" idea has evolved in American history.

In the 1770s, about 80 percent of England's land was in the hands of the aristocracy, and much of the population had little property ownership.[24] The American Revolution was partly a reaction to the feudal value system that England tried to impose on the colonies. To maintain their economic power, the aristocrats who dominated Britain tried to restrict business and trade in the colonial economy, interfere in the economic liberty of its residents, and design the tax system to benefit narrow economic interests.[25]

Wealth in the United States today is also highly concentrated. The top 5 percent of households control over half of all wealth in the nation, while the top 10 percent control almost three-quarters of all wealth and over 80 percent of all financial assets. Half of all households own no stock, many households have meager financial holdings, and a quarter of households have zero or negative net worth. The wealth of most middle-class families has declined since the 1980s. Only a very small propor-

tion of American families are growing richer.[26] Typical employees do not have nearly enough to retire on, much less buy the
things they want or need, such as education for their children.

How would the Founders have viewed such a concentration of wealth? On the basis of what they wrote about property
ownership in their own day, we think it is safe to say they would
have reacted with alarm. According to historian Lee Soltow,
a leading expert on income distribution in the early United
States, "Many of America's political leaders spent months, if
not years, in Europe and then recorded their sensitive feelings
about socioeconomic differences. Their expert opinions provide
broader insights into the broader ramifications in inequality.
Their thinking inevitably became embedded in the administrative and legal processes instituted in the new nation. Benjamin
Franklin, Thomas Jefferson, and James Madison, but most particularly John Adams, all had arrived at firm convictions about
these matters."[27] Their convictions centered on the importance
of expanding the ability of more citizens to acquire property
ownership.

Alexander Hamilton is famous for supporting the development of finance and arguing for manufacturing in the young
United States. But his argument for manufacturing was predi-
cated on the belief that the bulk of U.S. citizens would remain
independent farmers or proprietors, rather than wage earners
without any property, and that their expanding wealth would
cause the demand for goods and services in the economy to increase:

But it does by no means follow, that the progress of new
settlements would be retarded by the extension of manufactures. The desire of being an independent proprietor of land

is founded on such strong principles in the human breast, that where the opportunity of becoming so is as great as it is in the United States, the proportion will be small of those whose situations would otherwise lead to it who would be diverted from it towards manufactures. . . . The equality and moderation of individual property, and the growing settlements of new districts, occasion, in this country, an unusual demand for coarse manufactures.[28]

Today, the principal source of wealth is not land but capital ownership of different kinds of property, mostly ownership shares of businesses and financial assets such as stocks or bonds, along with real estate. Additional wealth comes from capital income that flows from this ownership, such as capital gains when the assets increase in value and interest, and dividends, and other shares. Capital income has always been more unequally distributed than labor income and has become more unequal in recent years. The share of capital income going to the top 1 percent of households increased from about a third of all such income in 1979 to about three-fifths in 2005. Ninety percent of all corporate stock is held by the richest fifth of households. Access to capital ownership and capital income now mostly determines both income and wealth.

The composition of personal income has shifted away from wage income to capital income. Citizens and those families whose income and wealth increased during recent decades did better because they had an income source other than their wages, such as capital income from shares of property or profits in businesses beyond their salary.[29] They also owned meaningful amounts of the capital in the country. The increased pay of executives has come almost entirely in the form of stock-related compensation, such as stock options or restricted stock grants—namely, capital ownership and capital income, such as dividends and different forms of profit sharing. Since this is payment for work, statistical agencies include it as part of labor income, but from our perspective it is also part of capital income. As an indication of just how much capital income has determined who has income, look at the trend from 1993 to 2010. Income for the bottom 99 percent, including capital gains, grew about 6 percent adjusted for inflation, while the income for the top 1 percent grew by 58 percent.[30]

Living at least partly off capital income and having meaningful capital ownership is similar to the Founders' concept of living from the property ownership of land and "reaping one's own harvest"—supporting oneself and one's family from owning a piece of the economy. The Founders wrote widely and debated about the distribution of capital ownership and income. Following American thinking about broad-based ownership and having a citizen's share in society from the eighteenth century to the current century can, we believe, help us develop a road map to increase the citizen's share of our economy. That is the purpose of this book.

1 THE AMERICAN VISION

Men are ever better pleased with laboring on their own farms, than in the workshops. Even the mechanics who come from Europe, as soon as they can procure a little land of their own, commonly turn Cultivators. . . . I rejoice in the belief that intellectual light will spring up in the dark corners of the earth; that freedom of enquiry will produce liberality of conduct; that mankind will reverse the absurd position that the many were made for the few and that they will not continue slaves in one part of the globe, when they can become freemen in another.

President George Washington, fragments from drafts of the first inaugural address, April 1789[1]

The property of this country is absolutely concentrated in a very few hands. . . . I am conscious that an equal division of property is impracticable. But the consequences of this enormous inequality producing so much misery to the bulk of mankind, legislators cannot invent too many devices for subdividing property, only taking care to let their subdivisions go hand in hand with the natural affections of the human mind. . . . But it is not too soon to provide by every possible means that as few as possible shall be without a little portion of land. The small landholders are the most precious part of a state.

Thomas Jefferson, letter to James Madison about France, Fontainebleau, France, October 28, 1785[2]

In a country where we have no wealthy incorporated companies of merchants—where we have no nobles with great estates, permanent in the family line—where we have no royal prerogative supported by an enormous civil list and numbers of dependents—I say in a country where we have no counterpose to correct its influence or control its enormities by their own—shall we grant such an institution? Shall we give such an artificial spring to concentrated wealth? By no means.

Representative William Findley, the General Assembly of Pennsylvania, 1786[3]

On Saturday, April 1, 1786, in Independence Hall in Philadelphia, the Pennsylvania General Assembly debated whether to give a corporate charter to the Bank of North America.[4] Benjamin Franklin chaired the meeting as president of the Pennsylvania Executive Council. The Bank of North America, one of the first banks in the United States, is where the Continental Congress held money to clothe and feed the army in the Revolutionary War and to pay the soldiers' wages. Its building still stands at the corner of South Sixth and Chestnut Streets near Independence Hall. This was one of the first debates about "the corporation" in U.S. history.

At issue was whether the bank was "compatible with public safety, and that equality which ought ever to prevail between the individuals of a republic." Representative William Findley of Westmoreland County, echoing Washington's and Jefferson's thoughts on the broad ownership of property, thought it was not. At that time, a corporation needed a charter from the legislature to operate, and even the great moral philosopher Adam Smith, later recognized as the father of modern economics, was suspicious of the corporation as an institutional form. When Smith published *The Wealth of Nations*, in 1776, most English firms were partnerships: each partner bore all the profits and losses directly. Smith doubted that managers of "other people's money" would treat it as carefully as they did their own funds.[5] Seeing the British government granting monopolies to entities like the royal charter trading companies, he viewed corporations as a danger to a market economy. The proponents of the Bank of North America's charter wanted the limited liability and protection from personal risk that a corporate charter would assure them.

Findley argued that allowing the bank to incorporate violated the state constitution because it promoted economic inequality. He feared that the bank would give "undue and impartial advantage to one set of men," who would "monopolize economic power and undermine the government because of its large concentrated economic power." A powerful corporation violated "the government, the laws, and the habits of the state."[6] If the assembly approved the charter of the bank, it would break the "great deed of trust between those in government and the citizens." In Findley's view, the purpose of democratic government was to make sure that everyone could "share in the fruits of their labor." Findley was not antibusiness, nor were the western Pennsylvania farmers and artisans he represented: they wanted to expand their commerce and enlarge their property. Like Washington and Jefferson, they favored an economy based upon what we today would call the middle class.

Born in Ireland in 1741 and educated in parish schools, Findley had immigrated to Philadelphia in 1763. During the American Revolution, he rose from private to captain in the Cumberland

County militia. He was a weaver, a farmer, a Jeffersonian Republican, and a Bible-toting Reformed Presbyterian; he was strongly opposed to slavery and "well-read in philosophical and scientific works." In 1783 he was elected to Pennsylvania's Council of Censors and became a member of the Supreme Executive Council, which managed the state government. One of the tasks of the Council of Censors was to watch for violations of the Pennsylvania Constitution, censure these violations, and, if necessary, call for a new constitutional convention. The Pennsylvania Constitution was drafted mainly by men from rural counties outside of Philadelphia. They fought to widen the base of voters by loosening the property ownership requirements for voting. This increase in the suffrage gave greater power to the western rural interests, and their voices were now heard in this raucous debate.[7]

That the debate took place in the commonwealth of Pennsylvania reflects that state's distinct position. The Pennsylvania Constitution of 1776 was the most democratic in the colonies. There was only one legislature, the General Assembly. There was no state senate, a body that in other states generally protected the interests of the wealthy. The assembly's Supreme Executive Council had a president, who acted as an executive but without the power of a popularly elected governor. Pennsylvania elected all its representatives annually. Laws enacted by the assembly became effective only after a year, so that "the people" could have a chance to form an independent opinion about them. The delegates to Pennsylvania's Constitutional Convention in 1776 had even seriously debated a clause that would allow the state to limit the amount of land any one person could hold in the city or on a farm. Even though Philadelphia's merchants had managed to defeat this clause, the merchants viewed the constitution as a radical document.[8] Moves to limit individual ownership in Pennsylvania were part of a trend that had also cropped up in other regions. Some of the early colonies, such as Jamestown in Virginia and the Plymouth Colony in Massachusetts, had been involved in failed experiments with communal ownership rather than individual property ownership and farming.[9]

Findley traced how the policies of the Bank of North America were harming the Pennsylvania economy. The bank charged excessive interest rates that pushed people into debt. Debt would cost them their houses. Vacant houses meant reduced tax rolls and less income for the government to make improvements. In addition, the bank financed importers who brought in consumer goods that encouraged citizens to overspend. It gave out credit to help pay for the imports, which added to the state's foreign debt. The bank's foreign investors did not have the nation's good in mind. A democratic government's purpose, Findley said, was to ensure that the "source and the support of feudal dignity are therefore taken away." "Feudalism" was a strong word to level at the bank.

It did not make sense to Findley that the bank would have a permanent charter whereas Pennsylvania's governments changed annually. The bank would become a "permanent society, congregated by special privilege," that would control the most profitable foreign markets and produce a corporate aristocracy harmful to democracy. He concluded his speech by stating that the legislature literally did not even have the power to give the bank a charter: "The laws are a common property. The legislatures are entrusted with the distribution of them. This house will not— this house has no right, no constitutional power to give monopolies of legal privilege—to bestow unequal portions of our common inheritance on favorites."

This banking debate resonates with today's economic problems. The revolving door between Wall Street and Washington, DC, in which politicians appoint bankers to top jobs who then return to the private financial sector after public service, fits Findley's fears of how concentrated wealth could create a privileged elite. The term "crony capitalism" did not exist in his day, but that was the underlying issue. The Bank of North America mainly served a very small group of wealthy individuals, who could abuse their power. The bank's accountant had in fact borrowed large sums for long periods to finance personal land speculation.[10]

Would the Pennsylvania General Assembly charter a bank corporation that would concentrate economic power? If it did, would the citizens be able to influence government decisions once the bankers and corporate leaders had amassed their power?

The record of the 1786 Pennsylvania General Assembly debate runs 130 pages. It shows that the early leaders of the American Revolution connected the American democratic ideal with citizens' ownership of property, so that the country would not be dominated by a small group of wealthy capital owners. While these ideas are associated with Thomas Jefferson and James Madison, who together organized the Democratic-Republican Party to stand for the common man, the views of the Federalists, such as John Adams, reveal similar concerns. Historian Drew R. McCoy explains why the founders of the new democracy considered it important that every citizen have an ownership stake in the economy, which in those days meant ownership of land:

American republicans valued property in land primarily because it provided personal independence. The individual with direct access to the productive resources of nature need not rely on other men, or any man, for the basic means of existence. The Revolutionaries believed that every man had a natural right to this form of property in the sense that he was entitled to autonomous control of the resources that were absolutely necessary for his subsistence. The personal independence that resulted from the ownership of land permitted a citizen to participate responsibly in the political process, for it allowed him to pursue spontaneously the common or public good, rather than the narrow interest of the men—or the government—on whom he depended for support. Thus, the Revolutionaries did not intend to provide men with property so that they might flee from public responsibility into a selfish privatism; property was rather the necessary basis for a committed republican citizenry. Property in land also served another crucial purpose in a republican society—it stimulated the productivity of an alert and active citizenry.[11]

At the Pennsylvania General Assembly debate, many others besides Findley spoke about the dangers of inequality to democracy. Robert Lollar, paymaster of the Pennsylvania forces during the Revolution, argued that the corporate charter would "destroy that equality which ought to take place in a commercial country." In an era when corporate charters were issued specifically for the public good—for civic projects such as turnpikes—Lollar could not fathom that the Bank of North America would have an unlimited charter to operate. What specific public good would it serve from day to day? Like Findley, he was alarmed that the assembly and its president were elected every year, while the charter of the bank would be indefinite and its directors could serve unlimited terms.[12] John Smilie, from Fayette County, later a congressman and early opponent of slavery, called the bank "an aristocratical idea" because it granted "exclusive rights" to concentrate large amounts of capital for which there would be no "counterbalance" in the people's commonwealth. Smilie thought the bank "would be totally destructive of that equality which ought to prevail in a republic."[13]

Similarly, Robert Whitehill, who helped write the Pennsylvania Constitution and, according to some historians, had drafted language that James Madison used in the Bill of Rights, called the bank "an engine of destruction" that would "enable a few men to take advantage of their wealth." He went on: "But the government of Pennsylvania being a democracy, the bank is inconsistent with the bill of rights thereof, which says that the government is not instituted for the emolument of any man, family, or set of men. . . . It [the bank] is inconsistent with not only the frame but the spirit of our government." Whitehill emphasized that the states encouraged broad holding of property through "long credits, and . . . slow methods for recovering debts." He favored the practice in which Americans "divide our estates, both real and personal, more equally among our heirs, than the laws or habits of any country that I know of" and therefore had "no kingly prerogative . . . no hereditary nobles . . . no feudal law." Whitehill tied a tight knot with his conclusion: "Enormous wealth, possessed by individuals has always had its influence and dangers in free states. . . . Wealth in many hands operates as many checks. . . . Every man in the disposal of his own wealth will act upon his own principles. . . . If our wealth is less equal than our kind of government, how absurd must it be for government to lend its special aid in so partial a manner to wealth. . . . Democracy must fall before it."[14]

Tench Coxe, later Hamilton's assistant treasury secretary, wrote a series of essays against the bank. Coxe came from a rich Philadelphia family and was a respected political economist. He criticized the Bank of North America as a monopoly and attacked its corporate governance as aristocratic. There is no question but that he was an interested party. The bank had blocked his own attempt to set up a rival bank that would be more open to small property holders—artisans and farmers—to whom the bank rarely gave loans.[15]

On the other side of the debate, the bank's directors lobbied the assembly and sought to convince the citizenry that the bank was necessary for economic development. The opponents intimated that the bank's allies engaged in bribery, but historians have found no evidence supporting that claim.

When the assembly voted on the corporation charter issue, the vote was 41–28 against the charter.[16] However, that was not the end of the matter. Pennsylvania elected assembly members every twelve months, and the charter fight became a major issue in the 1786 election. Supporters of the bank marshaled petitions, arguing that the bank would help finance economic expansion. They obtained the support of Benjamin Franklin and, in a stunning coup, that of Tom Paine, the legendary populist pamphleteer of the American Revolution. Paine believed that the bank would promote economic development that would eventually extend economic opportunity to all citizens.[17]

These arguments convinced voters that the benefits of the bank exceeded the dangers of the concentration of capital. Artisans split with farmers and supported the bank in the hope that it would give them financing. The electorate voted many of the charter's opponents out of office, replacing them with bank supporters. On March 17, 1787, the new assembly reversed the previous year's decision and approved the bank's charter. As it turned out, the artisans had made a sensible decision. Some years later, half of the bank loans were to artisans.[18] Arriving in Philadelphia only a few weeks later to chair the Constitutional Convention for the United States, which would also struggle over the issues of property, democracy, and equality, George Washington had dinner at the home of Thomas Willing, the bank's president.

The issues behind the bank debate went beyond a single corporate charter. Findley, Whitehill, and their colleagues were aligned with the proponents of the populist Pennsylvania Constitution, which sought to shift power in the state from a small group of propertied men to a wider body of citizens. The directors of the bank were aligned with the Federalist Party, which had opposed the 1776 Pennsylvania Constitution. These men of commerce were horrified by the discussion of allowing the state to limit property ownership.

The difficult economy that followed the end of the Revolutionary War strained relations between the two sides. Farmers wanted paper money, to make it easier to pay their debts, and easy credit to develop their commerce. Merchants wanted bank credit to allow them to expand their businesses. The broader fight was over whether the United States would maintain its land-centered economy of yeomen farmers or encourage a wider change that would shift the economy toward industry. The latter would necessarily concentrate wealth and increase the bankers' economic power.[19]

The ability of corporations to amalgamate huge sums of capital to invest in new economic activities was necessary for economic development, even when corporate charters did not specify their exact public purpose. Eventually, the laws regulating corporations relaxed: corporations did not have to ask permission to exist, and their years of operation were not limited. Different states competed with each other to attract corporations. These firms accumulated vast amounts of capital, which became another ocean of property beyond the country's vast lands. Citizens could acquire ownership stakes in corporations as they could in land, though corporate ownership was more concentrated among the few, with potential undesirable consequences for democracy. The tension between the concentration of capital for investment, presumptively necessary for rapid economic development, and the democratic ideal of equality of citizens (for those with the suffrage at a given point of time) that upset the Pennsylvania General Assembly is recurrent in U.S. history, from the founding of the United States to the present day.

PROPERTY, INEQUALITY, AND DEMOCRACY

On May 14, 1787, leaders from the thirteen states opened the Constitutional Convention to design a federal government for the United States. The convention was held in Independence Hall, where the Pennsylvania General Assembly had reversed its decision over corporations just weeks earlier, and it was just a short walk from the Bank of North America. Mindful of the effort to include a clause in the Pennsylvania Constitution for state limits on ownership of property and similar excesses in other states, some of the delegates feared that an enfranchised majority would violate property rights, and that was their focus.[20] Others were concerned that inequality in property was inconsistent with democracy and citizen support of those same property rights. On one side, those without property might seek to restrict private property rights, in the manner of the abortive Pennsylvania clause, or engage in disruptive social protests and demands for redistribution. On the other side, concentration of ownership might give the rich enough resources to undo democracy and create a new aristocracy. Broad property ownership was more likely to lead to wide citizen support for a republic and a stable democracy that operated on behalf of all citizens. All previous republics had been small and homogeneous, and some of the participants observed that "no federal or republican government had ever worked on so large a scale" as the United States.[21] Could the new country devise institutions and policies to balance the competing forces?

Appendix 1.1 conveys the concerns about inequality, property ownership, and democracy of some of the Founders in their own words.

The three presidents who followed George Washington—John Adams, Thomas Jefferson, and James Madison—each had a unique approach to the problem. Expecting inequality to increase as the economy evolved, they sought ways to make the acquiring and holding of property, especially land, as broad based as possible, although they could not overcome their blindness to slavery at the time. Similar views can also be seen in the writings of Benjamin Franklin and the leading pamphleteer of the Revolution, Tom Paine.[22] Broad-based ownership would give many citizens a stake in preserving the political and economic system.

John Adams

John Adams believed that a government could not protect liberty if it did not protect the right to property, but that concentration of property endangered democracy. (See Appendix 1.2.) One historian has observed "no subject interested Adams more than the nature and origins of inequality."[23] Adams focused on the problem throughout his life. The colony of Massachusetts distributed public lands to citizens as widely as possible and had minimal qualifications for property ownership for the right to vote. Adams fought repeatedly to distribute free land to American soldiers and foreign deserters during the Revolution as an incentive for their military service.[24]

After the American Revolution, he favored state laws to force families to divide their estates among all their children and thus prevent the large feudal estates that developed in Europe when property went only to the eldest (male) offspring. Regulating inheritance in this way would reduce inequality without touching the distribution of income between rich and poor families.[25] Like other Founders, Adams closely read the seventeenth-century political philosopher James Harrington, whose book *The Commonwealth of Oceana* linked broad property ownership to the distribution of power and liberty in a republic. As the principal author of the Massachusetts Constitution, Adams stressed the protection of property rights and the right to acquire property. He thought the concentration of wealth was bad for a society's political health and that extensive property ownership would be an important check on the emergence of a new aristocracy.[26] Recognizing that natural human differences lead to inequality, Adams opposed mechanical plans to distribute property, but he still wanted property ownership to be as widespread as possible.

Searching for institutions or mechanisms to avoid the twin dangers of property inequality and violations of property rights, Adams reviewed the experiences of dozens of past republics and federations. He published the results in a book, *A Defense of the Constitutions of the United States*, which appeared around the time of the Constitutional Convention. The design of the U.S. Constitution was consistent with many of his ideas. The three branches of government would check one another to best protect the right to property. A strong executive would help maintain the balance between the rich and the poor. Having two houses of Congress would help avoid the populist extremes. The Senate, he wrote, would be a place "to group the rich . . . to tie their hands." The goal was to create a society where individuals would be responsible for their own performance and improvement and where society would adopt institutions and policies that made the acquisition of property easy.[27] Adams "advocated a public policy that would encourage the broadest possible distribution of property" so that "the property of every man has a share in the government."

Toward the end of his life, Adams grew pessimistic about the future of republican governments. His fear was not that the propertyless majority would redistribute property, but that inequality would allow a new aristocracy to manipulate elections to sway democratic majorities. Fearing "a system of subordination of all to . . . the capricious will of one or a very few," he offered some guidelines for the future. The goal of a republic, he wrote, was not the enrichment of the powerful and wealthy but "the greatest happiness for the greatest number." The government should not only guarantee equality of rights but also enact "equal laws for the common interest." He hoped that the highly accomplished and wealthy, the "aristocracy of merit," would lead the way through their passion for the public good.[28] Historians generally portray Adams as the most traditional of the Founders, but he held strong views about broadening property ownership.[29]

Thomas Jefferson

Thomas Jefferson, Adams's successor, consistently argued for a policy of expansive property ownership. (See Appendix 1.3.) His draft of Virginia's Constitution in 1776 called for granting fifty acres of public land to each person without landownership. In his only book, *Notes on the State of Virginia*, he argued that as the proportion of citizen landowners went up, political corruption went down. He wrote to James Madison in 1775 that those excluded from property ownership needed to have this "fundamental right" returned to them. Like some other Founders, he believed property owners were more likely to protect liberty. His worry that the nation would run out of land, expressed in a letter to John Jay, sheds light on why he favored government support for the cod industry as well as the Louisiana Purchase. The independence of the fisherman was comparable to that of the farmer and thus to be strongly supported. Early drafts of the Declaration of Independence emphasized citizens' "acquisition" of property. Jefferson and others developed the Northwest Ordinance of 1787, which offered land for less than a dollar an acre in what would later become Ohio, Indiana, Michigan, Illinois, Wisconsin, and part of Minnesota, and is considered by some historians of this period among the most important legislative acts aside from the Constitution itself. Among other things, it outlawed primogeniture in the entire region.[30] In his 1801 inaugural address, Jefferson called for not taking "from the mouth of labor the bread it has earned." His stunning condemnation of the British landed aristocracy in a letter to Governor John Langdon of New Hampshire adroitly recalls the current political situation in the United States where two parties, close in power, use a variety of methods to get the propertyless masses to vote for them.

Jefferson went further than any Founder to implement his ideas. He supported granting land to soldiers during and after the American Revolution. He persuaded the Virginia legislature to outlaw primogeniture. The Virginia Constitution ensured not only the right to own property but also the right of "acquiring and possessing property."[31] Jefferson wrote President George Washington's first major report on distributing public lands. As president he set up land offices and hired surveyors to accelerate the distribution of land to citizens. Setting aside his own constitutional reservations, he made the Louisiana Purchase in part because this vast increase in the nation's territory advanced his vision of a homogeneous property-owning republic, "the empire of liberty." In a letter to Edward Bancroft in 1789, a year before Jefferson returned home to work on the cod fishery, Jefferson revealed that he intended to do a social science experiment that would show how landownership benefited human behavior as well as individual well-being. He wanted to import as many Germans as he had slaves, provide each group with fifty acres of land, and observe how they responded to this opportunity. He had "no doubt but that they [both groups] will be good citizens."[32]

While Jefferson's support of the broad middle class contrasts with Alexander Hamilton's interest in creating a financial elite closely tied to the central government, Jefferson's lack of interest in industry and finance can be exaggerated. He opposed, as cozying up to the financial elite, Hamilton's plan for the federal government to issue bonds for the entire Revolutionary War debt of the states and the Confederation. He opposed Hamilton's push to persuade Congress to provide substantial support for manufacturing. And he opposed Hamilton's plan to charter a Bank of the United States. But he relied on the outcome of Hamilton's investment banking prowess to raise the funds for the Louisiana

Purchase and was friendly to manufacturers during his presidency. He came up with creative financing ideas, not unlike today's employee stock ownership plans, to help people use leverage in their purchases of public land. He was open to European and American "land corporations" buying and distributing land to citizens. Herbert Croly, the founder of the *New Republic* magazine, said Jefferson achieved Jeffersonian ends through Hamiltonian means. In the end, Jefferson's yeoman farmers, his citizens, and his proposals were more market oriented than is often recognized.[33]

In *A Preface to Economic Democracy*, political theorist Robert Dahl writes that wide access to land allows the state to create broad property ownership. For the United States, buying land, pushing westward, and dividing up more and more land as the population grew seemed like a way to make Jefferson's vision of a homogeneous republican citizenry come true. Jefferson's first inaugural address described "a rising nation, spread over a wide and fruitful land." He repeatedly wrote that land would "in the end contribute most to real wealth" because self-labor would make the land more valuable and create independent capital owners across the nation. There is no question that blindness to the rights of Indians helped facilitate the land's availability.[34]

To support "a nation of citizens spread over vast tracts of land," Jefferson funded the Lewis and Clark expedition and spent $15 million on the Louisiana Purchase, acquiring almost a million square miles of land. As the historian Gordon Wood wrote, the purchase served to "fulfill the president's dream of having sufficient land for generations to come of his yeoman farmers" and was "the most popular and momentous event of Jefferson's presidency." Ironically, many members of the Federalist Party, which normally favored activist national government, opposed this expenditure, although Alexander Hamilton supported it. Jefferson clearly stated the connection between land and democracy: "By enlarging the empire of liberty, we multiply its auxiliaries, and provide new resources of renovation, should its principles at any time degenerate in those portions of the country which gave them birth."[35]

James Madison

James Madison, the fourth president, was more pessimistic than Jefferson about the ability of a vast supply of land to keep inequality in check. He worried more about how inequality might harm the political system. (See Appendix 1.4.) In *The Federalist*, he expressed the fear that a majority faction based on those without property would seek to cancel the property rights of the richer minority. Protecting liberty therefore meant protecting property rights. Yet allowing people with "unequal faculties to acquire property" would certainly generate more inequality. Madison opposed equalizing property through redistribution as "impracticable" and "unwise." His political solution was what he called "extending the sphere" by making the country so large that multiple factions, a large territory, a government of checks and balances, and a Senate made up of cooler heads would all help avoid the implosion that mounting inequality could produce if the majority tried to violate property rights.[36] Many scholars stress this aspect of Madison's thought because he gave so much attention to it at the Constitutional Convention and in *The Federalist*.[37]

Another dimension of Madison's thought was his support for broad-based property ownership and the right to acquire property. He wanted that right added as an amendment to the U.S. Constitution. Like Adams and Jefferson, he supported a program of tough laws to abolish primogeniture, which restricted how property would pass from generation to generation.[38] In a piece written for the Virginia Constitution Convention in 1829, near the end of his public career, he worried that the effect of "equalizing the property of citizens" by abolishing primogeniture would not be enough to keep property widely distributed. At the same meeting, he made a table of the likely U.S. population for the next one hundred years. By about 1930, he estimated, the United States would have 192 million people (the actual number was 123 million) and there would be 800–900 million acres to divide among the citizens. He feared that there would not be enough land to go around to sustain broad property ownership.[39]

Still, Madison held firm to his original idea that "the owners of the country itself form the safest basis of free government." Extensive property ownership was thus important to protect liberty and social order. He thought the government would be freer if the nation had a lot of property assets—that is, land—relative to the population and adopted laws that favored widespread property ownership. The more freeholders in a country, the more they would protect liberty compared to those who had no hope of acquiring property. The political economy problem was how to broaden property holdings while respecting property rights. He also believed that this type of broadened ownership-oriented economy probably provided more social control to calm the masses who were landless.[40]

Madison never elaborated a program for solving his political economy problem, but in a series of stark articles in the *National Gazette* in 1792, he offered some hints. He favored withholding unnecessary opportunities from the "few" that would lead to unmerited accumulation of riches. He favored laws that would extend the middle class by reducing extreme wealth without violating property rights. While he was against arbitrary restrictions on acquiring property, he strongly opposed monopolies and preferential treatment for the rich and powerful. He was against policies that would favor one interest at the expense of another, and he hoped that the rich and the poor would serve as a check on each other and produce an equilibrium of moderate inequality.

Madison's bottom line is as much a challenge to policy makers today as to his contemporaries: "To the effect of these changes, intellectual, moral, and social, the institutions and laws of the country must be adapted, and it will require for the task all the wisdom of the wisest patriots." It would require some very wise policies to meet this challenge. Looking forward to the future economy, he worried about a deficiency of capital "for the expensive establishments which facilitate labor and cheapen its products." Indeed, the corporation later emerged as a possible solution to his worry because it offered a new type of capital for "expensive establishments" that would not run out like land but could be broadly owned. We will consider whether the corporation is capable of creating the wide base of property stakeholders whom Madison considered so necessary.[41]

THE HOMESTEAD ACT

It has long been a cherished opinion of some of our wisest statesmen that the people of the United States had a higher and more enduring interest in the early settlement and substantial cultivation of the public lands than in the amount of direct revenue to be derived from the sale of them. . . . This policy has received its most signal and beneficent illustration in the recent enactment granting homesteads to actual settlers. Since the 1st day of January last the before-mentioned quantity of 1,456,514 acres of land have been taken up under its provisions.

—*President Abraham Lincoln, December 9, 1863, Annual Message to Congress*[42]

The land was not exhausted yet. During much of the nineteenth century the extensive territory west of the Mississippi made Jefferson and Madison's dream of increasing the independent landowning population of the country a plausible way to reconcile the dilemma between inequality and property. There were two competing views of what the federal government should do with its hundreds of millions of acres. The Hamiltonian view favored selling the lands to the highest bidder to raise enough revenue to balance the indebted nation's books. The Jeffersonian view called for distributing public lands to landless citizens, to give them a direct capital stake in society. The land-distribution policies of the Northwest Ordinance of 1787 and the Louisiana Purchase had begun the process in earnest. The early 1800s saw some additional modest programs along Jeffersonian lines. The Harrison Land Act of 1800, which created the Indiana Territory out of the Northwest Territory, sold land to citizens by means of a liberal system of credit to help them buy small amounts. In 1804 the federal government made access to land easier and gave land grants to military volunteers. In some areas, squatters pressured the government to sell to them. A congressional act of 1820 reduced the price of land to $1.25 an acre, less than the price immediately after independence. Treasury Secretary Albert Gallatin reflected the original "republican sentiment": "Every purchase is voluntary and advantageous to all parties: to the purchaser, who on the most easy terms, becomes a freeholder and secures for life an independent existence; to the community at large, which is enriched by the annual conversion of unproductive into most productive land; to every individual of that community, whose taxes are lessened in proportion to the amount received."[43]

This policy culminated in the Homestead Act, which President Lincoln highlighted in his Annual Message to Congress. The idea had long roots: its first mention may have been by Thomas Hart Benton, a Jacksonian Democrat, in 1809. Then serving in the Tennessee Senate, Benton called for a policy to give the first settler on public land who improved it the first option to buy it. He emphasized that settlers who were landowners were more self-sufficient and less likely to go to the poorhouse. The then standard practice of selling government land to the highest bidder was, he said, "a false policy." Benton's efforts were, according to his biographer, "thrust aside with ridicule as mere visionary dreams." Later, in the U.S. Senate, Benton regularly introduced bills to distribute federal land to citizens, citing George Washington, Alexander Hamilton, and Thomas Jefferson in support of his proposals. He asked the State Department to do a special census of freeholders to track the development of a broad-based proprietary economy. He attacked the federal government for having 70 million acres in areas where 140,000 non-freeholders lived. A land distribution bill he introduced in 1828 almost became law but got entangled in the battle over whether western lands should allow slavery.[44] Southern plantation owners wanted to buy new lands and operate them with gangs of slaves. Northerners wanted small free farmers to operate the lands. The result was a deadlock.

In the late 1840s, the idea of giving land to citizens who worked it gained more favorable attention than any other measure, other than cheap postage. The National Reform Association, allied with labor groups, stimulated the largest nationally coordinated petition drive in American history in favor of homesteads. Alvan Earle Bovay, secretary of the association, described homesteading as "an effort [for the worker] to redeem himself from the slavery of wages." Newspapers across the nation endorsed the petition. Many of them included petition forms that people passed around and mailed in to the government.[45] In 1848, citizens in the Midwest formed the Free Soil Party under the motto of "Free Soil, Free Labor, and Free Men." (See Appendix 1.5.)

In the early 1850s the Free Soilers joined other groups opposed to the spread of slavery to form the Republican Party. The Republicans' first candidate for president, former California senator John C. Frémont, ran on a slogan that was only slightly modified: "Free Soil, Free Labor, Free Men, and Frémont."[46] In response to the financial crash of 1857, Congress passed a homestead act in 1860. Initially the plan was to provide 160-acre farm plots for free to pioneers, in part to help workers who lost jobs in the crisis, but the eventual bill made lands available at twenty-five cents an acre, still a very good price. Industrialists opposed the bill for fear it would reduce the supply of labor. Southern plantation owners opposed the bill for fear that the lands would attract Free Soilers opposed to the extension of slavery. President James Buchanan vetoed it.[47]

The Civil War changed the political calculus. In 1862, with no representatives from the southern states, Congress passed the Homestead Act. House Speaker Galusha Grow, often called "The Father of the Republican Party," steered the act through Congress as promoting social and political equality, saying, "I want the government to protect the rights of men." Grow's words highlight the belief that among the basic human rights was the right to own property and that the right should extend to all persons.

The Homestead Act gave ownership of 160 acres of undeveloped federal land west of the Mississippi River to families for a small fee and five years of residency if they built a house and worked the land, or for $1.25 an acre with minimal improvements and a six-month residency. Veterans who had not fought against the Union could count their military service against the five years. It was the country's greatest effort to improve the wealth of citizens and carry out the Jeffersonian vision. The Homestead Act did not take property from any existing owners. The land was the common property of the United States. Though it was a government program, it was also, in the eyes of many, an antigovernment program, moving assets from the government to private ownership. By the 1880s, both political parties supported the homestead idea that the lands should go to citizen settlers and not corporations.[48]

The original Homestead Act eventually allowed some six hundred thousand Americans to get a property stake in society. Between 1860 and 1900 it created 4 million farms. It did not live up to its promise quickly because the government's administrative apparatus was not widespread or efficient enough to manage the program, because of fraud and favoritism. After the Civil War the government passed many additional homestead acts to allow for the different land needs associated with different types of farming. The Homestead Act continued until it was finally repealed in 1976. Similar legislation continued in the state of Alaska until 1986. The distribution of public lands through homesteading helped build many western states that today value rugged individualism and small government.

These laws represented a major implementation of the Founders' policy of broad-based ownership. Between 1862 and 1938, 10 percent of the landmass of the United States—nearly the area of Texas and California combined—was claimed and settled by 1.6 million homesteads under the different homestead acts. This represents about 20 percent of all public land and is comparable to all the land granted to states and sold or awarded to corporations and land grant colleges. While Congress granted four times more land to railroad corporations than it allotted under the original Homestead Act, railroads sometimes granted "homesteads" to citizens to encourage the building of settlements and create markets for their services.[49]

When the original Homestead Act became law in 1863, African Americans could not become citizens and so could not enjoy its benefits. On November 15, 1865, General William Tecumseh Sherman issued an order granting forty acres of land to free blacks on "the islands from Charleston, south, the abandoned rice fields along the rivers for thirty miles back from the sea, and the country bordering the St. Johns River, Florida" and offered the new settlers military protection. His field order was canceled by President Andrew Johnson. The Civil Rights Act of 1866 at least officially granted African Americans citizenship. Radical Republicans who wanted to reform the South tried after the Civil War to create a "Homestead Act for free blacks" by promising forty acres and a mule to every black family, but this was blocked. In 1866 the Southern Homestead Act was passed to open up 46 million acres of public land for former slaves. Southern opposition to black ownership led Congress to repeal that act in 1876.[50]

THE CORPORATION AS THE NEW LAND?

The ideology of agrarian democratic republicanism developed during a peculiar moment in American history, when farmland and small artisans could hold a large proportion of the country's property and capital, and inequalities among citizens were relatively modest. Historian Gordon Wood writes about this theme in *The Empire of Liberty*:

> Just as Americans lacked the corrupting luxury of Europe, so too, they constantly told themselves, they were without Europe's great distinctions of the wealthy few and the poverty-stricken many. Compared to Great Britain, America had a truncated society; it lacked both the great noble families with their legal titles and sumptuous wealth and the great masses of poor whose lives were characterized by unremitting toil and deprivation. In America, wrote Benjamin Franklin in one of the many expressions of the idea of American exceptionalism in these years, "a general Mediocrity" prevailed. . . . Commentators were eager to turn the general middling character of America into an asset. "Here," wrote Crèvecoeur, "are no aristocratical families, no courts, no kings, no bishops, no ecclesiastical dominion, no invisible power giving to a few a very visible one, no great manufactures employing thousands, no great refinements of luxury. The rich and the poor are not so far removed from each other as they are in Europe." . . . Nowhere in America, he said, ignoring for the moment, as most American social commentators did, the big houses of the Southern planters and the slave quarters of hundreds of thousands of black Africans, could one find "the hostile castle and the haughty mansion, contrasted with the clay-built hut and miserable cabin, where cattle and men help to keep each other warm and dwell in meanness, smoke, and indigence." . . . The fact that the great bulk of Americans were landowners radically separated them from the rest of the world. . . . Americans were a society, in

other words, suited for republicanism. . . . It was precisely the prevalence of all these independent farmers that made possible virtuous republican government in America.[51]

But the era of the independent farmers did not survive into the twentieth century. While the U.S. population did not grow as rapidly as Madison expected, it grew sufficiently to validate his belief that the Jeffersonian vision of a broad-based agrarian property class with fairly equitable holdings was not a plausible outcome. Instead, the share of workers in agriculture dropped from census to census as the population grew increasingly urban. Manufacturing increasingly drove the economy, along with the exploitation of natural resources such as coal and oil. Rapid industrialization and modernization after the Civil War produced the kind of economy that Findley and his allies in the Pennsylvania General Assembly feared: huge concentrations of capital; key markets controlled by monopolies or trusts; and a generation of superrich individuals with great influence and power. In the late 1800s and early 1900s, two thousand corporations were consolidated into fewer than two hundred huge concentrations.[52] Then, most of the population ended up working for someone else: first in the massive expansion of manufacturing, oil, and mining, and later in white-collar and retail businesses. Corporate capitalism generated great economic growth and huge pools of capital but also huge inequalities in the distribution of property.[53]

The problem of creating broadened ownership in the new industrial world was not something the Founders foresaw. James Madison worried about "capital for these expensive establishments," but no one came up with a way to turn the citizens in them into a new version of "proprietors." When Republican Speaker Galusha Grow finally retired from the House of Representatives in 1902, he gave one last speech on "Labor and Capital." Having seen both the successes and limitations of the Homestead Act, he proposed that profit sharing could be used to provide access to property rights to workers in the now industrialized economy. It was not, he argued, that corporations were themselves the problem—as Findley tried to convince the Pennsylvania General Assembly—but rather that business and political leaders had envisioned no way of organizing the finances of corporations that encouraged broadened ownership.[54]

Could the Founders' vision for widespread ownership be fulfilled with the new forms of wealth embodied in corporate property? Could the corporation that Findley and his colleagues saw as the enemy of liberty become instead the new source of broad-based property? How would firms that spread the benefits of ownership to all their workers fare in the marketplace against more traditional firms?

APPENDIXES
Appendix 1.1. The Dual Fears from Unequal Distribution of Property: Lack of Protection of Property vs. the Rich Control of Government

THE PROPERTYLESS COULD TRAMPLE PROPERTY RIGHTS

Suppose a nation, rich and poor, high and low, ten millions in number, all assembled together; not more than one or two millions will have lands, houses, or any personal property. . . . If all were to be decided by a vote of the majority, the eight or nine millions who have no property, would not think of usurping over the rights of the one or two millions who have? . . . The time would not be long before courage and enterprise would come, and pretexts be invented by degrees, to countenance the majority in dividing all the property among them, or at least, in sharing it equally with its present possessors. Debts would be abolished first; taxes laid heavy on the rich, and not at all on the others; and at last a downright equal division of every thing be demanded, and voted. What would be the consequence of this? The idle, the vicious, the intemperate, would rush into the utmost extravagance of debauchery, sell and spend all their share, and then demand a new division of those who purchased from them.

John Adams, *A Defense of the Constitutions of Government of the United States of America*, 1794[55]

There will be debtors and creditors and an unequal possession of property. . . . In England, at this day, if elections were open to all classes of people, the property of landed proprietors would be insecure. An agrarian [redistribution] law would soon take place. If these observations be just, our government ought to secure the permanent interests of the country against innovation. Landholders ought to have a share in the government, to support these invaluable interests, and to balance and check the other. They ought to be so constituted as to protect the minority of the opulent against the majority.

James Madison, Philadelphia Constitutional Convention, June 26, 1787[56]

All communities divide themselves into the few and the many. The first are the rich and well born, the other the mass of the people. The voice of the people has been said to be the voice of God; and however generally this maxim has been quoted and believed, it is not true in fact. The people are turbulent and changing; they seldom judge or determine right. Give therefore to the first class a distinct, permanent share in the government. They will check the unsteadiness of the second, and as they cannot receive any advantage by a change, they therefore will ever maintain good government. Can a democratic assembly, who annually revolve in the mass of the people, be supposed steadily to pursue the public good? Nothing but a permanent body can check the imprudence of democracy. Their turbulent and uncontrolling disposition requires checks.

Alexander Hamilton, Philadelphia Constitutional
Convention, June 19, 1787[57]

THE RICH COULD TAKE CONTROL

Are the citizens to be all of the same age, sex, size, strength, stature, activity, courage, hardiness, industry, patience, ingenuity, wealth, knowledge, fame, wit, temperance, constancy, and wisdom? The answer of all mankind must be in the negative. . . . There is an inequality of wealth; some individuals, whether by descent from their ancestors, or from greater skill, industry, and success in business have estates both in lands and goods; others have no property at all . . . The only remedy is to throw the rich and the proud into one group, in a separate assembly, and there tie their hands; if you give them scope with the people at large or their representatives, they will destroy all equality and liberty, with the consent and acclamations of the people themselves.

John Adams, *A Defense of the Constitutions
of the United States*, 1794[58]

If all power be suffered to slide into hands not interested in the rights of property which must be the case whenever a majority fall under that description, one of two things cannot fail to happen; either they will unite against the other description and become dupes and instruments of ambition, or their poverty and dependence will render them mercenary instruments of wealth. . . . In either case liberty will be subverted; in the first by a despotism growing out of anarchy, in the second by an oligarchy founded on corruption.

James Madison, *Observations on the "Draught of the Constitution
for Virginia,"* ca. October 15, 1788[59]

Do we imagine that our assessments operate equally? Nothing can be more contrary to the fact. Whenever a discretionary power is lodged in any set of men over the property of their neighbors, they will abuse it, their passions, prejudices, partialities, dislikes, will have the principal lead in measuring the ability of those over whom their power extends.

Alexander Hamilton, July 4, 1782[60]

Appendix 1.2. John Adams on Widespread Property Ownership

Property monopolized or in the Possession of a few is a Curse to Mankind: We should preserve not an Absolute Equality—this is unnecessary, but preserve all from extreme Poverty, and all others from Extravagant Riches.

John Adams, Fragmentary Notes for a Dissertation on the Canon
and Feudal Law, May–August 1765[61]

Our Laws for the distribution of Intestate Estates occasions a frequent Division of landed Property and prevents Monopolies of Land.

John Adams, letter to Abigail Adams, October 29, 1775[62]

Harrington has Shewn that Power always follows Property. This I believe to be as infallible a Maxim in Politicks, as that Action and Reaction are equal, as in Mechanicks. Nay, I believe We may advance one Step farther, and affirm that the Balance of Power in a Society, accompanies the Balance of Property in Land. The only possible Way then of preserving the Balance of Power on the side of equal Liberty and public Virtue, is to make the Acquisition of Land easy to every Member of Society: to make a Division of the Land into Small Quantities, So that the Multitude may be possessed of landed Estates. If the Multitude is possessed of the Ballance of real Estate, the Multitude will have the Ballance of Power, and in that Case the Multitude will take Care of the Liberty, Virtue, and Interest of the Multitude in all Acts of Government.

John Adams, letter to James Sullivan, May 26, 1776[63]

All men are born equally free and independent, and have . . . certain natural, essential, and unalienable rights: among which may be reckoned the right of enjoying and defending their lives and liberties; that of acquiring, possessing, and protecting their property; in fine, that of seeking and obtaining their safety and happiness.

John Adams, *Report of a Constitution or Form of Government for the Constitution of Massachusetts*, ca. October 28–31, 1779[64]

The general discontents in Europe have not been produced by any increase of the power of kings, for monarchical authority has been greatly diminished in all parts of Europe during the last century, but by the augmentation of the wealth and power of the aristocracies. The great and general extension of commerce has introduced such inequalities of property, that the class of middling people, that great and excellent portion of society upon whom so much of the liberty and prosperity of nations so greatly depends, is almost lost; and the two orders of rich and poor only remain. . . . The people find themselves burdened now by the rich. . . . In America, the right of sovereignty resides indisputably in the body of the people, and they have the whole property of land. . . . But if the whole people be landlords, or hold the land so divided among them, that no one man or number of men, within the compass of the few or aristocracy overbalance them, it is a commonwealth. . . . In America, the balance is nine tenths on the side of the people.

John Adams, in the *Boston Patriot*, 1811[65]

That all men are born to equal rights is true, Every being has a right to his own, as clear, as moral, as sacred, as any other being has. This is as indubitable as a moral government in the universe. But to teach that all men are born with equal powers and faculties, to equal influence in society, to equal property and advantages through life, is as gross a fraud, as glaring an imposition on the credulity of the people, as ever practiced by monks, by Druids, by Brahmins, by priests of the immortal Lama, or by the self-styled philosophers of the French revolution.

John Adams, letter to John Taylor, April 15, 1814,
Quincy, Massachusetts[66]

Appendix 1.3. Thomas Jefferson on Broad-Based Property Ownership

The political institutions of America, it's various [soils and climates opened a] certain resource to the unfortunate & to the enterprising of every country, and ensured to them the acquisition & free possession of property.

Thomas Jefferson, *Draft of the Declaration of Independence*,
June 1775[67]

Every person of full age neither owning nor having owned 50 acres of land shall be entitled to an appropriation of [fifty] acres . . . in free and absolute dominion. And no other person shall be capable of taking such an appropriation.

Thomas Jefferson, *Proposed Constitution for Virginia*, Section IV,
Rights, Public and Private, June 1776[68]

Generally speaking, the proportion which the aggregate of the other classes of citizens bears in any State to that of its husbandmen, is the proportion of its unsound to its healthy parts, and is a good enough barometer whereby to measure its degree of corruption. . . . The mobs of great cities add just so much to the support of pure government, as sores do to the strength of the human body. It is the manners and spirit of a people which preserve a republic in vigor. A degeneracy in these is a canker which soon eats to the heart of its laws and constitution.

Thomas Jefferson, *Notes on the State of Virginia*, 1784[69]

Whenever there is in any country, uncultivated lands and unemployed poor, it is clear that the laws of property have been so far extended as to violate natural right. The earth is given as a common stock for man to labour and live on. If, for the encouragement of industry we allow it to be appropriated, we must take care that other employment be furnished to those excluded from the appropriation. If we do not the fundamental right to labour the earth returns to the unemployed.

Thomas Jefferson, letter to James Madison,
October 28, 1785[70]

We have now lands enough to employ an infinite number of people in their cultivation. Cultivators of the earth are the most valuable citizens. They are the most vigorous, the most independent, the most virtuous, and they are tied to their country and wedded to its liberty and interests by the most lasting bands. As long therefore as they can find employment in this line, I would not convert them into mariners, artisans, or anything else. . . . This is not the case as yet, and probably will not be for a considerable time. As soon as it is, the surplus of hands must be turned to something else. I should then perhaps wish to turn them to the sea in preference to manufactures, because comparing the characters of the two classes I find the former the most valuable citizens. I consider the class of artificers as the panders of vice and the instruments by which the liberties of a country are generally overturned. However we are not free to decide this question on principles of theory only.

Thomas Jefferson, letter to John Jay, 1785[71]

As long as agriculture is our principal object, which will be the case while there remain vacant lands in any part of America. When we get piled upon one another in large cities, as in Europe, we shall become corrupt as in Europe, and go to eating one another as they do there.

Thomas Jefferson, letter to Uriah Forrest,
December 31, 1787[72]

A wise and frugal government . . . shall not take from the mouth of labor the bread it has earned. . . . It is proper you should understand what I deem the essential principles of our government[:] . . . Economy in public expense that labor may be lightly burthened.

Thomas Jefferson, first inaugural address, 1801[73]

What, in the nature of her government unfits England for the observation of moral duties? In . . . her king is a cypher; his only function being to name the oligarchy which is to govern her. . . . The real power & property in the government is in the great aristocratical families of the nation. The nest of office being too small for all of them to cuddle into at once, the contest is eternal, which shall crowd the other out. For this purpose they are divided into two parties, the Ins, & the Outs, so equal in weight that a small matter turns the balance. To keep themselves in, when they are in, every stratagem must be practised, every artifice used which may flatter the pride, the passions or power of the nation. Justice, honour, faith must yield to the necessity of keeping themselves in place. The question whether a measure is moral is never asked.

Thomas Jefferson, letter to John Langdon, March 5, 1810[74]

Appendix 1.4. James Madison on Extensive Property Ownership

I have no doubt that the misery of the lower classes will be found to abate wherever the Government assumes a freer aspect, & the laws favor a subdivision of property. . . . Our limited population has probably as large a share in producing this effect as the political advantages which distinguish us. . . . No problem in political Oeconomy has appeared to me more puzzling than that which relates to the most proper distribution of the inhabitants of a Country fully peopled.

James Madison, letter to Thomas Jefferson, June 19, 1786[75]

Those who contend for a simple Democracy, or a pure republic, actuated by a sense of the majority, and operating within narrow limits, assume or suppose a case which is altogether fictitious. . . . We know however that no Society ever did or can consist of so homogeneous a mass of citizens. . . . A distinction of property results from that very protection which a free Government gives to unequal faculties of acquiring it.

James Madison, letter to Thomas Jefferson, October 24, 1787[76]

Viewing the subject in its merits alone, the freeholders of the Country would be the safest depositories of Republican liberty. In future times a great majority of the people will not only be without landed, but any other sort of property. These will either combine under the influence of their common situation in which case the rights of property and public liberty, will not be secure in their hands; or which is more probable, they will become the tools of opulence and ambition, in which case there will be equal danger on another side.

James Madison, Suffrage Qualifications for Electing the House of Representatives, August 7, 1787[77]

In estimating the tendency of Governments to the increase or relaxation of their powers, particular causes . . . seem to have been overlooked or little heeded by the great oracles of political wisdom. A Government of the same structure, would operate very differently within a very small territory and a very extensive one . . . over a Society composed whole of tenants of the soil aspiring and hoping for an enlargement of their possessions and a Society divided into a rich and independent class, and a more numerous class without property and hopeless of acquiring a permanent interest in maintaining its rights.

James Madison, Note on the Influence of Extent of Territory on Government, ca. December 1791[78]

That is not a just government where arbitrary restrictions, exemptions, and monopolies deny to part of its citizens that free use of their faculties and free choice of occupations, which not only constitute their property in the general sense of the word, but are the means of acquiring property strictly so called.

James Madison, in the National Gazette, March 29, 1792[79]

The proportion being without property or the hope of acquiring it, cannot be expected to sympathize sufficiently with its rights, to be safe depositories of power over them.

James Madison, the Virginia Convention, 1829–1830[80]

In every political society, parties are unavoidable. A difference of interests, real or supposed is the most natural and fruitful source of them. The great objects should be to combat the evil: 1. By establishing political equality among all. 2. By withholding unnecessary opportunities from a few, to increase the inequality of property, by an immoderate, and especially unmerited, accumulation of riches. 3. By the silent operation of laws, which, without violating the rights of property, reduce extreme wealth towards a state of mediocrity, and raise extreme indigence towards a state of comfort. 4. By abstaining from measures which operate differently on different interests, and particularly such as favor one interest, at the expense of another. 5. By making one party a check on the other, so far as the existence of parties cannot be prevented, nor their views accommodated—If this is not the language of reason, it is that of republicanism.

James Madison, in the *National Gazette*, January 23, 1792[81]

Appendix 1.5. The Homestead Act[82]

The public lands of the United States belong to the people, and should not be sold to individuals nor granted to corporations, but should be held as a sacred trust for the benefit of the people, and should be granted in limited quantities, free of cost to landless settlers.

Eighteen fifty-two platform of the Free Soil Party that was absorbed into the Republican Party

As the means for sustaining life are derived almost entirely from the soil, every person has a right to so much of the earth's surface as is necessary to his support. To whatever unoccupied portion of it, therefore, he shall apply his labor for that purpose, from that time forth it should become appropriated to his exclusive use; and whatever improvements he may make by his industry should become his property and subject to his disposal. For the only true foundation for any right to property is man's labor. . . . The struggle between capital and labor is an unequal one at best. It is a struggle between the bones and the sinews of men and dollars and cents, and in that struggle it needs no prophet's ken to foretell the issue. . . . Is it not time you struck from your statute books its lingering relics of feudalism, wiped out the principles engrafted upon it by the narrow-minded policy of other times, and adapted the legislation of the country to the spirit of the age, and to the true idea of man's rights and his relations with his government. For if a man has a right on earth he has a right to land enough to rear a habitation on.

> Congressman Galusha A. Grow, former Speaker of the House
> of Representatives and Republican Party whip, speaking
> during the Homestead Law debate, March 1852

Free Homesteads. That we protest against any sale or alienation to others of the Public Lands held by actual settlers, and against any view of the Free Homestead policy which regards the settlers as paupers or suppliants for public bounty; and we demand the passage by Congress of the complete and satisfactory Homestead Measure which has already passed the House.

> National platform of the Republican Party, 1860

The freedom of the public lands to actual settlers, and the limitation of future acquisitions of land to some reasonable amount, are also measures which seem to us vitally necessary to the ultimate emancipation of labor from thraldom and misery. What is mainly wanted is that each man should have an assured chance to earn, and then an assurance of the just fruits of his labors. . . . Every new labor-saving invention is a new argument, an added necessity for it. And so long as the laboring class must live by working for others, while others are striving to live luxuriously and amass wealth out of the fruits of such labor, so long the abuses and sufferings now complained of must continue to exist or frequently appear. We must go to the root of the evil.

> Horace Greeley, former editor of the *New York Tribune* and congressman from New York, writing in the *New-York Weekly Tribune*

I agree with you, Mr. Chairman, that the working-men are the basis of all governments for the plain reason that they are more numerous. . . . I will simply say that I am for those means which will give the greatest good to the greatest number. . . . In regard to the Homestead Law, I have to say that in so far as the Government lands can be disposed of, I am in favor of cutting up the wild lands into parcels, so that every poor man may have a home.

> Abraham Lincoln, address to Germans at Cincinnati, Ohio, February 12, 1861

The homestead policy was established only after long and earnest resistance; experience proves its wisdom. The lands in the hands of industrious settlers, whose labor creates wealth and contributes to the public resources, are worth more to the United States than if they had been reserved as a solitude for future purchasers.

> President Andrew Johnson, December 4, 1865

In every country, and under every system of government, the ownership of land by the larger portion of the people has been a cause for congratulation, and the fact has been treated as evidence of stability in the government.

George S. Boutwell, secretary of the Treasury under President Grant; governor of Massachusetts; congressman and senator; first commissioner of the Internal Revenue Service under President Lincoln

The principle involved in this bill is one that has divided free democratic principles and aristocratic government for all past time.

Eugene Hale, Republican senator from Maine

2 EXAMPLES

Well, my philosophy is that if we're going to make a lot of money investing our dollars, employees who help us make that money should get some of the reward. And then when we set up Intel, we also gave stock options to the executive staff, but about a year later, Bob Noyce and Gordon Moore and I were sitting around trying to figure out where, if at all, in addition, we should give options and one of us, I think it was me but it's not important who it was, said, why don't we just give them to all the employees. And that seemed to strike a good note with the other two. . . . The culture in those companies was to work hard and to perform. . . . These companies that we're talking about, the early stage companies of Silicon Valley, all had a very strict work ethic and people were expected to work hard and work long hours and we thought we should reward them for that. . . . I think just trying to give people a little of the fruit that other people are receiving is the right thing to do. I expect the stockholders will benefit from all of this.

Arthur Rock, legendary venture capitalist; early investor in Intel and Apple; founder, with Robert Noyce and Gordon Moore, of Intel in 1968 and chairman of its board; and founder of Arthur Rock & Company[1]

This chapter is about examples. Some analysts dismiss examples as anecdotes—folk medicine tales that should be taken with many grains of salt. An example or two of corporations that operate successfully with a system of employee stock ownership or profit sharing or stock purchase does not prove that such systems work in general. Perhaps there is something unique about a company or its CEO or history or workforce that makes broad ownership or profit sharing succeed, whereas such a system would not work in general. We disagree. Validated examples or case studies in the more formal business school sense are evidence. They are what mathematicians call a proof of existence: that under some conditions a given policy or practice works or does not work. If we did not have cases of businesses that succeeded with broad-based ownership and profit sharing, we would not have written this book.

The examples in this chapter come from firms that exist today. Some formed recently. Others formed much earlier in U.S. history. Just as we relied on the words of the Founders to show their concerns about the relationship between the distribution of property and democracy, we rely on the words of the founding entrepreneurs and leaders of firms and of their employees to show that broad-based shares and a culture of employee participation can contribute to economic success. We focus on a small number of cases, but we also cite additional examples to demonstrate that broad-based capitalism succeeds under a wide set of circumstances. To keep from giving a Pollyannaish picture, we also report on cases in which firms with broad-based shares have failed or in which they have produced socially undesirable outcomes.

GOOGLE

Google is not a conventional company. We do not intend to become one. . . . Now the time has come for the company to move to public ownership. . . . As a private company, we have concentrated on the long term, and this has served us well. As a public company, we will do the same. . . . Our business environment changes rapidly and needs long-term investment. We will not hesitate to place major bets on promising new opportunities. We encourage our employees, in addition to their regular projects, to spend 20 percent of their time working on what they think will most benefit Google. This empowers them to be more creative and innovative. Many of our significant advances have happened in this manner. For example, AdSense for content and Google News were both prototyped in "20 percent time." . . . We have transferred significant ownership of Google to employees in return for their efforts in building the business. . . . Our employees, who have named themselves Googlers, are everything. Google is organized around the ability to attract and leverage the talent of exceptional technologists and business people. We have been lucky to recruit many creative, principled and hard working stars. We hope to recruit many more in the future. We will reward and treat them well. . . . We provide many unusual benefits for our employees, including meals free of charge, doctors and washing machines. We are careful to consider the long-term advantages to the company of these benefits. Expect us to add benefits rather than pare them down over time. We believe it is easy to be penny wise and pound foolish with respect to benefits that can save employees considerable time and improve their health and productivity. The significant employee ownership of Google has made us what we are today. Because of our employee talent, Google is doing exciting work in nearly every area of computer science. We are in a very competitive industry where the quality of our product is paramount. Talented people are attracted to Google because we empower them to change the world; Google has large computational resources and distribution that enables individuals to make a difference. Our main benefit is a workplace with important projects, where employees can contribute and grow. We are focused on providing an environment where talented, hard working people are rewarded for their contributions to Google and for making the world a better place.

—*Letter to the public from Google founders Larry Page and Sergei Brin, 2004*[2]

Everyone knows Google. Everyone uses Google products. Gmail. YouTube. Google Search. Google Maps. Google is one of the most important innovative firms in the information world, the nation's seventy-third-largest corporation. Its policies about free speech on the Internet and its search engine algorithms help determine what we see about the world. As Larry Page and Sergei Brin's letter shows, from its inception Google was devoted to employees sharing in the corporation's economic outcomes and in decision making. The Google founders, like many leaders of successful firms with broad-based ownership structures, view workers having a role in the business's ownership or profits and participating in decisions as two sides of the same coin of company success. Indicative of Google's labor practices in 2012, it won the first position on *Fortune* magazine's "Hundred Best Companies to Work For" list, in part for its commitment to broad-based employee ownership. The company also has a significant profit-sharing program based on company-wide and individual performance. Google is continuing a long American tradition since Albert Gallatin (later to be Jefferson's secretary of the Treasury) instituted a profit-sharing plan to attract skilled European craftspeople to set up his glass factory in 1797 in New Geneva, Pennsylvania.[3]

Sergei Brin and Larry Page created Google in the late 1990s at Stanford University. They set themselves up in the garage of Brin's sister-in-law, Susan Wojcicki. In ten years the company grew from eight employees to almost twenty thousand. Google is in a long line of high-technology companies using shares, dating as far back as Intel in 1968.[4] Brin and Page owned 100 percent of Google in the beginning. But to develop more products and services that would make a huge difference in the world, they needed scores of worker teams to pioneer ideas and products that no one had previously imagined. Paying workers with stock options and grants of stock significantly diluted the founding partners' ownership of Google, but the payoff was that Google could attract superior talent and motivate those workers to make the pie much bigger. Until 2004, Brin and Page and Google employees and some private investors owned the company in its entirety.

At Google, employee stock ownership is part of a corporate culture that attempts to empower workers and encourages them to participate in decisions. When that culture works, a company can expect employees to give more discretionary effort to the company, to be more innovative, to be more likely to stay with the company, and to build the business. Google views its compensation policy of sharing stock options with workers as "crucial to our ability to motivate employees to achieve our goals." It is one of the few corporations that details in its annual reports to shareholders its policy and practice of creating and maintaining a corporate culture based on broad-based capitalism. The company touts its mode of operation:

> We take great pride in our culture. We embrace collaboration and creativity and encourage the iteration of ideas to address complex technical challenges. Transparency and open dialog are central to us, and we like to make sure that company news, whether about product launches, industry news and innovations, or organizational changes, reaches our employees first through internal channels like weekly TGIF (Thank God It's Friday) meetings, Tech Talks, blogs, and messages from leadership. We have evolved into a software, technology, internet, mobile, advertising, and media company all rolled into one. We take technology innovation very seriously and compete aggressively for talent across the globe. We strive to hire the best computer scientists and engineers to help us solve very significant challenges across systems design, artificial intelligence, machine learning, data mining, networking, software engineering, testing, distributed systems, cluster design, and other areas. We work hard to provide an environment where these talented people can have fulfilling jobs and produce technological innovations that have a positive effect on the world through daily use by millions of people. Despite our rapid growth, we still cherish our roots as a startup, and we give employees the freedom to act on their ideas regardless of their level within the company.[5]

In the years after Google went public, the ownership stake of Brin and Page and former CEO and executive chairman Eric Schmidt has been reduced to about 20 percent. With a workforce of about fifty-five thousand employees and stock now traded on the NASDAQ exchange, Google has thus far maintained its culture of financial employee involvement and participation. To protect the firm from the short-termism of the stock market and Wall Street pressures for squeezing workers in favor of shareholders, Brin and Page instituted a controversial—but so far workable—plan where their shares have ten times more votes than everyone else's. As a result, at every annual Google shareholder meeting, they control about 60 percent of the votes. Shareholders gain monetarily from their investment in the firm but cannot challenge the founding partners' commitment to investing in longer-term innovation and operating through a broad-based system of employee sharing and participation.[6]

Google's commitment to shares can be seen by how and with whom it shared ownership. As the company says, "All of Google's employees are also equity-holders, with significant collective employee ownership."[7] A conservative estimate is that Google is about 5 percent owned by its nonexecutive employees and has reserved almost 5 percent of its shares for future stock and stock option grants for the workforce. Thus, Google has made about a 10 percent employee ownership commitment to its employees. Just for perspective, all of Google's outside board members own less than 1 percent of the company, and the mutual fund companies Fidelity and Black Rock own only 7 percent and 5 percent, respectively, of Google. With other sources of employee ownership not publicly reported, the total staff ownership could perhaps be as high as 15–20 percent or more.

The commitment involves an annual decision to provide a "share homestead" to each Google worker. Each year a stock pie is cut up at Google. Less than 1 percent goes to the top executives. The other 99 percent goes to the broad group of workers.

In addition, Google rewards special individual and team accomplishments with shares. Google does not say what its total employee stock ownership is; however, with its commitment to doling out shares annually, and assuming Google workers buy some of its stock on the open market, there is no question that the company keeps replenishing the worker shares. If Google does well, the employees do well. As the company's sales and profits increase, Google employees can take part in that success. Google is a corporation that is a kind of federation of its original entrepreneurs, a broad group of workers, and stock market investors. Google is not just one story, because its combination of stock options and employee stock ownership represents one of the main broad-based capitalism combinations used in the country today, which is becoming increasingly common in science-based corporations.[8] The company goes to great lengths to assess the value of these ideas. One no-holds-barred analytical study of Google's share program found that the corporation's broad-based ownership significantly reduces turnover, improves some aspects of work performance that can be measured (this is certainly difficult in a software problem-solving company), and helps the company select better workers.[9]

Thus far Google has been one of the great successes of the Internet economy and seems likely to continue its success into the future. But whether based on broad-based ownership and employee participation or not, successful firms invariably run into problems as they deal with a dynamic changing market environment. Companies are not, nor should they be, immortal. The lesson from Google is that from its founding to its current prominence, it has relied on a sharing of capital ownership with its employees and that it attributes a good deal of its success to its broad-based ownership and employee decision making. The founders are astonishingly wealthy, but its workers have also done extremely well. Google's employees collectively have turned out to be exceptionally good entrepreneurs. The Global Equity Organization, a worldwide association of multinationals that share ownership broadly with their employees, gave Google a prize as a leader in using technology to share ownership and developing financial education programs for its associates.[10] The founders of Google invented many things, but they did not invent the share idea in the corporation. The most long-term sustained example of broad-based capitalism in a major corporation got its start with William Cooper Procter, who used it to transform his family's soap company into a giant in household products.

PROCTER & GAMBLE

Procter & Gamble is not a high-tech firm formed in recent years by West Coast entrepreneurs with technical degrees from Stanford. It was founded in Cincinnati, Ohio, in 1837 by William Procter, a candle maker, and James Gamble, a soap maker, to produce soap and candles—products that date back to ancient Babylon and Egypt. During the Civil War, P&G supplied the Union army with those products, which gave it a national brand name. In the 1880s it developed its signature product, Ivory Soap, which became one of most recognized brands in the world. Throughout this period P&G was an archetypical family-owned company, with ownership and control passed on to family descendants. When it went public early in its history, the company developed a widespread employee ownership program after years of pioneering the use of profit sharing. Many of its products are produced in small manufacturing facilities around the world. Yet, as the ultramodern firm it has become, P&G says that its research and development arm has more PhDs working in core areas than Yale, MIT, and the University of California-Berkeley because the corporation is so dependent on permanent innovation.

Today Procter & Gamble is the country's twenty-seventh-largest corporation, with 129,000 employees, making consumer products that all Americans use every day. In fact, it is the dominant household products maker in the nation. It has 20 percent of the world toothpaste market, 25 percent of the world fabric-care market, 30 percent of the feminine-care market, 35 percent of the baby-care market, and 40 percent of the paper towel market. Through its 2005 purchase of Gillette, which itself had a long history of employee stock ownership, it dominates the razor blade and shaving industry. It also sells foods of all types. P&G has profit sharing and broad employee stock ownership and is conservatively estimated to be about 10 percent employee owned, although it is possible that total employee ownership is as high as 20 percent or more. This corporate culture has withstood the test of repeated external evaluations. In 2012 *Fortune* magazine ranked P&G at ninth place on its list of the "World's Most Admired Companies." The company boasts that every single CEO of P&G started at the entry level. P&G made the Glassdoor list of the "50 Best Places to Work in the US" from 2009 through 2012, and has achieved many other accolades for its labor practices and commitment to operating as a socially responsible corporation.[11]

The notion that P&G might operate better if it shared profits with its workers came from the grandson of the Procter side founder, William Cooper Procter, who introduced the practice in 1887. Cooper Procter had learned about the potential value of broad-based profit sharing and employee ownership as an undergraduate from a required course in political economy at Princeton University in 1883. The course was given by Professor Lyman Atwater, one of the university's leading moral philosophers, who for years had been steering students through the understanding of broad ownership of property as the way to organize industry. We can document the influence of the course on young Procter because Professor Atwater's lecture notes survive. The press releases from Procter & Gamble when Procter first introduced broad-based profit sharing to the company in 1887 read practically like Professor Atwater's lecture notes.

But more went into the decision to introduce profit sharing than the transmission of knowledge from university to business. When Procter returned to Cincinnati from Princeton, he worked alongside the workers for a few years and then became general manager of the corporation. He brought to his management job an understanding of the attitudes and skills of the workforce. He came from a conservative Episcopalian family who hewed to the classical American ideal of the "yeoman farmer" and Judeo-Christian ideals of social justice. The family was active in the Republican Party. As leader of P&G, Procter struggled with ways to broaden the access to capital and capital income in huge growing manufacturing corporations. He saw the massive accumulation of capital in corporations as a possible solution to the growing inequality that William Findley and his compatriots feared would endanger democracy. Procter believed that corporations could become a mechanism to finance the accumulation of capital in which citizen-workers could share ownership. The corporation could use its dividends to fund purchases of share ownership for workers while sharing short-term profits with them. Early in the century he developed "Employee Conference" committees to solicit workers' suggestions and ideas. His speeches over the years are peppered with the republican ideology of the importance of ownership to the individual in society:[12]

> Our employees have been called "working capitalists." Perhaps the title is not too far afield. But to me it is of more significance to know that they are contented and happy. . . . Many of our innovations were born more of the earnest desire to foster this spirit of content, and to give our workers freer opportunity to express themselves, than of the mere wish to improve their finances. . . . The Employees' Conference Plan was, I believe, the first move of its kind in business history. . . . Together with the profit sharing, group insurance, and pension and benefit plans, it is simply in line with our conception of the square deal. . . . We thought that if we could create the idea of ownership or proprietorship, we would get that interest that would justify the profits. And so we adopted the plan of stock ownership. The chief problem of "big business" today is to shape its policies so that each worker, whether in office or factory, will feel he is a vital part of his company, with a personal responsibility for its success, and a chance to share in that success. . . . Such a step may be looked upon by other employers of labor as a doubtful experiment. . . . I myself have no fear of the result. . . . I believe that on the whole the efficiency of the plant has been increased.[13]

In the early 1900s, Ida Minerva Tarbell, renowned as one of the great muckraking journalists of her time, brought to national attention the story of William Cooper Procter and the P&G effort to increase workers' ownership stake in the economy. Tarbell, born in a log cabin in Hatch Hollow near Erie in western Pennsylvania, had been sufficiently angered at the business practices of the early Standard Oil, which had destroyed her father's small business, to research and write in 1904 *The History of the Standard Oil Company*, a classic piece of investigative journalism on American corporations. Her book was serialized in *McClure's Magazine*—the *Time* magazine of its day—where she served as the editor.

But she was more than a critical muckraker. She was also on the lookout for solutions to the problem between labor and capital created by the role of corporations in economic development. In 1916 she published *New Ideals in American Business*, which told the story of Procter & Gamble's policies to increase the worker's share in capitalism and provided a hardheaded evaluation of them. Workers making less than $1,500 a year in the 1920s could buy shares of Procter & Gamble stock financed mainly with cash profit-sharing payments and dividends. Workers contributed only very modest amounts from their weekly paycheck, so that the riskiness was kept within reasonable bounds. This is how William Cooper Procter applied the ideas of his teacher Lyman Atwater to finance the acquisition of property ownership by regular workers. Tarbell wrote:

> No successful stock ownership plan in the country is based on a longer experience or a firmer determination to find something practical than that of Procter & Gamble of Cincinnati. The scheme as first worked out was put before the employees of the concern—then between 450 and 500 persons—early in 1887. The firm believed it was possible to increase profits if they could increase "the diligence, carefulness, and thoughtful cooperation" of their employees. They

hoped to do this by sharing profits. . . . When this plan has been in operation 50 years the "wage earner" ought to have a respectable share in the business. . . . The present general superintendent of the manufacturing plants began as an office boy. . . . All the men who have risen and all who are acquiring stock are emphatic in their conviction that the policy makes for efficiency. . . . "Do you suppose I am going to let a new man come in an[d] loaf on his job or that I don't watch the leaks? It's my profits that I'm looking out for now," a man told me. . . . It's the old and tried American scheme for making a man brought up to date. But it does take brains, freedom from isms, humanity and a large firm sense of responsibility.[14]

The systems that Procter devised to help workers accumulate shares in their firm resonate with the approaches in place today. Selling shares to workers at a discount lies at the heart of employee stock purchase plans that many corporations offer workers. Procter combined cash profit sharing, dividends, and gradual payment plans with modest long-term investment programs to help workers become owners. His early approach reflects current practices of offering all employees stock options or grants of restricted stock that require no worker payment and the mechanism of financing employee stock ownership plans (ESOPs), which are not based on using worker savings at all. Procter was one of the first industrialists to experiment with employee suggestion committees and later set aside three seats on the firm's board of directors for worker-shareholders. He devoted a good deal of attention to personally appraising the effectiveness of the share ideas in his company.[15]

SOUTHWEST AIRLINES

Southwest Airlines is famous for being one of the great successes of the policy of deregulating the airline industry. From a small regional airline in 1971, it has become the largest low-cost carrier in the United States, with forty-six thousand employees around the country. Southwest is number 167 on the Fortune 500, with annual sales of about $16 billion. It wins awards for good service and for treating its workers well, and makes good profits to boot. Decade after decade, for thirty-nine years running, it has been the only consistently profitable U.S. airline.[16]

Southwest is also famous for being one of the most highly unionized firms in the United States and for having the most amicable relations with unions in the airline industry. It is the archetype special case in which broad-based employee sharing in company outcomes and collective bargaining work hand in hand to produce success. From 2010 to 2012, Glassdoor.com ranked Southwest Airlines as one of the twenty "Best Places to Work," giving it the number one spot in 2010. What is fascinating about Southwest's compensation philosophy is that the company says its system of rewards for executives, nonunion workers, and union workers is basically the same, that only the levels are different, depending on the person's responsibilities and his or her contract. The company does not report its total employee ownership, but it is estimated to be quite significant, close to 10 percent and possibly much more, given its long history of granting worker shares and the information that it does reveal.[17]

The story recounted in the *New York Times* of Southwest employee Mike Mitchel, who collected boarding passes and helped passengers into planes, illustrates how employees benefit from working at the firm and the way in which the airline operates. Mike helped start Southwest over forty years ago with eight flight attendants, five operations workers, and four executives. As he said in his newspaper interview, he is a multimillionaire because he received cash profit sharing from Southwest Airlines every year on top of his salary. "I could retire tomorrow. I like to save. I'll pick up a penny." His Southwest stock was worth almost $1 million in 2006, just a quarter of his portfolio. Every worker at Southwest from the chief executive officer to the ramp attendant owns a piece of the airline and shares in its profits. Each has stock in the company and cash profit sharing, and many have stock options, which Southwest awarded broadly for many years. Along with a capital stake in the airline, Southwest workers have what are widely considered in the industry to be generally fair wages. Another early employee, Deborah Stembridge, who began as a flight attendant, put the workers' situation this way: "My friends who left early at Southwest regret it so much." Dan Johnson started as a ramp worker in 1971. "This place has pushed employees to the breaking point. It's part of why we're successful. I don't need to work. In fact, I paid off the house two weeks ago."

Southwest has been committed to building capital ownership for all its employees, on top of negotiating with its unions for fair wages. The firm has a profit-sharing system through which workers receive profit-sharing payments that have ranged from 10 to 15 percent of their pay annually. Until recently, Southwest traditionally gave stock options to all its employees and not solely to executives, as many firms do. As a result, 90 percent of the company's outstanding stock options have been held by employees below the top executive level. Southwest also has a separate 401(k) pension plan where it does not allow workers to invest in company stock, thus giving them diversification in their retirement assets.

The reason Southwest has operated in this way is that management views employees as its greatest asset in the highly competitive air transportation industry. In his long career as head of Southwest, cofounder Herb Kelleher continually stressed the connection between a dedicated, satisfied workforce and shareholder value, which included workers as shareholders' partners. "If they're happy, satisfied, dedicated, and energetic, they'll take real good care of customers. When the customers are happy, they come back. And that makes shareholders happy." His successor, CEO Gary Kelly, has stated succinctly, "Our people are our single greatest strength and most enduring long-term competitive advantage." When passengers walk down the Southwest ramp to the airplane, they see the walls filled with the photographs of employees who also star in its commercials.

The company encourages a sense of ownership through what might be called freedom-based management—a term coined by former executives and business writers Bill Nobles and Paul Staley.[18] The airline brands itself as a "symbol of freedom," with freedoms for workers at the core of its culture: the freedom to create financial security, the freedom to pursue good health, the freedom to learn and grow, the freedom to make a positive difference, the freedom to work hard and have fun, the freedom to create and innovate, and the freedom to travel, which underscores, the free unlimited travel every Southwest worker and some family members have.

Freedom at Southwest means less hierarchical control, managers who share the vision for success with employees and act as aggressive coaches. It means organizing workers into small teams where everybody pitches in. It is not uncommon to see a pilot helping to clean an airplane. The company website says this about its culture: put others first, be egalitarian, follow the golden rule, desire to be the best. Researching her book *The Southwest Airlines Way*, which documented these practices and how many of these goals are realized, Brandeis University professor Jody Hoffer Gittell interviewed scores of workers and managers and compared Southwest to other airlines. She found that the culture of participation and the shared fates went hand in hand in the company. Workers acted like partners. They reduced costs because teamwork allowed them to achieve a high level of coordination. Teammates tended to monitor each other. Supervisors have frequent and intense interaction with teams and focus on coaching and feedback.

Workers are involved in selecting new employees through an intensive hiring process that tries to identify the relationship competence necessary to work well with coworkers and serve customers. Through its University for People (U4P) educational program, Southwest invests in intensive training to teach workers to develop strong working team-based relationships. U4P helps workers learn how to solve problems and manage their performance and that of their team. It provides leadership training, and offers courses on subjects such as team building, communications, and running effective meetings. One outcome is that Southwest's workers quit the company at a much lower rate than at other airlines.[19]

NOT THE ONLY BIG FISH IN THE OCEAN

Google, Procter & Gamble, and Southwest Airlines are exemplary firms in terms of business success and finding ways to share ownership with employees, but they are not the exceptions that "prove the rule" that skeptics of broad-based capitalist arrangements often make—that firms represent a small niche that cannot be expanded to spread capital ownership and capital income widely (Box 2.1).

BOX 2.1. CITIZENS' SHARES AMONG THE FORTUNE 100[1]

Exxon Mobil, the country's largest corporation, in oil and
energy, has had broad-based employee ownership plans
for decades, since John D. Rockefeller established one
of the earliest and most generous employee ownership
plans in 1919.

Chevron, the country's third-largest corporation, in
energy exploration, oil, natural gas, and chemicals, has
had broad-based employee ownership plans for decades, including an employee stock ownership plan.

ConocoPhillips, the country's fourth-largest corporation,
exploring and marketing crude oil and gas, has an
extensive broad-based employee stock ownership plan
and profit-sharing plan and has received the Global
Equity Organization Prize for creatively using technology to manage employee shares.

GM, the country's fifth-largest corporation, the bailed-out
and restructured automaker, has cash profit sharing and
broad-based stock options, while its unionized workers
and retirees' health plan owns a significant chunk of its
stock.

Ford Motor Company, the country's ninth-largest corporation, has an employee stock ownership plan and a
deferred profit-sharing plan for its salaried and hourly
employees, along with cash profit sharing, and is at
least 13 percent owned by its employees.

(continued)

BOX 2.1 *(continued)*

Apple Computers, the country's seventeenth-largest corporation, has a generous employee stock purchase plan that allows employees to buy up to $25,000 of the stock annually at a 15 percent discount. Apple employees who bought stock for the last seven years realized a reported 869 percent return on their investment. Apple reportedly also compensates some employees with meaningful grants of equity in addition to wages.

IBM, the country's nineteenth-largest corporation, an information technology company offering business solutions, encourages shares through its employee stock ownership plan, a deferred profit-sharing plan, and an employee stock purchase plan.

Procter & Gamble, the country's twenty-seventh-largest corporation, making consumer products, pioneered many of the forms of equity and profit sharing during the late 1880s as big business was first emerging and has a large employee stock ownership plan.

Microsoft, the country's thirty-seventh-largest corporation, a leader in software and the Internet, beginning in 1986, pioneered broad-based employee ownership in the software industry, has continually updated these benefits, is ranked number seventy six on *Fortune*'s "100 Best Companies to Work For" list in 2012, and has been a winner in that competition in several recent years.

Johnson & Johnson, the country's forty-second-largest corporation, has a long history of offering workers a share of the profits and ownership as a result of the writings of Robert Wood Johnson II early in the twentieth century and has a significant employee stock ownership plan.

Intel, the country's fifty-first-largest corporation, making the chips that power computers, has broad-based employee ownership and profit sharing (and pioneered the idea early in Silicon Valley's history), received the Global Equity Organization Prize for financial education of workers and the most effective ownership plan, ranked number forty six on *Fortune*'s "100 Best Companies to Work For" list in 2012, and has been a winner in that competition in several recent years.

United Parcel Service, the country's fifty-second-largest corporation, the delivery and logistics company, has substantial broad-based employee ownership with a long history.

Amazon.com, the country's fifty-sixth-largest corporation, an online retailer and information and hardware seller, has had broad-based employee ownership since its founding and gives restricted stock to most employees. Its spokesman says, "Employee ownership is part of our DNA. We're not going to do anything to subtract from that."[2]

Coca-Cola, the country's fifty-ninth-largest corporation, has a broad-based profit-sharing and employee stock ownership plan for both its nonunion and union employees.

Cisco Systems, the country's sixty-fourth-largest corporation, maker of the technology that runs the Internet, has broad-based profit sharing, gain sharing, and

(continued)

BOX 2.1 *(continued)*

employee ownership, with a president and CEO, John Chambers, who has been one of the most vocal executives discussing such ideas in the media. It ranked number ninety on *Fortune*'s "100 Best Companies to Work For" list in 2012 and has been a winner in that competition in several recent years.

Morgan Stanley, the country's sixty-eighth-largest corporation, in financial services and investment banking, has substantial broad-based employee ownership and identifies itself as a corporation where employee share ownership is a central value.

Abbott Laboratories, the country's seventy-first-largest corporation, maker of pharmaceutical and nutritional products, has broad-based profit sharing and employee stock ownership and won a Global Equity Organization Prize for establishing one of the world's leading financial education program for its workers.

Google, the country's seventy-third-largest corporation, has broad-based employee ownership and profit sharing, is a repeated winner of the Global Equity Organization Prize, and ranked number one on *Fortune*'s "100 Best Companies to Work For" list in 2012 and has been a top winner in that competition for several years.

Honeywell, the country's seventy-seventh-largest corporation, which invents and manufactures diverse technologies, has broad-based employee stock ownership and profit sharing.

Goldman Sachs, the country's eightieth-largest corporation, an investment bank, has substantial broad-based
employee ownership and a gain sharing plan, ranked
number thirty three on *Fortune*'s "100 Best Companies
to Work For" list in 2012 and has been a winner in
several recent years.

General Dynamics, the country's ninety-second-largest
corporation, has significant broad-based employee stock
ownership and has a long history of encouraging
employee stockholding.[3]

1 Because of the extent of these employee stock ownership plans
nationwide, most of the largest financial service corporations in the
United States have "employee stock plan services" divisions that help
companies administer the plans. They are affiliated in the American
Coalition of Stock Plan Administrators at: http://www.acspa.info
/members.html. The Fortune 500 was developed by *Fortune* magazine
and is available online at: http://money.cnn.com/magazines/fortune
/fortune500/2012/full_list/ (accessed September 29, 2012). The
criteria for inclusion on our list are : (1) detailed public information
on the company's website (beyond simple mention) about employee
stock ownership or share plans; (2) detailed public documentation of
the plans in either the company's U.S. Securities and Exchange
Commission filings or public media reports in Dow Jones & Company's dataset of newspapers and newswires which goes back twenty
years (called Factiva); and (or) (3) public information on the plans at
Brightscope (www.brightscope.com), a financial information
company that provides public information on employee investment
plans based on filings on those plans made by the corporations
themselves to the federal government. Where Brightscope is the sole
basis of the listing, evidence of a significant role of employee stock

(continued)

BOX 2.1 *(continued)*

ownership relative to the size of the employment base was required along with a "Highest Rating in Peer Group" score or close to the highest score by Brightscope or high scores on most components of the plan. Brightscope evaluates each plan by describing the role of employee stock ownership and then grading it in terms of company generosity, participation rate of employees, whether the assets accumulated by employees are meaningful, the total cost of the plan, and other features. A key criterion is that these sources indicate that the plan is broad-based, namely, includes most (more than 51%) of the company's employees. Joseph Blasi also conducted supplementary management interviews for: Procter & Gamble, Microsoft, Intel, Cisco, Morgan Stanley, and Abbott Laboratories. Some company websites provide additional relevant detail. For ConocoPhillips, see http://www.conocophillips.com/EN/careers/cop_careers/benefits/ additionalbenefits-us/pages/index.aspxhttp://www.conocophillips. com/EN/susdev/ourpeople/compensation/incentives/Pages/index .aspx. On ConocoPhillips award for Best Use of Technology, see http://globalequity.org/geo/geoawardrecipients for 2011. On Johnson & Johnson, see Robert Wood Johnson II, *People Must Live and Work Together or Forfeit Freedom* (Garden City, N.Y.: Doubleday, 1947); Lawrence G. Foster, *Robert Wood Johnson—The Gentlemen Rebel* (State College, Pa.: Lillian Press, 1999), 403, 527. On Intel, see Blasi, Kruse, and Bernstein, *In the Company of Owners*, 3–30. See also, Intel Corporation, *Intel Proxy Statement* (Washington, D.C.: U.S. Securities and Exchange Commission, April 4, 2012), 33, for the firm's statement on employee stock ownership. On Intel's receiving the GEO Prize for Best Plan Effectiveness and Financial Education, see http:// globalequity.org/geo/geoawardrecipients for 2011 and 2008. On the Abbott Laboratories GEO Prize, see http://globalequity.org/geo /geoawardrecipients for 2012. On IBM, see the company benefits brochure, 14–15 at: http://www-01.ibm.com/employment/us /benefits/2012_Benefits_Brochure.pdf. On Apple, see http://www .apple.com/jobs/us/benefits.html and Troy Onink, "$1.6 million for

Apple Employees, Up $500,000 in Six Months," *Forbes*, March 14, 2012, available at http://www.forbes.com/sites/troyonink/2012/03 /14/1-6-million-for-apple-employees-up-500000-in-six-months/. Estimates of the amount that employee ownership "at least" consti- tutes for Ford Motor Company and for IBM are based on the authors' analyses of the U.S. Department of Labor's 2008 Form 5500 filed by these corporations with the federal government on the stock holdings of their employee benefit plans. The authors would like to note that the public reporting for share plans needs to be simplified and standardized given the wide variation between corporations in the level of detail made public above the minimum required. This table is based on our best efforts to analyze and to report publicly available data given the quality of those public data. The authors would also like to thank Ilona Babenko of Arizona State University for her input.

2 Quoting Amazon.com spokesman Bill Currey in Jeff D. Opdyke and Michelle Higgins, "What the New Option Rules Mean for Your Pay," *Wall Street Journal*, August 7, 2002.

3 On General Dynamics, see http://www.generaldynamics.com /careers/benefits/. See also "General Dynamics Boosts Dividend, Remains Mum on Big Payout," *Aerospace Daily and Defense Report*, March 12, 1992, 411.

The case evidence is not limited to these firms. About 10 to 20 percent of the 4,500 corporations whose stock is traded on the New York Stock Exchange and the NASDAQ exchange have meaningful employee stock ownership. We estimate that among the Fortune 100, twenty-one companies, or about 20 percent, emphasize broad-based capitalism in their business cultures. These include leading firms in technology, finance, transportation, energy, retail, and consumer products. Some of their stories resemble those of Google, Procter & Gamble, and Southwest Airlines, while others represent more modest commitments. We estimate that about 10 percent of the companies in the Fortune 500 have employee stock ownership of between 5 percent and 20 percent. Other estimates suggest that about 20 percent of the largest thousand corporations on stock markets have broad-based share ownership plans, although almost half of them have modest employee ownership programs. Some have employee stock purchase plans that allow workers to buy stock at a discount. Some have lower-risk employee stock ownership plans that finance the purchase of stock for workers through loans or company contributions and grant stock to workers for which the workers do not pay. Sometimes ESOP stock matches employee contributions to 401(k) plans. Some plans allow workers to buy stock with wages in 401(k) plans. Others have stock options where workers obtain the right to buy stock into the future at today's stock price, thus sharing any increase in the stock. Now more common than stock options are other plans that grant workers restricted stock that they receive as long as they stay with the company.[20]

In addition to firms on the stock exchanges, the United States has many privately held large companies, a substantial number of which have also chosen some form of worker ownership or profit sharing with their employees (Box 2.2). Seventeen of the one hundred largest private corporations in the country that *Forbes* magazine ranks annually in "America's Largest Private Companies" have meaningful citizen's shares. Some of them are also in the Fortune 500. While each company is seeking a "partnership culture" with its employees, another major reason these companies use employee ownership is that it allows them to stay off the volatile public stock markets. New and departing employees create an internal market for the stock, allowing the original family investors to occasionally turn part of their ownership into cash and making it possible for departing employees to sell their stock to new employees. In one study, J. Robert Beyster recounts the story of building such an employee-owned company, SAIC, and the challenges of keeping it private versus going public.[21] Cargill, a major producer of agricultural products, is another major privately held company with a broad-based system of worker ownership or profit sharing with its employees. Other leaders doing forms of profit sharing are Fidelity Investments, a major provider of mutual funds and administrator and broker for employee stock plans, and Bloomberg News, which has become one of the most successful and innovative sources of news on business and government activities and owns and publishes *Business Week* magazine.

Many of these corporations have won repeated national and regional prizes for their company cultures. Each year *Fortune* magazine sponsors the "100 Best Companies to Work For" competition. The companies are identified through employee surveys based on a sample of workers, and management-practice surveys administered to managers conducted by the Great Place to Work Institute. Corporations with broad-based employee ownership or profit sharing regularly represent about half of the national

BOX 2.2. CITIZENS' SHARES AMONG AMERICA'S LARGEST PRIVATE CORPORATIONS[1]

Cargill, the country's largest privately held corporation, an international producer and marketer of food with 127,000 workers and $110 billion in annual sales, has broad-based employee ownership through an employee stock ownership plan, which has helped keep the company private.

Mars, the country's third-largest privately held corporation, a producer of chocolate, candy, and other foods, with 65,000 employees and $65 billion in annual sales, has a form of profit sharing.

Publix, the country's sixth-largest privately held corporation and number 106 on the Fortune 500, is a supermarket chain with 148,000 employees and annual sales of $27 billion; it has been named one of *Fortune* magazine's "100 Best Companies to Work For" from 1998 to 2012 and is 100 percent worker owned through an employee stock ownership plan.

Fidelity Investments, the country's twentieth-largest privately held corporation, an international provider of financial services with 38,000 employees and $38 billion in annual sales, has broad-based profit sharing.

S. C. Johnson & Sons, the country's twenty-ninth-largest privately held corporation, a maker of household, storage, pest control, and auto care products, with 12,000 employees and an estimated $9 billion in annual sales, has broad-based profit sharing, has been one of the leaders of the Council on Profit Sharing Industries in the country since the 1950s, and has been a regular winner of *Fortune*'s "100 Best Companies to Work For" competition since 2006.

Bloomberg, the country's forty-fourth-largest privately held corporation, a supplier of business and financial news information, with 13,000 employees and an estimated $7 billion in annual sales, has a broad-based form of profit and gain sharing.

Wawa, the country's forty-seventh-largest privately held corporation, an operator of convenience stores and gas stations in the Middle Atlantic States, with 18,000 employees and $7 billion in annual sales, is about a third employee owned through an employee stock ownership plan.

Hy-Vee, the country's forty-eighth-largest privately held corporation, a Midwest supermarket and retail store chain, with 56,000 employees and an estimated annual sales of about $7 billion, is majority employee owned through an employee stock ownership plan and was an early innovator in the country with employee bonuses and profit sharing.

Wegmans Food Markets, the country's fifty-fifth-largest privately held corporation, a regional supermarket chain with 42,000 employees and about $6 billion in annual sales, has broad-based profit sharing and has been recognized by placing in the top five in *Fortune*'s "100 Best Companies to Work For" competition every year since 2006.

(continued)

BOX 2.2 *(continued)*

CH2M Hill Companies, the country's fifty-sixth-largest privately held corporation and number 440 on the Fortune 500, a full service engineering, construction, and operation firm, with 23,000 employees and about $6 billion in annual sales, is majority employee owned through an employee stock ownership plan and has been on *Fortune*'s "100 Best Companies to Work For" list in 2006, 2008, 2009, and 2011.

Sheetz, the country's fifty-eighth-largest privately held corporation, with 14,000 employees and an estimated $5 billion in annual sales, has a broad-based employee stock ownership plan.

WinCo Foods, the country's sixty-sixth-largest privately held corporation, a supermarket chain in the western part of the United States, with 14,000 employees and about $5 billion in annual sales, is majority employee owned through an employee stock ownership plan.

Graybar Electric, the country's sixty-ninth-largest privately held corporation and number 451 on the Fortune 500, an electrical equipment wholesaler, with 7,000 employees and about $5 billion in annual sales, is majority employee owned through an employee stock ownership plan.

Edward Jones, the country's eighty-third-largest privately held corporation, with 37,000 employees and about $4 billion in annual sales, is a partnership with a third of the employees being partners and has won *Fortune*'s

"100 Best Companies to Work For" competition every year from 2006 to 2012.

Hallmark Cards, the country's ninety-fifth-largest privately held corporation, a maker of greeting cards, paper, and party supplies, with 13,000 employees and estimated annual sales of about $4 billion, has had broad-based profit sharing for many decades, is widely considered to be a leader in that area, and was one of the first members of the Council on Profit Sharing Industries.

1 "America's Largest Private Companies" was developed by *Forbes* magazine and is published online at http://www.forbes.com/lists /2011/21/private-companies-11_rank.html (accessed on January 24, 2012). Estimates of sales were provided by *Forbes* or by the company for *Forbes*. Information on the companies is from the websites of the companies and the National Center for Employee Ownership's "Employee Ownership One Hundred: America's Largest Majority Employee-Owned Companies" at http://www.nceo .org/main/article.php/id/11/printable/y/ (accessed on January 24, 2012). Private companies tend to give more detail on their websites about their commitment to employee ownership and profit sharing. Some books have been written about these companies. Cargill's ESOP is also discussed in detail in Wayne G. Broehl Jr., *Cargill: From Commodities to Customers* (Hanover, N.H.: Dartmouth University Press, 2008): 113–120, 182–189, 204, 210–212. The Cargill ESOP is called the Cargill Partnership Plan. It is highly rated by Brightscope for employee participation and large account balances and is a major investor in Cargill's common stock. On Mars, see http:// www.mars.com/global/about-mars/mars-pia/working-at-mars/pay -and-benefits.aspx and http://www.mars.com/global/careers/your -mars/us-experienced-hire/rewards-and-benefits.aspx. On Publix, see Joseph W. Carvin, *A Piece of the Pie: The Story of Customer Service at Publix* (Lakeland, Fla.: Publix Supermarkets, 2005) and http://

(continued)

www.publix.com/about/PublixHistory.do and http://www.publix.
com/careers/whypublix/OurBenefits.do. On Fidelity, see http://jobs
.fidelity.com/benefits/retirement/benefits_retirement.shtml. On S.
C. Johnson, see http://www.scjohnson.com/en/Careers/culture
/benefits.aspx. On Wawa, see http://www.wawa.com/wawaweb
/WhyJoin.aspx. On Hy-Vee, see http://www.hy-vee.com/company
/about-hy-vee/default.aspx. http://www.hy-vee.com/company
/careers/benefits.aspx. On Sheetz, see http://sheetzjobz.com/great
-benefits.html. http://www.ch2m.com/corporate/about_us
/employee_ownership/default.asp. On WinCo, see http://www.win-
cofoods.com/about/. On Edward Jones, see http://careers.edward-
jones.com/us/boa/BenefitsCompensation/index.html and http://
careers.edwardjones.com/us/headquarters/BenefitsCompensation
/index.html. On Hallmark, see http://corporate.hallmark.com
/OurCulture/Beliefs-And-Values and http://www.hallmark.com
/careers/benefits/. The authors would like to note that the public
reporting for share plans of large private companies needs to be
simplified and standardized given the wide variation between
corporations in the level of detail made public. This table is based
on our best efforts to report publicly available data given the
quality of those public data.

winners. Each year the Global Equity Organization, a group of
multinationals with broad employee ownership plans, also se-
lects companies considered leaders in this area by their peers.[22]
In short, well-known corporations with widely shared employee
financial participation have taken their place among all these
groups of major corporations.

SMALL AND MEDIUM ESOP BUSINESSES:
THE CASE OF COMSONICS

Today, almost all majority employee ownership and 100 per-cent employee share plans are done through an ESOP. Workers receive grants of stock from their company that they do not have to purchase with their savings or wages. Typically, the company sets up a trust that accumulates company stock for employees through company contributions or loans that the company takes out to buy the stock. A bank or other lender has to approve the loan based on an evaluation that the company can pay it back. The stock is granted to most workers based on salary. Because workers do not pay for the stock with their wages, this form of employee ownership has lower risk. The ComSonics Corpora-tion in Virginia, with over two hundred workers, is one example of an ESOP story.[23]

In the 1930s Warren Braun and his friend Norman Baird were called "the mad scientists." Braun's local Virginia news-paper, the *Valley Business*, in the historic Shenandoah Valley, put it this way: "The friends always seemed to be making gadgets or fixing radios for free. In the 1930s, they invented a score-board and operated it from the bleachers at high school basket-ball games." Over the years Braun's local paper chronicled his story and the variety of capitalism that he built with his fellow employees.

Braun is an electrical engineer who built the first cable TV system in Harrisonburg and managed a TV station there as a young man. When he was fired, he started a consulting practice to support his family. He collected a few friends, whom his wife called "the boys in the basement." They tried to use their smarts to find solutions to technical problems that customers brought to them, while continuing to work out of Braun's basement. Braun had a knack for making history. In 1968, he was working on an invention that could stitch together multiple callers on a telephone line for a popular TV call-in show, *Night Calls*. On April 4, when Martin Luther King Jr. was assassinated, the producers of *Night Calls* thought Warren's invention could help quiet the violent reaction that began to spread across the country. Braun drove to a radio station in Harlem and used his machine to help a national network of four hundred radio stations take calls from black leaders in communities around the country and help these key community leaders stay on the air for two days.

Braun and his colleagues went on to invent other technologies and manufacture other machinery for the cable TV industry and other industries. Soon Braun moved from the basement and founded a company. He had strong views about companies. "I've always had the tremendous feeling . . . [that companies] were throwing away a lot of talent by not allowing employees to participate. I really believe that part of what people earn by doing their jobs is the right to participate in the ownership of the company. I felt the employees made the company. I believed the managers made the company go, but in the end it's the employees that made the company what it is, the employees and managers working together as a team." Like the Google founders, Braun started off owning 100 percent of his little company, but he wanted to develop it and build it.

Warren Braun found that there was no easy way to develop far-reaching broad-based employee share ownership in the corporation in 1972. By 1975, the employee stock ownership plan, part of the first congressional legislation to address this problem, had been written into federal law, based on the work of its creator, lawyer and investment banker Louis O. Kelso, and the influential legislator Senator Russell Long of Louisiana. Braun decided that his company, ComSonics, would be one of the first ESOPs in the nation and sought Kelso's counsel.

The company set up an ESOP. The ESOP initially took out a loan to buy 20 percent of Braun's stock, then another 19 percent, and finally the ESOP took out a loan in 1985 to buy the rest of the stock with an eight-year repayment term, making the company 100 percent ESOP owned. This was not redistribution of wealth. Braun received payment for his stock. The local banker's belief in the business plan of the enterprise, which showed that the ongoing profits could pay back the loan, enabled the workers to become owners. Braun liked the idea that workers did not have to buy the stock with their savings. In the Com-Sonics case, bank credit for an ESOP to buy the company stock was the answer, with collateral provided by the company itself. As the loan was paid back, workers received a stake in American capitalism, and the value of the stock went up as the sales of the company increased. Since ComSonics was a closely held corporation, it was insulated from many of the ups and downs on the public stock markets. This was just another advantage for a regional firm with national sales but focused on doing its work rather than being followed on public stock markets.

ComSonics today has locations in Virginia, California, and Indiana. It also has a subsidiary in Weyers Cave, Virginia, that does manufacturing for the business as well as other companies. Braun, who retired in 1990, believed that employee-owners to some extent could become their own managers. The current chairman and chief executive officer, Dennis Zimmerman, sees the employee ownership as stabilizing the culture and providing local control. "Warren Braun wanted to empower employees as owners, but it was also a way to sell the company without seeing the culture destroyed. It provides a common currency from employees to managemen—the stock. It's a flattening of the debate." Like Google, Procter & Gamble, and Southwest Airlines, ComSonics developed a distinctive culture. The company went on to use profit sharing, too. Employees are encouraged to take courses at company expense to upgrade their skills. The company has an award-winning employee communications committee. The elected chair of the committee becomes a full voting member of the board of directors.

Over the years, the local newspaper, the *Valley Business*, continued to follow the company. "We are controlling our own destiny," Miles Sandin, a management information systems administrator at ComSonics, told the paper. "It's worth it for all of us to bust our backsides to make the stock value go up. . . . It's an interesting environment to work in. . . . People tend to look out more, because it's their company." The former chief financial officer, Bill McIntyre, explained the company's view of information sharing: "Basically, we just started giving employees a lot of information. You give each person in the company the information they need to make the decisions needed for their job. That was at a minimum. We also made total company financial information available to everyone." McIntyre is now a program coordinator at the Ohio Employee Ownership Center, which works with small manufacturing companies across Ohio to support many employee ownership plans and help companies convert to employee share ownership.

At the end of 2009, the average ComSonics employee had an ESOP account worth about $85,000. Workers also have a separate 401(k) plan not invested in company stock, to provide diversification. Many companies like ComSonics have gone on for decades; some build up a lot of value and are sold, with employees getting paid handsomely for their stakes. ComSonics is not just one story. Many of the workers in the United States with broad-based capitalism have the ComSonics combination of worker-owned stock and some cash profit sharing.[24]

By 2013, there were an estimated 10,300 corporations with ESOPs and similar plans, mostly small- and medium-size businesses, with just over 10 million workers and almost a trillion dollars in total value. They are a test bed of broad-based capitalism. Several features are distinctive about ESOPs. One is that the workers do not buy the shares with their wages or savings, but the company typically borrows money with federal tax incentives to buy shares that are distributed to workers as the loan is paid back. If the company does well, workers share in the value of that performance. ESOPs sort companies for management ability. They make possible purchases of companies by existing managers and workers where a management team is already in place or by a new management team has been approved by lenders.

Given the volatility of public stock markets, the fact that most ESOPs are not on stock exchanges provides some insulation. Finally, an increasing number of ESOPs are majority or completely worker owned by managers and rank-and-file employees, unlike the smaller or more modest employee ownership stakes we find in stock market corporations.[25]

Every year *Fortune* reports on the results of the competition to be named to its "100 Best Companies to Work For" list. Indicative of the way firms with ESOPs or other forms of broad-based ownership or profit sharing treat their employees, as we have seen, a significant proportion of the winners in each years' contest have ESOPs and other forms of broad-based capitalism. Peer groups of these firms also recognize the exemplars and leaders among them with national and state awards.[26] Some of these companies' names are easily recognizable because they have national sales markets. For example, Herff Jones sells class rings and yearbooks in all fifty states. Its name is noticeable on products in middle schools and high schools throughout the country. Majority employee-owned Parsons, an engineering and consulting company, has built some of Newark's new public school buildings, NASA's Goddard Space Flight Center, the Sheraton Phoenix, and the Interstate 90 bridge over Biloxi Bay in Mississippi. These are the larger ESOPs. Box 2.3 shows some examples of ESOPs of all sizes in different regions of the country.

A smaller yet notable part of the small business sector are companies organized as cooperatives. One example, showing how versatile the worker cooperative form can be, even in a high-technology industry, is Isthmus Engineering and Manufacturing in Madison, Wisconsin, where skilled workers design custom automation solutions and equipment. Worker cooperatives have also proven effective in jump-starting community-based economic development in some of the poorest neighborhoods in the country. The Evergreen Cooperatives of Cleveland have started out small, but they are oriented to build and create jobs in the community and work closely with anchor institutions like the Cleveland Clinic as customers. They are the most important model in helping vulnerable populations.[27]

ENTREPRENEURIAL START-UPS

Giving workers a piece of the pie is central to the culture of start-ups. The form of broad-based capitalism perhaps closest to the yeoman farmer developing a new plot of land into a workable farm is the entrepreneurial start-up. This is when an innovator comes up with a new idea and starts a business from

BOX 2.3. EMPLOYEE STOCK OWNERSHIP PLANS (ESOPS) AROUND THE COUNTRY[1]

Acadian Ambulance (Lafayette, LA), a 100 percent employee-owned emergency medical transportation company

Bobs Red Mill (Milwaukie, OR), a 100 percent employee-owned seller of whole grains

Burns & McDonnell (Kansas City, MO), a 100 percent employee-owned engineering, architectural, construction, and environmental consulting firm

Chart Rehabilitation (Honolulu), a 100 percent employee-owned provider of physical and occupational therapy services

Dansko (West Grove, PA), a 100 percent employee-owned maker of footwear

EBO Group (Sharon Center, OH), a 100 percent employee-owned manufacturer of mining equipment, motorized medical stretcher-chairs, photovoltaic solar systems, and drive modules for electric vehicles

Eileen Fisher (Irvington, NY), a 33 percent employee-owned designer of women's fashions

Entertainment Partners (Burbank, CA), a 100 percent employee-owned production management company for Hollywood film productions

King Arthur Flour (Norwich, VT), a 100 percent employee-owned flour and baking products corporation

(continued)

BOX 2.3 *(continued)*

New Belgium Brewing (Fort Collins, CO), a 33 percent
  employee-owned maker of Fat Tire beer

Padilla Speer Beardsley (Minneapolis and New York City),
  a 100 percent employee-owned public relations firm
  handling social media, media relations, public affairs,
  crisis management, consumer marketing, and business-
  to-business marketing

Pre-tech Precision Machining (Williston, VT), a majority
  employee-owned manufacturer of precision biomedical,
  environmental, aerospace, and semiconductor industry
  applications

Rable Machine Company (Mansfield, OH), a 100 percent
  employee-owned high-tech custom machining
  company

S&C Electric (Chicago), a 100 percent employee-owned
  global provider of equipment for electric power systems

Scot Forge (Spring Grove, IL), a 100 percent employee-
  owned manufacturer of custom forgings in a variety of
  industries, including the nuclear submarine sector

Sun Automation (Sparks, MD), a 100 percent employee-
  owned automation equipment manufacturer

W. L. Gore & Associates (Newark, DE), a majority
  employee-owned inventor of Gore-Tex that manufactures fabric laminates, medical implants, and diverse
  fiber technologies

Will-Burt Company (Orrville, OH), a 100 percent
  employee-owned manufacturer of telescoping mast and

tower elevation technology for surveillance, communications antenna, and scene lighting systems

1 This list is based on a selection of majority and 100% employee-owned ESOPs around the United States by the authors in order to be representative of service, manufacturing, and high-technology industries, different regions of the country, and privately held corporations with Employee Stock Ownership Plans that had websites where the corporation self-identified as majority and 100% employee-owned. The authors would like to thank the ESOP Association and Loren Rodgers, the executive director of the National Center for Employee Ownership, for helping us identify some of these firms by region and industry and Trevor Young-Hyman, a PhD candidate in the Department of Sociology at the University of Wisconsin at Madison for helping us identify some of these firms that are in the high-technology manufacturing field.

scratch. The use of broad-based profit sharing in Silicon Valley was pioneered by William Hewlett and David Packard in 1938 with the founding of their little electronics company in a Palo Alto garage.[28] Typically, as Princeton University entrepreneurship expert Martin Ruef has found in his book *The Entrepreneurial Group,* an entrepreneur uses savings, loans from family and friends, and some small bank and government loans to get started until the product or service creates enough profit to grow on its own.[29] Early in the process, the entrepreneur assembles a small group that helps create the firm and discusses how to divide up shares, and it usually uses shares to recruit new employees into the very risky and unpredictable project. Apple and Google started in a garage in Silicon Valley. The Procters and the Gambles stumbled upon the recipe for Ivory Soap by accident. Start-ups have limited funds to pay wages in the beginning, so they offer employees shares of the firm in lieu of higher compensation.

Start-ups typically begin as a sole proprietorship or a partnership of two or three people. The story of Bill Gates and Microsoft is an informative case. Gates's first product was the invention of a tic-tac-toe game that could be played between a computer and a person. As a math student at Harvard, he had worked out a solution to the mathematical "pancake sorting problem" in which one tries to flip a stack of pancakes into a particular order, with the smallest number of reversals. Gates and his mathematics professor published the paper, and for thirty years it stood as the best solution to the problem.[30]

After Gates dropped out of Harvard, he and Paul Allen formed Microsoft, which began by paying lower wages to early employees but added annual profit-sharing bonuses. When the firm incorporated in 1975, Gates owned 53 percent and Paul Allen owned 31 percent, with the rest split among Steve Ballmer—later to become CEO with 8 percent—and a few others. To attract more workers, the firm used grants of stock options. Gates explained his feelings about spreading employee ownership this way: "We never thought that offering stock options to all of our employees—instead of just to executives, like other companies did—was really that innovative. It seemed totally natural to us. Even back then I felt that great programmers were just as important as great management. If we gave all the options to management, we couldn't hire the best developers." While not all start-ups turn into large stock market companies, Microsoft illustrates how sharing equity was a seamless part of the story. By 2012 Gates owned about 6 percent of the firm, and Ballmer, the new head of the company, owned about 4 percent. But the total market value of the company was over $230 billion.

Over many decades, Microsoft developed and then perfected an extensive program of broad-based employee ownership. Each year the company has granted over 90 percent of its stock options and stock to its nonexecutive employees. As Gates granted more stock options to Microsoft's workers over the years and sold stock to the public, his ownership interest went down, but he ended up owning a smaller percentage of a much larger pie. Talking about employee ownership, Ballmer told us that it "has been a successful practice for our company," and added, "It's clear that a sense of ownership seems to be strongly linked to corporate success in many industries." Microsoft now uses stock grants rather than stock options to give workers a direct ownership stake. Today, Microsoft is about 5 percent owned by its employees and has reserved shares to distribute another 8 percent of ownership to its workers. With other sources of employee ownership not publicly reported, we estimate that the company's worker ownership could be as high as 15 to 20 percent.[31]

It is hard to get information on start-ups, but they are a nursery for employee ownership. When some schoolkids set up their lemonade stand in the summer, this start-up will surely fall beneath the nation's statistical radar screen. But once firms reach some status, they will surface on government and other data sets. They have to hire people, pay taxes, and so on. A national source of information on such small firms is Dow Jones VentureOne, which keeps track of about ten thousand entrepreneurial start-up firms that have some form of venture capital investment, possibly from investors like Arthur Rock & Company. A venture capitalist collects funds from investors to buy stock in these companies early, before they hopefully go public. One survey indicates that about three-quarters of these firms give stock options to about 90 percent of their workers, while more than three-quarters of start-ups say that all their workers receive stock options. Another survey finds that nonfounder employees own about 15 percent of start-up companies and gain ownership in about half of them. Others give actual grants of stock broadly, rather than options. If these companies find a product or service that attracts a market, they are likely to continue to practice wide employee share ownership, and they may eventually go public and turn into a Google or a Microsoft. Some of them want to stay away from the volatile public stock markets forever.[32]

Two of this book's authors, Joseph Blasi and Douglas Kruse, and former *Business Week* associate editor Aaron Bernstein, in their book *In the Company of Owners*, took a closer look at the one hundred corporations emerging from start-ups that survived into the early 2000s. These corporations invented, wrote software for, made equipment for, and sold products or services on the Internet. This was a case where an entire industry moved rapidly toward citizens' shares. These hundred survivors of the risky start-up stage ultimately listed their shares on the New York Stock Exchange or the NASDAQ. Virtually every corporation shared ownership with most of the workers. In interviews we conducted with entrepreneurs in two start-up regions, Silicon Valley and the Seattle area around Microsoft, we found that many of the founders spoke of creating a work culture that encouraged collaboration and wide responsibility for results. By 2003, nonexecutive employees had about one-fifth of the equity of these companies, in most cases, as the Microsoft story shows—more than the founders, the board, and any individual venture capital or institutional investor.

Start-ups are not for the risk averse or lighthearted. Many Internet start-ups failed along the way, and some of the companies were bought by other companies, with the workers turning their stock into wealth before the firms ever went public, so only about a small fraction actually went public. Once these corporations were more mature and their stock was growing at a slower clip than booming companies like Google, they tended to switch away from stock options to cash profit sharing and whole grants of company stock to the workers. This pattern is now being repeated in the fields of biotechnology, nanotechnology, and other emerging technologies. Early on, workers take lower fixed pay and settle for stock options or grants of stock as a reward, if the company survives. The core founding members do invest their own money and that of their friends and family, all of which can be lost. These companies are the nurseries of new technologies, they are where those medium and large corporations sprout, yet they represent the most perilous form of citizens' shares.[33]

FAILURES AND CHALLENGES

The successful examples highlighted in this chapter do not mean that increasing the property stake of workers through employee stock ownership, profit sharing, or broad-based stock option systems invariably succeeds in improving economic outcomes. Firms that use shares can fail, just as do more traditional firms (though, as we see in Chapter 5, at a lower rate). Moreover, sometimes when employee share ownership, profit sharing, all-employee stock options, or stock grants lead a firm to perform better, its success may also come at the expense of the rest of society. Pirates have a long tradition of sharing the loot that they seize from other vessels and creating nothing of value for society. It is possible for workers to invest too much of their assets in their firm and become overly dependent on the performance of the firm for their own basic economic well-being. The cases of failures of broad-based capitalist arrangements that we examine next show that these are not abstract concerns.

Enron, WorldCom, and Lehman Brothers

This House of Horrors has the following names in big lights: Enron, WorldCom, and Lehman Brothers. These three firms encouraged workers to buy company shares with their wages and savings while misleading them about the risks that the company faced. According to government investigations and numerous books, the managements of Enron and WorldCom committed fraud on their employee-owners and other shareholders, on their suppliers, and on their customers. Lehman Brothers got deeply involved in very risky markets while playing with huge worker stakes in the firm without a truly independent and objective system of corporate governance at the board level. Its mode of compensation allowed management and shareholders to profit from short-run changes in the share price while its worker-owners did not have that opportunity.

Enron began as a holding company that dealt with energy and energy-related products, transmitting and distributing electricity and natural gas, owning power plants and pipelines throughout the United States. From 1996 to 2001, *Fortune* magazine named Enron "America's Most Innovative Company." The CEO and later chairman of the firm, Kenneth Lay (who later faced trial and conviction but died before any sentence was issued, so his conviction was abated), played a large role in attempting to get government to let the industry operate as it wished. Enron did a remarkable job fooling other businesses, the financial press, its own employees, and Washington officials that it was a profitable, successful firm, when in fact many of its recorded assets and profits were inflated or fraudulent. The firm encouraged its thousands of employees to buy company stock in their 401(k) retirement plans with a generous matching program. This is the riskiest form of employee stock ownership.

But the most innovative company was all sham. Spurred by a critical *Fortune* article by young reporter Bethany McLean, investigators discovered Enron's fraudulent practices of exaggerating profits and hiding losses in off-the-books special-purpose vehicles. In 2001, Enron went bankrupt—the biggest bankruptcy in U.S. history at the time it was filed. When the firm was on the verge of collapse, the top managers, who were unloading their shares as fast as they could, held an all-employee public meeting to encourage employees to buy more shares, although the same managers made it impossible for employees to sell their company stock in the employee 401(k) plan. The sordid details were the subject of a best-selling book and a movie documentary based on the book titled *Enron: The Smartest Guys in the Room*. Thousands of employees lost their jobs and were in danger of losing the bulk of their contracted severance pay as well. Many had so much of their retirement savings invested in company stock that they lost a large chunk of their retirement. Although Enron's white-collar workers were nonunion, the AFL-CIO campaigned for the bankruptcy court to give the workers their severance pay and won about $80 million for them. One very unfortunate set of victims was the entire workforce of eighty-five thousand employees of Arthur Andersen, at the time a Big Five accounting firm, who lost their jobs as a criminal conviction of the entire firm started a series of events that led to its bankruptcy. It is unlikely that any but a small proportion of Arthur Andersen's workers were involved in the wrongdoing. The

U.S. Supreme Court subsequently overturned the collective conviction of the entire firm and this case of collective punishment that unfortunately extended to scores of innocent employees.

WorldCom was a huge communications company that merged in 1998 with phone giant MCI and then sought to monopolize most of the telecommunications market by purchasing Sprint as well (an action blocked by regulatory agencies). Like Enron, it used shady accounting methods to appear to be growing and earning huge profits, when in fact it was highly indebted and losing money. It capitalized current expenses to reduce reported expenses and listed revenues that did not exist. Its CEO, Bernard Ebbers, was subsequently convicted on securities charges of fraud and conspiracy after enriching himself by borrowing money from the firm for personal investments. The case involved one of the largest accounting scandals in U.S. history. WorldCom encouraged its employees to invest in company stock. Over half the employee 401(k) retirement plan was in company stock, and employees lost most of this.

On September 15, 2008, the fourth-largest investment bank in the United States, Lehman Brothers, declared bankruptcy and helped set off the implosion of Wall Street and the financial markets that partly led to the Great Recession and that still underlies many of the economic problems of the United States. An archetypical Wall Street firm, Lehman Brothers was a complicated enterprise. About 2,300 legal entities acted in its name in different financial markets. It did investment banking, sold stocks and bonds, traded in U.S. Treasury securities, did private equity, and had a large subprime mortgage business. Like Enron and WorldCom, Lehman used accounting gimmicks to make its finances appear less shaky than they really were—for instance, reporting repurchase agreements with other financial firms as actual sales when in fact Lehman contracted to buy back the securities. The *Wall Street Journal* reported that Lehman was 25 to 30 percent employee owned and that employee ownership was at the core of Lehman's culture. Workers lost an estimated $10 billion in paper value when these investments went down the tubes. Unlike Enron and WorldCom, however, all of Lehman's employee ownership was not concentrated in the 401(k) plan where workers bought the shares with cash. Much of it was reportedly based on grants of stock, which workers could not sell until they remained with the firm for many years.[34]

Enron, WorldCom, and Lehman had substantial numbers of worker owners, but those workers did not have the information or the corporate governance role that might have allowed them or independent board members to prevent top management from engaging in fraudulent accounting irregularities and/or taking huge risks with the company's assets. The companies had passive boards of directors and auditors and audit committees of the boards that did not do their job. With nonexecutive workers owning major blocks of the stock, not one of these boards of directors had even one member representing the nonexecutive employees exclusively. The incentives for top management were to take large risks with the firm's investments and the capital of public shareholders and then to try to cover up losses in the hope that some risky investment paid off. Holding large amounts of employees' 401(k) retirement assets in company shares and encouraging employees to invest more reduced workers' diversification of their assets.[35]

United Airlines: Hard Challenges to Overcome

The most famous example of failure of employee ownership is United Airlines. There is much to be learned from what it did wrong. It is different from the previous cases. This was not the case of a dishonest management investing money in high-risk financial deals or fraudulently reporting revenues and costs. United became employee owned when the company needed wage, benefit, and work rule concessions from its workers to compete with younger airlines like Southwest that had lower labor costs. In 1994, pilots, mechanics, ticket agents, and other employees, with the exception of the flight attendants, took reductions in their compensation of 15 to 25 percent to obtain majority ownership of the firm. Seats on the new board of directors went to the pilots and machinists and to nonunion workers. United was one of the small number of employee ownership plans where workers bought stock through wage concessions and it was not a traditional ESOP—although as one of America's major brands, it came to represent the employee ownership story in an outsize way for those who followed it on TV, radio, and in the newspapers.

United Airlines made two mistakes.

First, it based worker shares on drastic cuts in worker wages and benefits without establishing any short-term profit sharing. Basing shares on cuts in wages and benefits was against the ESOP idea of not financing worker shares with wages or savings or reductions in income but rather providing less risky grants of stock to workers. There was no cash profit-sharing plan so that workers could see some wealth returning to them as the company turned around. This might have softened the blow of the large wage reductions, when the firm did better. Management and shareholders aside from workers gained, while workers would benefit mainly when they retired or left the firm. Without the cash profit sharing to reward workers for the improved profitability of the firm, the unions felt they were in a position to only bargain with the management of their own company for wage increases that the company's management believed it could not afford. Union leaders reverted to conflict-oriented tactics.

Second, United failed to develop a cooperative ownership culture after it became employee owned, but rather operated much as it had before. Employee stock ownership cannot do well in an atmosphere of toxic labor-management relations, and United had had decades of it. Under Gerald Greenwald, the first chairman and CEO of the employee-owned corporation, United initially started to turn itself around and began to make some progress on undoing a difficult company environment. But many of United's managers did not get behind creating a more participatory corporate culture. Just when employee involvement started to work, a different CEO stepped into place, and the new CEO and the new union heads were very suspicious of the idea. United based the ownership on concessions that workers resented, and built in no way for workers to share in the performance of the company when shareholders made money. Neither management nor the unions that had negotiated majority employee ownership invested in developing a participatory corporate culture. Advertisements for United stressed that the workers owned the firm, but, save for a brief honeymoon period after the change in ownership, United never operated differently enough from how it had in the past. And one major group of workers, the flight attendants, who were the face of the company to customers, had chosen against participating in the employee ownership plan.

The slowdown of the airline industry that followed the 9/11 terrorist attacks weakened United so much that it filed for bankruptcy in 2002. The workers with 401(k) plans that were not invested in company stock maintained their retirement benefits, but workers lost all of the stock they bought with their wage and benefit and work rule concessions. The failure was that United set up its ownership system in ways that ran against what successful employee-owned firms have learned over decades of experience.[36]

The examples in this chapter show that corporations with widely spread shares can operate successfully in the U.S. market economy. The examples also show such enterprises can fail. For broad-based capitalism to be a realistic solution to promote more wealth independence, limit inequality, and help democracy flourish in the vision of the Founders of the country, it is essential that the successes far exceed the failures, and that broad-based capitalism extends to enough workers and firms to be a substantial and potentially growing presence in the U.S. economy. We turn next to statistical evidence on the proportion of American workers that have some form of broad-based capitalism.

3 CITIZEN SHARES IN THE UNITED STATES

How many employees in the United States today share in the ownership and profits of the corporation for which they work? How much of their income comes from profit sharing and ownership stakes? How do citizens' shares differ among persons?

Until recently neither the government nor any private group could answer these questions with any certainty. National surveys did not comprehensively ask a representative group of citizens whether they had a property stake in the business for which they worked through profit sharing, gain sharing, employee stock ownership, or stock options or stock grants, nor the amounts of those stakes. The only way to answer questions about employees' shares in their firm was to cobble together responses from separate surveys of different forms of equity and profit sharing obtained at different times with different approaches by different groups.[1]

To fill this gap in the nation's knowledge about the extent of shared capitalism, in 2002 we applied to add a supplement on employee share ownership and profit sharing to the University of Chicago's National Opinion Research Center General Social Survey. We applied to repeat the survey in 2006 and 2010. The

General Social Survey has great virtue for estimating the extent and amount of share arrangements. It is a nationally representative survey conducted every two years whose sample size of about 1,500 adults is sufficiently large to provide reliable estimates of the extent of worker stakes in their firms for the entire nation. Supported by the National Science Foundation to increase information on the social and economic situation of the population, the survey collects data on the economic and demographic aspects of citizens and on a range of topics—from group membership and participation, to life satisfaction, to political attitudes—that allow us to identify many of the factors associated with shares.[2]

The General Social Survey obtains its information by face-to-face interviews in the homes of randomly selected adults. This is generally superior to mail surveys and to opinion polls that use telephone calls. The interviewer can ask more detailed questions than are possible through telephone or mail and can clarify the meaning of questions. The interviewee can check personal records to answer questions accurately. While response rates for telephone and mail surveys have been declining in recent years, raising concerns over how valid the data are, the General Social Survey gets responses from more than 70 percent of the people approached.

The National Opinion Research Center asked private wage and salary workers if their income depended on company performance: profit sharing and closely related gain sharing; ownership of shares; and holding stock options. They also asked about the cash payout or value of profit and gain sharing and share ownership.

By profit sharing we refer to situations in which some of the worker's cash pay depends on company profits. If the company makes a profit, it pays a part of the profits to workers. If the company loses money, workers do not get the profit sharing. Worker income through profit sharing generally varies over the business cycle. In good times profits are high and workers obtain sizable profit-related shares. In bad times profits are generally lower and workers get less. Profit sharing is inherently unpredictable. Gain sharing refers to situations in which a firm agrees to make a cash payment to workers when the sales or financial performance of a department or division of a company improves or when workers reduce the cost of production or meet some other company-determined target. It is less risky than profit sharing since it depends on worker effort in meeting the sharing goal independent of the business cycle. We asked workers with profit- or gain-sharing plans how much, if at all, they earned from their participation in these share approaches.

Employee stock ownership refers to situations in which a worker owns a share of stock outright. Employees commonly receive company stock through grants from an employee stock ownership plan (ESOP) or restricted stock. Or they may buy the shares as part of their 401(k) plan or other type of retirement plan. Or companies matched their contributions to 401(k) plans in company shares. The workers might have bought the shares on a stock exchange at the market price, or, more likely, they bought the shares at a lower price through an employee stock purchase plan operated by their company. More and more companies grant shares to workers though stock grants.

Stock options refer to the right of someone to purchase stock at a given price in the future regardless of the market value in that period. Many stock options in the United States allow a worker who received, say, one stock option on January 1, 2014, when the stock was trading at $10 a share, the right to buy the share for $10 for the next ten years, and pocket the increased value of the share as a cash profit. It is not the same as owning a share of stock. If the stock price increases in the future relative to its value when the firm granted the option, and if the recipient has held the option for a sufficient amount of time to exercise it, the recipient can buy the share at the specified price (the "strike price") and then sell it immediately at the higher price and earn a profit. If the stock price goes down, the recipient does not exercise the option to buy shares and does not lose any money from the decline in price.[3]

The General Social Survey has one other virtue that makes it an exemplar of survey research. Each survey, including our supplements, can be downloaded by students, researchers, or any person who wants to examine the General Social Survey evidence to analyze and contribute to our knowledge of broad-based capitalism.[4]

WHAT WE LEARN FROM THE NATIONAL SURVEY

The big surprise from the General Social Survey is that about 47 percent of private-sector full-time wage and salary workers have some form of share in the firm where they work (Figure 3.1). Finding that these arrangements cover so many workers demolishes the skeptics who dismiss broad-based capitalism as a niche form of business practice with the refrain, "If this really works, why isn't everyone doing it?" Nearly half the private-sector workforce is far too large for anyone to dismiss this form of capitalism as a niche phenomenon. Firms and workers throughout the United States have experience with employees participating in the financial performance of their firms. The answer to James Madison's question whether some form of "proprietorship" and ownership beyond land would emerge to

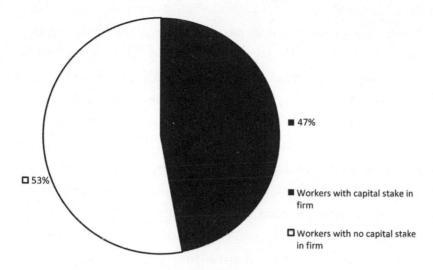

Figure 3.1. Citizens' Shares in the United States

allow large numbers of workers to have a property stake in the economy is yes.

The biggest part of citizens' shares consists of profit or gain sharing. About 40 percent of workers receive profit sharing or gain sharing in the company where they work. This is nearly twice the 21 percent who have employee stock ownership in the company for which they work and four times the 10 percent who report having stock options in their employer. The sum of these percentages exceeds the 47 percent in Figure 3.1. The reason is that many workers have more than one type of stake in their firm. About a third of all workers with shares have a combination of forms: 12 percent of all workers have profit sharing and employee stock ownership; 4 percent have profit sharing and stock options; 5 percent own shares and hold stock options; and 12 percent of all workers have all three forms together.[5]

Corporations combine profit or gain sharing that gives short-term rewards for current performance with employee stock ownership or options that pay off when a firm does well for years. The idea is to motivate workers to try to improve performance in the near term and in the more distant future.[6]

Employee share ownership and profit sharing are sufficiently widespread to meet Madison's wish for a form that can increase ownership stakes in society, but the survey data show that most worker shares are generally too small to make a big contribution to income or to reduce economic inequality for a large segment of the population at this time.[7]

Figure 3.2 shows the dollar amount that workers receive through profit and gain sharing in a year, and the value of their employee stock ownership. The chart tells us the value of these forms of shares in two ways. The light bar is the mean of all the values reported by workers on the survey—the standard definition of an average. The shaded bar is the value of profit/gain sharing or employee stock ownership for the median recipient of that form of shares—the income that the person in the middle of all those who have these shares would receive.

The figures for profit/gain sharing and for ownership in the chart are not directly comparable. This is because the amounts that workers report for these different kinds of shares are not in the same units. Profit and gain sharing are annual income that give the amounts workers receive each year. The employee ownership stake measures current wealth, namely the value of all employee stock ownership the day the workers took the survey. A worker who earned $2,000 per year for five years in profit sharing would have obtained about the same wealth (ignoring, for simplicity's sake, the return on those earnings each year) as

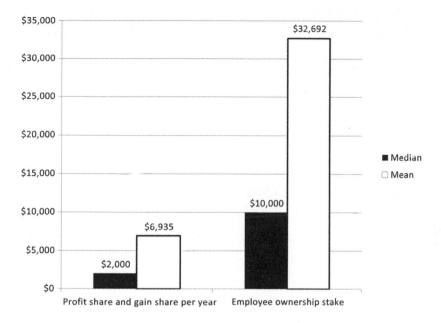

Figure 3.2. How Much Is the Typical Citizen's Share?

a worker who had accumulated $10,000 of capital in employee share ownership.

The average value of both the profit-sharing and the gain-sharing income exceeds the median by a substantial amount. The average value of profit shares, for instance, is $6,935. But the median worker receives just $2,000. This reflects the fact that workers in highly profitable companies will obtain larger amounts than those in less-profitable companies, and that workers in particular positions in the same company (managers, salespersons) may obtain larger profit sharing than workers in other positions. Similarly, the average value of employee stock ownership is also larger than the median value of employee share ownership ($32,692 compared to $10,000). Some workers—for example, workers in companies with ESOPs that own a large portion of the company—may have quite significant stakes. Also, those in management jobs or with higher levels of pay or longer tenure at a company are granted more shares of stock in the business than others. Employee stock purchase plans invariably offer all workers a discount when they buy shares from a corporation, but only about half of workers in corporations take the firm up on the offer. Some workers have too little extra cash or are risk averse, or are too likely to leave the firm in the near future, to purchase shares even at bargain prices.

We do not include worker income from stock options in Figure 3.2 because there are many technical complexities about valuing options. The value depends on the terms of the option— the number of years a worker must hold the option before he or she can exercise it (usually three to five years, but with some options requiring one or two years or even less. and with some requiring more years)—the number of years before the option expires (almost always ten years), and the volatility of the stock. Options are more valuable when share prices vary a lot, because the holder of the option can choose when to exercise it. If the share is volatile, there is a greater chance it will rise above the exercise price and be profitable than if the share is very stable. Financial economists use the famous (at least on Wall Street and in finance classes) Black-Scholes formula to approximate the value of options based on these factors.[8]

One easy and straightforward way to put a number on how valuable stock options are *to a worker* at any point in time is to ask how much money a worker would make if he or she cashed in the stock options today at today's stock price. We call this the potential value of stock options today. Given differences in the terms of options among firms and the size of the General Social

Survey sample, we did not ask about the potential value of stock options. To obtain information on this potential value of stock options, we used information from the National Bureau of Economic Research Shared Capitalism survey that we describe later in this book. The National Bureau for Economic Research survey did ask workers to estimate the value of all stock options that the employee held if all those options were exercised on the day of the survey.[9] As with profit sharing and employee share ownership, the average value workers would make if they cashed in their options on the day of the survey ($249,900) is higher than the median value ($75,000), indicating that some workers had very high potential values of stock options, but that the middle worker also has a significant stake. The lesson we draw from this information is that many workers receive broad-based capitalism forms of shares, although most workers have only modest amounts.[10]

THE LOCUS OF EMPLOYEE OWNERSHIP

Ownership of shares in the corporation for which an employee works, as opposed to profit sharing or having a stock option, is arguably closer to the ownership of the land by independent farmers that Jefferson, Madison, and the other Founders viewed as critical to resolving the tension between inequality and democracy. Share owners can exercise their ownership stake in ways that persons whose pay depends in part on profits or who receive options cannot do. In principle, share owners can have a vote on the way the firm operates. In practice their ability to exercise their ownership depends on the structure of corporate governance.

Figure 3.3 shows the percent of all workers in each group who have employee stock ownership.

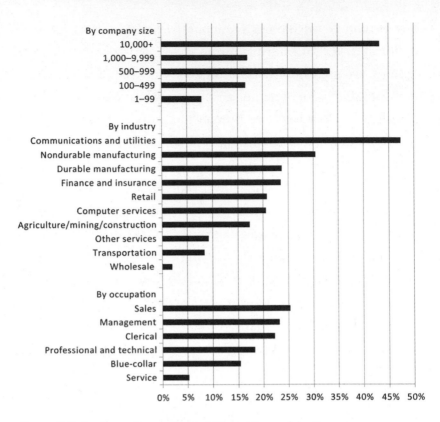

Figure 3.3. Employee Ownership in Different Parts of the Economy

The evidence on employee ownership in the General Social Survey demolishes three myths about the locus of employee ownership. The first myth is that ownership is found almost exclusively in the large firms like Google, Procter & Gamble, and Southwest Airlines, highlighted at the beginning of Chapter 2.[11]

The upper part in Figure 3.3 shows that employee stock ownership is most common in the largest corporations, which are more likely to have shares on the stock exchanges than smaller firms. Forty-three percent of all workers in firms with more than 10,000 workers own some company stock. There is a huge drop in the proportion of workers with shares in firms with 1,000 to 9,999 employees. But the proportion of workers with shares increases in companies with 500 to 999 employees and is as common for firms with 100 to 499 employees as for firms with 1,000 to 9,999 employees. This reflects the many thousands of smaller and medium-size corporations that we spoke about in Chapter 2 with Employee Stock Ownership Plans, but whose stock is not traded on public stock markets.

The second myth is that share ownership is disproportionate in high-tech sectors compared to traditional industries. The second part in the chart shows that the industries with the most employee stock ownership are communications and nondurable manufacturing, where 30 percent or more of all workers in those industries have some employee stock ownership. Twenty percent or more of workers in durable manufacturing, finance and insurance, computer services, and retail also have some employee stock ownership. The industries with the least employee stock ownership are wholesale, other services, and transportation.[12]

The third myth is that only executives and managers have share ownership. The third panel in Figure 3.3 shows that while over 20 percent of all managers in the country have some employee stock ownership, more sales employees than managers have an ownership stake, and nearly as many clerical workers as managers also have employee stock ownership. Nationally, 15 percent of blue-collar workers have an ownership stake. The group that has the least ownership stake is service workers. Companies that have broad-based employee ownership and profit sharing tend to include everyone or almost everyone.

JUST THE SUPERRICH?

Figure 3.4 focuses on ownership stakes and examines the extent to which ownership stakes add to the wealth of workers for those workers with different levels of salary who actually have employee stock ownership. The dollar amounts on the left are the total value of employee stock ownership a worker possesses. The income groups at the bottom represent the annual salary range of the workers in that group, for full-time workers who report being paid at or above market level (so the employee ownership is on top of regular fixed pay).[13]

The black bar tells us about the typical employee with share ownership. The typical employee making a salary of less than $50,000 a year has at least about $20,000 in employee stock ownership that he or she has accumulated. The typical employee making a salary of $50,000 to just under $90,000 a year also has about $20,000 in employee stock ownership that

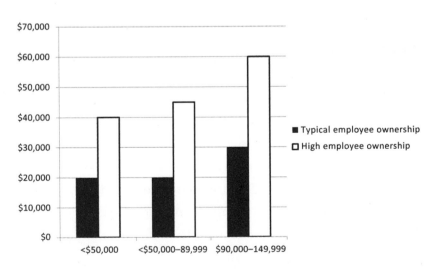

Figure 3.4. Employee Ownership and Income Levels

he or she has accumulated. Finally, the typical employee making a salary of $90,000 to just under $150,000 a year has at least about $30,000 in employee stock ownership accumulated. These are modest amounts of capital ownership for a typical worker.

The white bar shows the capital ownership of workers in firms with much greater employee share ownership—those in the top quarter of the value of those with employee stock ownership in their income bracket. Among these workers, those making a salary of less than $50,000 a year have at least about $40,000 in employee stock ownership that they have accumulated. Those making a salary of $50,000–$89,999 a year have at least about $45,000 in employee stock ownership that they have accumulated. Those making a salary of $90,000 to just under $150,000 a year have at least about $60,000 in employee stock ownership that they have accumulated. An ownership stake equal to between a half year and a year's pay is substantial, but not so great as to create a huge risk for workers if share prices fall. Some of these workers also have access to profit sharing and stock options in addition to owning stock in their companies. Among workers who have access to profit sharing and gain sharing and report being paid at or above market level, the typical bonus is $1,200 for those earning less than $50,000; $5,000 for those earning $50,000–$89,999 a year; and $10,000 for those earning $90,000 to just under $150,000 a year. As with the employee ownership stakes, these typical bonuses are large enough to make a meaningful difference in worker incomes, but not so large as to create a huge risk for workers. Worker shares can have a meaningful impact for workers at different salary levels.

CONCLUSION

Broad-based capitalism practices are more common in the U.S. economy than many Americans would expect. Almost half of all private-sector workers have one or more kind of share. Profit-related earnings are the most widespread. Employee stock ownership stakes are less widespread in general, but a valuable part of employees' financial involvement in their firms. These forms of shares are found throughout the economy—in different industries and occupations and among workers with different levels of pay. We conclude that citizen shares are widespread and meaningful enough that they could be the backbone of a different kind of future economy. Workers of different income groups with generous employee stock ownership plans can accumulate meaningful capital ownership. U.S. firms and workers have enough experience implementing shares that the approaches could be expanded relatively easily if the citizens decided this was an appropriate way to reform our economy and meet the challenge that the Founders set for us.

4 HOW IT EVOLVED

When the American Economic Association was formed about a quarter of a century ago, the prevailing system of economics taught that the state or organized society as such had nothing to do with economics. The sole function of the state was to preserve law and order, and to prevent physical violence to persons and injury to property. The philosophy did not provide for a condition of affairs in which the mass of workmen were unskilled, working for wages, and the instruments of industry were owned by another class of society for the most part devoid of technical knowledge. But it was not until the days of capitalistic industry and the enormous surplus resulting therefrom, with the consequent class cleavage and the creation of the great wage-earning, non-propertied classes, that we began to discover that the majority of personally free adult males, because of economic conditions, were quite [as] unfree economically as many of those whose personal freedom was limited by law. Should the present decline in real wages continue for many years, the tension is likely to become very great, for inequality, with the consequent lack of bargaining ability, tends to increase at an ever accelerating rate. Our free land has heretofore obscured the real tendencies of our economic development. On the other hand, it offered opportunities to vast numbers of people to make individual fortunes, and thus rise to the capitalistic class. This kept alive that speculative spirit and hope so conducive to energy, enterprise, and economic efficiency and production. Whatever the final outcome may be it must accomplish two important results: it will give the workman a conscious share in the direction of the industry; and it will also . . . give him a share in the speculative gains and profits of the industry. With our concentrated wealth and large-scale production, in the absence of a wise and conscious social policy, increased population and consequent rise in rents will tend to shut out an ever increasing part of the population from dominion over or ownership in the natural resources and implements and tools of production.

Professor John H. Gray, president of the American Economics Association, annual address, 1915[1]

The evidence in the last chapter that almost half of American wage and salary workers are involved in some form of broad-based capitalism, albeit at relatively modest levels, may have surprised you. We were surprised and so too were others, including social scientists, when we showed them the results. They run counter to three widespread skeptical views about the potential of corporations in which workers have some ownership stake and profit share to offer a way to address the issues of inequality and property ownership that concerned the Founders. The first view, associated with the notion that people only pursue their personal short-run interests, is that free riding will ultimately undermine profit sharing and employee ownership in large organizations. The second view, which stems from a Social Darwinist perspective, is that there is a tiny group of "wealth creators" who have the information, expert knowledge, and ability to run large businesses, and whose orders the rest of society should just follow. The third view, which stems from a class conflict perspective, is that employer-employee relationships are inherently a zero sum game, in which executives and managers will do almost anything to control firms and gain wealth and power for themselves at the expense of others.

The facts do not support these views. Business leaders and managers throughout U.S. history have established broad-based capitalist arrangements that have benefited workers as well as firms, and that have succeeded in meeting the market test of surviving in a competitive economy. This chapter provides a brief history of how broad-based capitalism has developed into a real and seemingly permanent feature in an economy in which industry and business capital and knowledge capital, rather than land, are the predominant forms of property.[2]

INDEPENDENT CRAFTSPERSONS AND MECHANICS VERSUS WAGE SLAVERY

The country did not have an easy time developing the industrial counterpart to the "yeoman farmer" and homestead concept. The model closest to the yeoman farmer was the independent craftsman or mechanic. Initially, many of the first manufacturers in colonial America were master craftsmen and craftswomen in small shops doing baking, carpentry, shoemaking, barrel making, printing, metal trades, bookbinding, dressmaking, gown making, wig making, and other crafts. These independent craftspeople typically had individual "worker ownership" of their businesses and complete "profit sharing" of the capital income. The master craftsperson would often train an apprentice, who would later graduate to being a full-fledged owner/master.

A struggle over the share in ownership and profits of these crafts workers came to a head as regional and national markets expanded in the young country. Some master craftspeople found it profitable to divide up tasks they had given to apprentices among several lower-paid, less-skilled workers who did not have the prospect of learning enough to become independent craftsmen on their own and thus became wage earners rather than worker owners. Persons who held to the "yeoman farmer" ideal viewed wage earning as "wage slavery."

Employee-owned companies set up by workers in 1791 and 1806 in Philadelphia were founded to provide an alternative for these craftspeople or mechanics or artisans who refused to become "wage slaves" rather than become masters themselves as this emerging factory system developed by fits and starts. They wanted to continue to own their jobs and enjoy the full benefit of their own profits.[3] The beginning of certain craft unions in the United States and a number of the first strikes in the late 1700s were partly about the decline of the right to capital ownership and capital income by these workers and their fervent attempt to defend that right.[4] Some of these frustrated citizen craftspeople actually lobbied for the homestead idea and then went west as homesteaders.

THE FIRST GIANT CORPORATIONS: RAILROADS

After the Civil War, the country experienced another massive change in direction away from realizing the republican ideal of ownership. Sociologist Charles Perrow tells this story in his analysis of the railroads. A new superclass of bankers emerged "flush from profits on their war loans," and the New York money market attracted national and international pools of capital of astounding amounts. The first huge corporations in America were the railroads that got access to much of this credit. The railroads went in many directions that the naysayers in the Pennsylvania debate on the corporation could only imagine. Because the government was anxious to rapidly develop a massive national transportation system, railroad companies received enormous amounts of land and capital from both federal and state governments as subsidies for monopolies. The federal government showered the railroads with resources and favors. Legal rulings removed local and regional oversight from the railroads and centralized much of the decision making in Washington. President Andrew Johnson called the railroads "an aristocracy based on nearly two and one half billion in national securities . . . to assume that political control which was formerly [only] given to the slave oligarchy."

The corruption was massive. Free stock was sometimes issued to politicians and to allies of management in order to increase control relative to other investors. Most of the railroads went bankrupt on a regular basis and sometimes overbuilt trackage where no real markets existed. Historian David Nasaw tells how the executives of the Pennsylvania Railroad would raise capital from investors for the railroad corporation, sign a sweetheart contract with a separate construction company that in fact the executives and their families themselves secretly owned, and then milk both. The front construction corporation would build the railroad at a huge profit to its secret owners, who were the managers of the original railroad corporation. The original railroad corporation would then go bankrupt. In a huge skimming operation, the original shareholders lost, the executives and their families and related politicians enriched themselves as a result of the generous construction contract, and often the workers had to make do with a less-profitable company and demands for lower wages.

The Crédit Mobilier scandal of 1872 was one of the most famous examples of nineteenth-century corrupt crony capitalism.

The officers of the Union Pacific Railroad set up a sham company to do the construction that was supposedly objectively selected. Crédit Mobilier of America was a corporation chartered in Pennsylvania with a name chosen to sound solid but actually having no connection to the French bank of the same name. In fact, the Crédit Mobilier construction firm was owned by the corporate officers, and a colluding congressman, Oakes Ames, was distributing cash bribes and shares in the company to his fellow congressmen. The scandal sullied the administrations of Presidents Andrew Johnson, Ulysses S. Grant, and James Garfield. This was precisely the vision of the corporation that William Findley so feared, and it illustrated everything that the Founders meant by monopoly and the opposite of the broad-based-property approach to political life.

Railroads became the polar opposite of the republican idea. The firms were giant centralized national "organizational powerhouses." Ownership was dispersed around the country, and nonowner managers tended to control the companies, often with banks. Through holding companies they gobbled up all kinds of other companies. While they were "the biggest and richest organizations in the country," they were often inefficient as a result of their corruption and lack of transparency. Many profits came from construction and mergers rather than from careful operations. The massive increase in railroad trackage came in the 1870–1890 period just after the Homestead Act. The federal government might have applied the philosophy of the Homestead Act and encouraged the railroads to have some broad-based employee stock ownership and profit sharing and citizens' share ownership in return for gaining monopoly powers, but it went down the corruption route instead.

The largest New York investment banking firm of Jay Cooke and Company was behind the Northern Pacific Railroad and many other lines. Cooke's firm led a speculative frenzy of overinvestment of depositors' funds before the entire market collapsed. When the firm failed, the New York Stock Exchange closed for over a week, and many companies nationwide went out of business. This Panic of 1873 led to double-digit unemployment. The railroads reacted with deep wage cuts, which led to widespread strikes and the calling out of the federal and state militias in the great railroad strike of 1877. There were riots and massive fires and damage to equipment and stations in Baltimore, Pittsburgh, Philadelphia, Reading, Chicago, and other cities. Nearly fifty years earlier, Madison had worried about the anger of citizens without property creating troubles "which would lead to a standing military force, dangerous to all parties, and to liberty itself." After the uprisings, National Guard armories were set up in many American cities to prepare for more conflict.

As Perrow continues the story, the centralized capital markets looked for another place to invest huge pools of capital after the overinvestment in railroads. The money went to mining and manufacturing industries and helped finance mergers. From the 1890s to 1910 about three hundred separate firms merged each year into giant trusts and monopolies. Some of the giant corporations of the present were formed, such as U.S. Steel, General Electric, Nabisco, DuPont, and International Harvester, while over 1,800 smaller firms disappeared.[5]

THE BEGINNING OF AN INDUSTRIAL SHARE MODEL
The same person is often capitalist and laborer, too. This is almost universally so with small farmers, mechanics, and

tradesmen. . . . Of course in such cases there can be no conflict between labor and capital. And this affords a clue to our
solution of the problem before us: that in all great manufacturing establishments requiring an aggregate of capital
vastly beyond the accumulations of laborers, as far as possible, the laborer should in some form and degree, however
small be made a capitalist or sharer in the fortunes of the
business.

—*Professor Lyman Hotchkiss Atwater, William Cooper Procter's
teacher in the required course in "political economy" at Princeton
in 1883*[6]

From the end of the Civil War in 1865 to about 1910, employees,
social observers, university researchers, and managers tried to
articulate and develop a business model where workers owned
part of the industry and shared in its profits as a continuation of
the "yeoman farmer" idea. These individuals did not believe that
economic inequality could be eliminated, only that the extreme
inequality in ownership of the industrial system was neither
necessary nor inevitable. Many had read the writings of Charles
Babbage and John Stuart Mill.[7] Workers tried to start their own
companies. Early on, some little-known experimentation took
place at the Waltham Watch Company in Waltham, Massachusetts in the 1850s, and at the Baldwin Locomotive Works, the
dominant producer of railroad engines, in Philadelphia in the
late 1800s.[8]

Workers such as stove makers, barrel makers (coopers), shoe-
makers, and other artisans decided that simply starting worker-
owned businesses was preferable to strikes and labor unrest in
various industries where their wages were coming under pressure. These groups started approximately four hundred worker

cooperatives. As William H. Sylvis, the president of the Mould-
ers Union that made stoves, said, "The cause of all these problems is the wages system. . . . We must adopt a system which
will divide the profits of labor among those who produce them."
These workshops were generally started with very little capital.
From 1884 to 1887, the Knights of Labor, which was briefly the
dominant labor organization in the United States, officially opposed strikes and favored members starting companies to address the failure of firms to share the fruits of labor with workers.
But many of these companies were poorly managed, they did
not appreciate the place of professional managers, and they refused to pay the salaries that professional managers required.
The failures led unions to turn entirely to collective bargaining
instead in a very difficult environment for workers.[9]

As a sidelight that reflects his remarkable prescience and
intellectual curiosity, James Madison had over sixty years earlier
participated in a serious discussion about worker cooperatives
with Robert Owen, the Welsh social reformer credited as one of
the founders of the cooperative movement, about ways to remake
the U.S. economy in the direction of broader property ownership. Madison purportedly judged that Owen had an overly
idealistic view of human nature, presumably for how much social involvement he envisioned in the organizations. The fact
that Madison had the meeting at all indicates he remained open
to exploring another format for shares.[10]

Social observers of the rising tensions over wealth inequality and horrible industrial working conditions brought the share
idea to the level of a national discussion. Three nationally publicized violent confrontations between workers and corporations
took place involving Madison's predicted shows of police or military force. They were the railroad riots in 1877, the Haymarket

riot in Chicago in 1886, and the Homestead (Pennsylvania) battle between Carnegie Steel and its workers in 1892. These helped motivate a focused discussion about how industry might be structured. At that time, economics and sociology as fields scarcely existed in colleges, and the foremost role in turning the discussion of profit sharing and employee stock ownership into a national affair was played by social observers based in Christian churches. Some denominations had been deeply involved in opposing slavery, and churches became important centers for moral dialogue on other important social and economic issues of the day. A few pastors became nascent "social scientists."

Thoughtful pastors and professors of moral philosophy read of British examples of profit sharing and worker share ownership and began to analyze the economic transformation taking place. Congregational pastor Washington Gladden preached from influential pulpits in Springfield, Massachusetts, and Columbus, Ohio, and authored many books on the share system. In his book *Working People and Their Employers*, Gladden suggested that the solution was what he called cooperation "by making the laborer his own capitalist." Gladden predicted that the idea would lead to better productivity and employee loyalty. He called the current system "industrial feudalism" and was proud that the Statement of Principles of the 17-million-parishioner-strong Federal Council of the Churches of Christ demanded "the most equitable division of the products of industry that can ultimately be devised." These ideas spread far and wide as a result of the Social Gospel movement in Christianity.[11]

Christian theologian and Baptist pastor Walter Rauschenbusch, who taught at the Rochester Theological Seminary, was the undisputed leader of the Social Gospel movement. His book *Christianity and the Social Crisis* explicitly discussed profit sharing and worker share ownership as the successor idea to the "mass of independent farmers that have been and still are the moral backbone of our nation" and echoed the analysis of American Economic Association president Gray.

Professor Lyman Atwater came to the College of New Jersey (later Princeton University) from Yale College in 1854 to teach moral philosophy and began teaching the first course on political economy in 1869, covering the same ideas every semester. He presented profit sharing and worker share ownership as the solutions of the conflict between labor and capital. The final essay exams of Atwater's class included questions asking the students to discuss how profit sharing and employee stock ownership could be applied to solving the labor-capital conflict and management problems. Sitting in Atwater's class was William Cooper Procter, who, as we have noted, implemented Atwater's ideas in Procter & Gamble, down to the last detail.[12]

In the late 1880s, social science researchers analyzed cases in which companies adopted profit sharing and employee ownership. The head of Johns Hopkins University's new graduate school in the social sciences divided up the entire country into five regions and assigned a doctoral student to study when and where the share idea was appearing and how and why it was performing in each of these areas of the country. The Johns Hopkins studies showed that most of the numerous smaller companies set up by unions failed because of poor quality of executive management and a lack of capital, whereas well-capitalized larger corporations that had committed executive managers with business acumen, supportive corporate cultures, and a history of sustained interest in sharing progressed. John Bates Clark, the second president of the American Economic Association, advised the Hopkins research group and wrote a book, *The Philosophy of*

Wealth, arguing for employee share ownership financed by profit sharing over and above fair wages, with competent professional managers running the companies. In 1885, several of the professors and graduate students working on the Johns Hopkins study along with Washington Gladden founded the American Economic Association, which published these doctoral theses on employee stock ownership and profit sharing in the first few issues of its journal.

Carroll D. Wright, the commissioner of labor statistics for the commonwealth of Massachusetts and later the first U.S. commissioner of labor, reported on what businessmen were doing with the share idea in their companies in Massachusetts. Wright linked the experience of the New England cod fishery with the newer industrial examples. He reported that workers "develop the whole group of industrial virtues: diligence, fidelity, caretaking, economy, continuity of effort, willingness to learn, and a spirit of cooperation."

Harvard graduate Nicholas Paine Gilman, one of the first members of the American Economics Association, a clergyman, and later a professor of sociology and ethics, wrote a wide-ranging analysis of the phenomenon of employee stock ownership and profit sharing—a study that was so carefully executed that when he died, John Maynard Keynes wrote Gilman's obituary praising the study's thoroughness. Gilman found in his case analysis that profit sharing was feasible, tended to increase productivity and quality and reduce wastefulness and the need for supervision, but required a steadfast and patient management team and educated workers whose efforts could actually make a difference.[13]

Francis Amasa Walker, head of the U.S. Census, a Yale economist, the first president of the American Economic Association, and then president of the Massachusetts Institute of Technology, wrote his take on the conclusions from these studies in his text-book for economics students, *Political Economy*. Social science quickly turned to studying the share idea. Walker tied the share idea to the old republican idea of broad-based ownership in American history. He expected the worker share ownership and profit-share ideas to be successful and lead to more productivity, but thought that the new model required a specific appreciation of the need for a solid executive management. Walker wrote that the "simple cooperation" experiments sometimes failed because they attempted to "eliminate" management, "the entrepreneur," the person who put the capital and the administrative discipline of the firm together, made it work, and took responsibility for build-ing the firm. The ideas had to be implemented in established companies with reliable business plans, not as part of attempts "to eliminate the entrepreneur." Whether companies were set up as cooperatives or stock companies, with profit sharing or worker stock ownership, they had to have serious management talent. He believed even pure worker cooperatives could work under the right circumstances.[14]

What did these very early and preliminary studies reveal? The nationally comprehensive initial Johns Hopkins studies, albeit of very recent and modest attempts, confirmed yet again that most of the numerous smaller companies set up by unions, despite occasional successes, failed because of poor quality of executive management, a lack of capital, an unwillingness to bring in competent managers, and a refusal to pay them well. The most notable exception were the small barrel-making co-operatives in Minneapolis. By contrast, several long-standing, well-managed, and well-capitalized larger corporations that had committed executive managers with business acumen, supportive corporate cultures, and a history of sustained interest in the ideas were making some progress.

In 1892, Walker, Caroll Wright, Nicholas Gilman, and several prominent CEOs of profit-sharing companies formed the American Association for the Promotion of Profit Sharing, which went on to publish a substantive high-level newsletter for executives, *Employer and Employed*, to guide managers step-by-step through the ideas and the execution of actually implementing the share idea. Many profit-sharing companies used profits to finance employee stock ownership, so the ideas were merging. At Walker's death, MIT celebrated his work on shares as one of his seminal public roles.[15]

INDIVIDUAL "ENTREPRENEURS" TAKE THE LEAD

The implication of Francis Amasa Walker's take was that if the share idea was to become the basis of the economic system, the leaders of corporations would have to step forward. The practices would become widespread only if they were put into operation by established corporations with solid ongoing plans to sustain their businesses.

Indeed, in the late 1880s and 1890s, major industrial titans swung behind the idea of broad-based capitalism. Ironically, they were pushing against the railroad model of organization that was typified by conflict between absentee owners and worker nonowners.

Charles A. Pillsbury

In 1882, Charles A. Pillsbury's flour mill in Minneapolis was the leading grain miller in the world, with half of the flour barrels being exported to Europe. Pillsbury had put together a four-part winning business strategy: close contact with a farming region that produced the high-quality grain his mills could best market; access to the energy of the powerful St. Anthony's falls to run the mills; the benefit of a national rail nexus connecting to a global export transportation system; and subcontracting one essential but non-flour-milling function of Pillsbury—namely barrel making to package its products—to others, namely the Minneapolis worker cooperatives. All Pillsbury needed to conquer the global market, besides his unquestioned reputation for quality, was for his mills not to explode over and over again, in a repeat of industrial accidents that had earlier wiped out a massive amount of Pillsbury family capital on several occasions. Pillsbury's strategic decision making is a good example of the need for an entrepreneur.

When the Johns Hopkins researchers interviewed him about profit sharing, Pillsbury "was emphatic in saying that he regards the system as advantageous to the firm." He said that "bad results caused by negligence are hard to trace to the culpable individual. The habitual attention to one's own work and to the work of one's fellows that is developed by a personal interest in the business is a great advantage in the modern manufacture of flour." With these words Pillsbury clearly stated his view on the free-rider shirking question: he expected workers to supervise one another. His entire theory was built on the notion that coworkers under profit sharing were more responsible and partly practiced self-management.

The Pillsbury family was simply determined to create a different kind of corporation. Charles's uncle, who was co-owner of the firm and governor and later senator from Minnesota, stood right behind him. In the first three years of profit sharing, workers received capital income equal to 33 percent, on top of their already fair wages. By 1886, the Pillsbury share system was the most publicized and longest lasting at any major firm. It has now come to light that Charles Pillsbury not only gave long-term supply contracts to the worker cooperatives that made all those barrels for his company's product, but that he advised them as well, and that they reported that they believed he played some role in their success. Unfortunately, Pillsbury was forced by sudden bad market conditions to sell majority control to British investors in 1889 to rescue his firm. The British capital did briefly save the firm, but the British canceled the profit sharing and then ran the corporation into the ground. But that was not the end of the share idea.

The Pillsbury family, who had regularly written about how proud they were of their profit-sharing legacy, got control of the firm back again and invented a novel approach to the employee stock ownership idea, spreading ownership broadly as the firm prospered again. Years later, Charles's grandson, George Sturgis Pillsbury, who served in the Minnesota legislature, would introduce the first state legislation to encourage employee stock ownership. State senator George S. Pillsbury's speech harked back to the republican share ideal and Madison's old fears: "An ancient Greek historian, Diorus Siculus, declared, 'It is absurd to entrust the defense of a country to men who own nothing in it.' "[16]

Nelson O. Nelson

In 1886, Nelson O. Nelson's plumbing goods factory was one of the most widely discussed industrial experiments in the entire country. He built Leclaire, Illinois, as a model town with a clean factory, sports fields, and lovely worker-owned homes that attracted visitors from far and wide. He named the town after the French painting contractor who some credit for inventing the modern corporate practice of profit sharing. Nelson saw his firm as a partnership between capital and labor. The deal was that as a supplier of capital he would get 6 percent interest on his capital in the firm, and the remaining profits would be split between the owners of capital—initially him—and the workers. For the first seven years, the company paid an average of 8 percent above market wages in profit sharing each year. Nelson's innovation was to invite workers to use part of their cash profit sharing to buy shares in the company that also paid dividends. His firm ran into the problem that it was not profitable every year.

Nelson focused on the broader issues of employee participation in the job and the health of the surrounding community. Each good year, some of the profits funded a disability and health plan and a kindergarten. In order to extend the share idea, the company bought property and allowed workers to build and buy private homes on an installment plan. The installment plan, using credit, gaining property by responsibly managing borrowing money and paying it back, was on its way to becoming one of the main methods for workers to acquire property. Committees of employees helped manage these various activities. Nelson and the employees appointed a joint auditor to confirm to everyone that the accounting of the profits was objective and fair. The company frequently asked groups of employees to solve production problems. To develop a sustainable partnership, Nelson combined short-term profit sharing with longer-term employee stock ownership and begin to develop some new approaches to personnel management and employee benefits. Workers did not have to finance ownership with their savings, so it was less risky.[17]

Andrew Carnegie

In 1886 and later, Andrew Carnegie, now one of the top three industrial titans in the nation, with John D. Rockefeller and J. P. Morgan, publicly embraced profit sharing and employee share ownership in a series of widely publicized interviews that shocked his peers and the public. About the worker, Carnegie said, "I believe cooperation [the word for employee share ownership at the time] is his hope." Initially, he proposed that the wages of steelworkers should be tied to the price of steel, with no floor as to how much wages could fall—a kind of sliding scale. He proposed this idea just when he understood steel prices were about to dive.

After several labor-management conflicts, one of the most violent labor confrontations in American history broke out at the ironically named Homestead (Pennsylvania) steelworks. Company-hired Pinkerton guards and steelworkers killed and injured each other in a melee that did indeed require Madison's imagined militia. Carnegie Steel won in its determination to drive wage rates down and have its union-free environment.

At the time, Carnegie was in the United Kingdom preparing a new book calling for cooperation and profit sharing as the solution to the labor-capital conflict. This book was never published, and his biographer found the dusty manuscript tucked into a folder. Years later, in a totally new 1908 book that laid out the share idea again, Carnegie said "labor as shareholders" and profit sharing was the answer to how capitalism must be redesigned.

Carnegie argued that studies showed "profit sharing and stock-owning plans have been vindicated by unusual success from every point of view, particularly in improving the relations between employers and employees." Carnegie cited the Filene Stores in Boston as an example, quoted Professor Nicholas Paine Gilman's book, and reminded readers of the cod fishery example, which he knew well! Showing a capacity for learning from experience, Carnegie now abandoned the idea of using profit sharing to reduce wages. He recommended federal tax incentives for employee stock ownership and, harking back to the yeoman farmer notion, spoke about "the beginning of . . . the reign of the working-men proprietors." The Carnegie lesson was that proprietary capitalism would be a nonstarter if it was mainly a strategy to drive down regular wages and substitute shares for fair wages. The idea could not be considered or implemented if labor and management were at loggerheads or, worse still, at war.[18]

George Eastman

In 1912, George Eastman of Eastman Kodak fame introduced broad-based profit sharing and would later offer workers a form of employee ownership akin to today's stock options. The profit-sharing plan was unique in that it powerfully stressed the partnership between workers and public shareholders. Eastman assumed that for shareholders, "cash dividends up to 10 percent are the equivalent of the employees' fixed wage." He believed that dividends above 10 percent were extraordinary, so Eastman told shareholders and employees that they would both share any dividends over the 10 percent paid to shareholders. For example, an employee working for the company for five years at $15 a week in the early 1900s would get capital income in the form of a dividend of $81.90, or just over five weeks' pay, about 10 percent on top of what was considered to be Kodak's generally fair fixed wages.

So as not to lose the skilled and unskilled workers on which Kodak's rapid innovation and growth depended, Eastman then went a step further and created what was the first stock option program in a high-tech corporation in the United States. He did it in the early 1900s. If workers stayed with the company, they could keep the shares. Employees could purchase a share for $100 and cash it in for almost $600—Kodak's Apple-like and Google-like stock price at the time—if they remained with the firm.

The company had a unique corporate culture, comprising what was widely viewed as fair fixed wages, generous employee benefits, and a high expectation that each supervisor was personally accountable for maintaining good employee relations, including an effort to do everything possible to avoid layoffs (as the company did during most of the Depression). Eastman left several generations of trained managers to carry on his plans. In the late 1930s, Kodak's turnover was 11 percent versus 45 percent in manufacturing overall; in 1956, turnover was 13 percent versus 50 percent in comparable firms—related, many managers contended, to the company's share system and culture.

George Eastman's contribution to broad-based capitalism was putting its practical application on the map for science-based companies, making it part of executive management's regular discussion with outside shareholders, and demonstrating—in the eye of the public and the mass media, including the *New York Times* and the *Wall Street Journal*—an unabashed enthusiasm for the idea as central to the operation of a large corporation. Eastman pioneered the determined presentation of the idea of broad-based capitalism to shareholders, the stock market, and the public.[19]

WILLIAM COOPER PROCTER: A PRESIDENTIAL CAMPAIGN FOR SHARES

Now, General, one word will make you President of the United States.

—*John Lattimore Himrod, confidential secretary to General Leonard Wood, proponent of profit sharing and employee share ownership and former army chief of staff, on Wood's being offered the Republican presidential nomination by corrupt boss Senator Boies Penrose of Pennsylvania in return for control of three cabinet departments*[20]

It was 1919. The 1920 presidential election year was looming. General Leonard Wood, former U.S. Army chief of staff, the first commander of the Rough Riders volunteer Cavalry regiment in the Spanish-American War, and strong supporter of Teddy Roosevelt, decided to run for the Republican nomination. His chances looked good. The *Wall Street Journal* reported that Wood was the hands-down favorite to beat President Wilson in the election, though in fact Wilson was too ill to run again, and the Democrats picked William Cox of Ohio, who lost in a landslide. In January 1920 William Cooper Procter, the owner of Procter and Gamble devoted to profit sharing, agreed to become Wood's national campaign manager after heading one of the Leonard Wood Leagues springing up around the country. Procter financed the campaign with almost $800,000 of his funds. He organized a plethora of field offices. He planned a modern, well-financed campaign to bring Wood's ideas to the nation using advertising, books, articles in newspapers and magazines, mass mailings, and lecture tours by Wood advocates, just as he had done with Ivory Soap. The goal was to win primaries and the minds of unpledged delegates so Wood could sweep the Republican National Convention in Chicago.

In February 1920 the national media gave attention to a cover-story interview by General Wood in a leading weekly magazine, *The Outlook*, asserting that profit sharing and employee share ownership were the solution to the industrial problems of the nation. *The Outlook* was owned by the corporation that published *The Independent*, where young Procter and his relatives had read about profit sharing in the 1880s; the February *Outlook* issue carried its typical full-page Ivory Soap ad sixteen pages before the Wood piece. Teddy Roosevelt, the Procter and Wood hero, had approved of the share idea as the new policy to advance. In his eighth annual message to Congress, December 8, 1908, Roosevelt had endorsed workers obtaining a greater share of ownership of the firms for which they worked: "I believe in a steady effort . . . to bring about a condition of affairs under which the men who work with hand or brain . . . shall own a greater share than at present of the wealth they produce, and be enabled to invest it in the tools and instruments by which all work is carried on. As far as possible, I hope to see a frank recognition of the advantages conferred by machinery organization, and division of labor, accompanied by an effort to bring about a larger share in the ownership by [the] wage worker of railway, mill, and factory."

Both Wood and Procter had issues with Wilson. President Wilson had passed over the very senior General Wood to command U.S. forces when the war in Europe had started and gave Wood only a minor training post. Procter had a history of run-ins with the current U.S. president, Woodrow Wilson, dating from a disagreement between the two men over the site of the proposed Princeton Graduate College when Wilson was the president of

Princeton University. Procter had participated at a summer training camp in Plattsburg, New York, for potential military officers,
an effort backed by Wood. The goal of the camp was to make the
case for a citizens' army based on universal conscription, an idea
with which President Wilson disagreed. General Wood was
committed to the profit sharing and employee ownership that
were the heart of Procter's vision for American business.

Some elements of the Republican establishment did everything they could to undermine the thought-to-be-inevitable
Wood candidacy. Before the convention, partly because of some
delegate vote buying by one of Wood's opponents for the nomination, the Senate conducted hearings on campaign financing
and subjected William Cooper Procter to unending questioning,
though there was no evidence that Procter had broken any laws.
Going into the convention, Wood was leading in primaries won
and delegates. Subsequent testimony before the Senate featured
evidence that Pennsylvania Republican "boss of bosses," U.S.
Senator Boies Penrose offered to swing the remaining delegates
behind Wood so the general could secure the nomination, if
Wood would give Penrose and his oil interest friends control of
three business-related cabinet posts. Penrose's view of the relation between government and business was simple. "I believe in
the division of labor. You (business) send us to Congress; we pass
laws under which you make money . . . and out of your profits
you further contribute to our campaign funds to send us back
again to pass more laws to enable you to make more money."
Wood's deputy presented old Penrose's offer to the general, "Now,
General, one word will make you President of the United States."

Wood said no. The establishment Republicans swung votes
to Ohio's Senator Warren G. Harding, who ended up receiving
the nomination and winning the presidency. The result was one

of the most corrupt administrations in U.S. history. While Harding was never implicated in securing personal financial benefit, his administration imploded in scandals, resignations, investigations, and suicides. Cabinet departments awarded sweetheart deals for oil companies to drill in Wyoming's Teapot Dome on federal property, leading to the famous Teapot Dome scandal. Harding could not say no to his friends and financial backers in a government dominated by his "Ohio gang." This was the nightmare vision of William Findley and other opponents of corporations in the Pennsylvania debates at the outset of the Republic.

Following Wood's loss of the nomination, Procter reduced his role on the national scene. He continued perfecting the P&G model, which would remain an enduring example of the share idea over a hundred years later. Had Wood and Procter managed to overcome the crony capitalists of their day, the country would almost certainly have taken at least a few steps down the road toward broad-based capitalism. An extraordinary opportunity was lost.[21]

CORPORATIONS TRY REDESIGNING CAPITALISM

But the effort to improve U.S. capitalism did not die with the demise of the Wood Progressive Republican candidacy. Apprehensive that tensions between workers and corporations would continue to erupt in strikes or worse, worried about Socialist parties which won elections in some cities and states, and concerned about the 1917 Bolshevik Revolution in Russia and the growth of communism in Europe and communist rhetoric in the United States, many corporate leaders were stunned. The extreme wealth inequality gap between the owners and the non-owners in American society and publicity of horrible work conditions were too stark to be ignored. Executives who opposed unions realized that many workers saw unions and collective bargaining as a way to address the fair-share issues. Progressive business leaders and thinkers, including Henry Ford, believed that they could create an alternative to unions in the form of sharing ownership and profits.

At hearings before the 1916 Federal Industrial Relations Commission, George W. Perkins—a J. P. Morgan partner, Progressive Party colleague of Teddy Roosevelt, and accomplished deal maker who had helped create the U.S. Steel and International Harvester trusts—said the capital-versus-labor conflict simply could "never" be solved by the wage system alone but required "a fair solution by coupling profit sharing with wages." Former Harvard University president Charles W. Eliot testified that both ownership and profit shares were the answer and stressed that both "must always be associated with cooperative management" to work well. MIT graduate and noted business forecaster Roger W. Babson, who founded Babson College, argued that labor's income could double with profit sharing and recounted to the commission the well-known Dennison Manufacturing case, where one of Massachusetts's most respected families was working with these ideas. In extensive testimony, Henry Ford said "profit sharing" led to a 20 percent rise in efficiency and a 90 percent drop in turnover in Ford's factories.

While organized labor as a whole was opposed to such ideas, soon after the hearings several key national railroad union leaders offered to operate the railroads under U.S. government ownership on a profit-sharing basis. Former railroad executive Walker Hines, who ran the railroads when they were nationalized by President Wilson during World War I, also proposed a plan of profit sharing. At the same time, the U.S. Department of Labor published a wide-ranging report with evidence from many case studies showing that profit sharing and employee stock ownership plans improved work relations and reduced turnover, although there was some debate as to the conditions under which the ideas actually improved efficiency. The idea had bubbled up.[22]

The National Civic Federation

Corporations themselves decided to press the issue in a big way. The National Civic Federation pulled together a critical tripartite mass of powerful representatives from corporations, labor, and the public who were able to attract huge coverage by the media and get the attention of influential economic leaders. The federation's goal was to find a cooperative solution between capital and labor on an array of national policies. The Federation had extraordinary presence and influence. At first its leadership included labor leaders as well as industrialists. Financier Lyman Gage, a former Treasury secretary under Teddy Roosevelt, served as president of the organization twice. American Federation of Labor leader Samuel Gompers was an initial vice president, and United Mine Workers president John Mitchell was one of its founders. While the group initially cooperated somewhat with unions, union leaders subsequently opposed all its recommendations on profit sharing and employee ownership plans, which in the end were mainly set up by nonunion companies. George W. Perkins, the J. P. Morgan investment banker, was head of its profit-sharing department, with other senior business leaders heading up a wide range of high-profile policy initiatives that resulted in reports, books, press, and some real changes in policy in Washington and the states. Now they pushed a head-on attempt at a redesign of capitalism.

In 1921, the group published as a book a systematic, 426-page report dealing with profit sharing and employee stock ownership. The report looked at what hundreds of U.S. corporations were doing and reported on developments in the business sectors in England and France, where these innovations had gotten under way several decades earlier. Because of the National Civic Federation's prestige, its staff managed to get company executives to report directly on their plans in long letters that included their attitudes about the plans and views of the results—surely a professor's dream! The first page of the book was unabashed in stating that the share idea was not just a personnel technique and that the goal was to "find some means of securing a wider distribution of wealth." Perkins wrote a long, carefully argued scholarly summary saying that a successful profit-sharing plan gave real financial benefits to employees on top of their fixed wages, that the profit-sharing formula had to be spelled out in advance, that it should not simply pay out cash but make the workers partners in the business by granting workers employee ownership shares funded by the profit sharing. Perkins favored profit sharing, but he did not paper over its problems: some firms abandoned the scheme due to the administrative burden of executives having to create a custom plan for every firm.

Perkins wanted corporations to provide employees with an honest and fair annual financial report so that they could understand the business, see how they could get involved in improving it, and trust the transparency of the profit-sharing formulas. In the companies where management was patient enough to adopt a careful approach to profit sharing, Perkins reported that the available evidence suggested lower turnover, higher productivity, more loyalty, and employee-initiated improvements that benefited shareholders. He reported that unions rejected the entire idea of shares for many reasons, to some extent because of the same fairness issues Perkins himself raised. In the end, Perkins liked profit sharing but could not ignore the many abandonments of plans and the great amount of personal attention that creating each plan took. Perkins saw employee stock ownership as having a more solid future, since every corporation had the mechanism for sharing the stock it already had in place.[23]

The National Industrial Conference Board

Then, another powerful group came forward. The National Industrial Conference Board (today the influential Conference Board) was organized by several dominant manufacturers and related industry associations. The National Industrial Conference Board published two influential reports on profit sharing and employee stock ownership focused solely on manufacturing operations. Executives of the firms reported on the impact of many of the plans and offered thoughtful analyses. The group's 1920 profit-sharing report and book found that most profit-sharing plans were successful when they were tried, that they promoted lower turnover, greater cooperation between employees and the company, and higher loyalty. Workers typically received 5 to 15 percent on top of wages through shares, and most workers were included. On the negative side of the ledger, profit-sharing plans were often abandoned because firms did not invest in them long enough, workers got apathetic, the company did not have profits, or unions opposed the plans. Again, this report stressed that using profit sharing to finance longer-term employee stock ownership promoted a closer tie to the company and more satisfaction. The group repeated that there appeared to be a more rapid growth in employee stock ownership plans, that these plans were easier to set up since the stock mechanism already existed in the companies, and that they were cheaper to operate since cash profits did not have to be paid out. Analyzing the preference for share ownership, historian Sanford Jacoby has stressed that employee stock ownership did not involve the grand promises Pillsbury and Nelson and Procter made in the 1880s, that it involved management giving up less control, that it used the stock market to distribute the shares, and that employee share plans could even raise some new capital in the process.

The National Industrial Conference Board's next foray was its 1928 employee ownership study and book. The report covered almost four hundred plans where the corporations made it easy for workers to buy stock on the installment plan at some discount and fund the purchase with dividends or cash profit shares. Expanding the distribution of wealth was an issue that this corporate group spoke about with no shyness. The group reported that the growth of employee stock ownership was tied to the general uptick in stock ownership in the American population and was viewed as a form of distinctively American "popular capitalism." Both companies and Wall Street realized that extending share-based capitalism was possible when they witnessed how easily and enthusiastically the American public responded to buying the Liberty Bonds used to fund World War I. Small investors had flocked to the idea, so maybe a "popular capitalism" was now possible. If farmers and workers would buy war bonds so easily, they could be educated to buy shares, too.

By 1928 there were 1 million workers with $1 billion in employee stock ownership investments in broad-based plans that included most levels of workers and which owned about 5 percent of the total stock of many corporations. In half of the cases, workers got preferred stock that was less risky. The report said it was not far-fetched that employee share ownership could become truly significant in the economy. The company association reported that the firms expected lower employee turnover, although the researchers thought that the amounts of stock needed to be much larger in order to have more of an efficiency impact on company operations. The risk to workers was underlined as a major concern. Again, the group put together an exhaustive review of the working parts of the employee ownership plans showing in meticulous detail what mechanisms made the idea workable, reduced risk, and made shares accessible for the greatest number of workers. Many of these mechanisms became the basis of federal laws on employee stock purchase plans and stock options that are the forms of broad-based capitalism in the United States today.[24]

John D. Rockefeller Jr. and the Special Conference Committee

The titans were not done yet. The most activist and forceful and resourceful corporate group, yet little known and secretive, was the Special Conference Committee founded by John D. Rockefeller Jr. in 1919. After the embarrassment and bad press of the violent and tragic Ludlow Massacre over worker rights at the Rockefeller Colorado Fuel & Iron Company, the Rockefeller organization decided to spearhead its own redesign of American capitalism. In a thinking-out-of-the-box move, John Rockefeller Jr. hired former Canadian minister of labor William Lyon Mackenzie King as a special adviser on the effort and head of industrial research for the Rockefeller Foundation. (The widely admired King subsequently became the longest-serving prime minister of Canada.) With a doctorate from Harvard, King had written a book called *Industry and Humanity* on the idea that capital and labor were natural allies.

The Special Conference Committee was made up of CEOs and heads of industrial relations for many of the largest corporations in the country, namely AT&T, Bethlehem Steel, DuPont, GE, GM, Goodyear, International Harvester, Irving Trust, Standard Oil of New Jersey, U.S. Rubber, U.S. Steel, and Westinghouse. Led by Standard Oil personnel relations executive Clarence Hicks, the group helped spearhead the "welfare capitalism" movement whereby corporations would continue to focus more on employee welfare in order to gain employee trust and loyalty and cooperation. The companies were encouraged to implement improvements in working conditions, paid vacations, sickness and injury insurance, profit sharing, employee stock ownership, and nonunion forms of company-sponsored employee representation, along with cafeteria, recreational, and educational programs.

The Special Conference Committee was for many years little publicized and coordinated most of its activities through informal meetings and dinners and what today might be called "benchmarking." Each of these leading corporations put a broad-based employee stock ownership program into practice. To spread its influence, the group held regular conferences through the YMCA and the National Association of Manufacturers. But, clearly, this group had no time for unions and was committed to electing nonunion, management-coordinated work councils that the labor movement considered "sham unions." Rockefeller set up a group called Industrial Relations Counselors, a consulting firm that helped corporations implement the plans.[25]

The Role of Princeton University and the Wharton School

Princeton University played an outsize role in the employee stock ownership story because of the early role of Professor Lyman Atwater in its political economy course and the large public role of William Cooper Procter. In 1922, the Rockefellers funded the Industrial Relations Unit in the Department of Economics at Princeton, along with other college programs to study these ideas and educate the rest of academia about them. The Industrial Research Department at the University of Pennsylvania's Wharton School (now the Department of Management) grew out of similar initiatives and played an important role. Altogether, Rockefeller put forth a coordinated effort.[26]

In 1926, the head of the Rockefeller program at Princeton University, economics professor Robert Foerster, came out with a report and book surveying the experience of corporations implementing employee stock ownership plans. He could not have made the connection between this effort and the Madisonian share idea in American history any more clear-cut. Those who appreciated the larger issues of employee ownership "would deplore the permanent growth of a wage earner caste, the coming of a class counterposed to another, the owning class, the acceptance by the workers of a status which has always bred discontent." He proposed that "from ancient times men have attacked the principle that the few should own and the many should serve, holding it to be a principle of instability, tending to subvert the state." The question was how to apply the idea of "scattered ownership . . . by the many" to the large corporation.

The new Princeton book on employee stock ownership again used the privileged perch of the Special Conference Committee network and a respected national university in order to collect detailed information on about four hundred corporations. The Standard Oil of New Jersey plan was considered the model lower-risk plan, with the company generously contributing half of employee payments for stock and selling the stock at one-third off the market price, with dividends on the stock being used to pay the stock off more rapidly. Employees had now become 44 percent of all shareholders at Standard Oil, owned almost 5 percent of the company, and elected company-sponsored nonunion works councils by 1926. The study found that the plans spread quickly and easily and included virtually all employees. The machinery of having employees buy stock at a discount on installments spread over a long period worked smoothly. Using dividends to pay off the stock and less-hazardous preferred stock helped reduce the risk.

Professor Foerster reported that employers were generally satisfied with the plans, typically seeing better employee-employer relations, and that the employee "consciously or unconsciously takes a deeper interest, works a little harder, wastes less." Some firms pointed to lower turnover. The researchers thought that some form of worker board representation made sense. Foerster found that a number of companies, like Procter & Gamble, had elected worker representatives on the board of directors, and that others had special worker shareholder meetings. This landmark study made clear that the corporations expected employee stock ownership to lead to greater efficiency and productivity. There was no question, however, that both the National Industrial Conference Board and the Special Conference Committee were more favorable to employee stock ownership than to profit sharing.

Rockefeller's initiative grew and peaked just before the stock market crash of 1929 and the Great Depression. The Princeton study raised the issue of excessive risk to workers if stocks were to go down significantly. That is exactly what happened. In Rockefeller's defense, the Standard Oil employee ownership plan, as noted, sold workers stock at a 50 percent subsidy and at a third of the price, financed partly by dividends—a meaningful hedge against just the crash that happened. The plan had many grant-like qualities. During the Depression, the Princeton University Industrial Relations Section again looked at employee share ownership, with a new book by Eleanor Davis in 1933, *Employee Stock Ownership and the Depression*. It concluded that basing the redesign of capitalism on employee stock ownership funded partly or completely by worker savings, in spite of the discounts offered, was too risky an approach, given the unprecedented level of this crash and the unpredictability of crashes.

TAXES, THE ROLE OF GOVERNMENT, AND INDUSTRY ASSOCIATIONS

The interest in employee share ownership initially waned after this period. Unions were legalized in the 1935 Wagner Act, employer-coordinated nonunion work councils were made illegal, and unions consolidated their pathway to argue for "fair shares" through collective bargaining about wages. Over the next fifty years, both union and nonunion companies gave workers a share of increased productivity in fixed pay packages. Cash profit sharing and gain sharing became far more acceptable to some unions after collective bargaining was legalized and they could negotiate the terms in order to be sure the accounting for the plans and the benefits was really fair. Sanford Jacoby has documented how many nonunion companies continued to foster employee stock ownership and profit sharing in the 1940s and 1950s, a phenomenon that exists right up to this day.[27]

For most of American history, corporations that had employee stock ownership or profit sharing simply did not look to the government for any leadership whatsoever. Various states amended their corporate laws in the early 1900s in order to make employee stock purchase plans easier to do. After the Sixteenth Amendment to the United States Constitution in 1913 legalized a federal income tax, the federal government began to levy both corporate income taxes and individual income taxes, and some government opinion on the tax status of the share plans became absolutely necessary. The corporations advocating profit sharing and employee stock ownership argued for and received tax incentives so that both the corporations and any worker contribution to these plans were exempt from corporate and individual income taxes under the Revenue Act of 1921. Shortly thereafter, as the capital gains tax rate differed from the ordinary income tax rate, employees could benefit from lower capital gains rates for employee stock ownership. As a result, after the period of corporate experimentation with profit sharing and employee stock ownership from the 1880s to 1920, most of the subsequent new formats to promote shares for workers were defined in federal law and continued to receive some tax regulation and benefits. The tax benefits were modest because they mainly allowed deductions for the share idea that were similar to deductions for all forms of compensation. In the end, the share idea did not really gain substantially different deductions.

Associations of corporations and individual companies (and a few unions taking a different tack) continued to implement the ideas themselves. While the Conference Board continued publishing studies, the most influential group since the 1950s was the Council of Profit Sharing Industries and its Profit Sharing Research Foundation, later the Profit Sharing Council of America (now the Plan Sponsor Council of America). It conducted educational and research programs on profit sharing and related employee share ownership plans from the 1940s straight through to the present day, with annual conferences and surveys. The council's thorough reports described how some corporations continued to intensively practice both profit sharing and employee stock ownership by providing substantial capital income and stock ownership to workers using profit shares to fund employee stock ownership. An Opinion Research Corporation survey in 1957 and a Dun & Bradstreet survey in 1961, both commissioned by the council, established that some large corporations and small businesses were practicing profit sharing, many with employee ownership as a goal, as a result of these determined efforts by the companies and their associations.[28]

Developments to encourage broad-based capitalism continued to expand. Philip Murray and Clinton Golden of the United Steelworkers Union espoused the idea of gain sharing, and it has been practiced by many union employers up to the present time. The idea was that teamwork and employee suggestions would increase productivity, and the gains would be shared with workers. Also, Ray Carey, the former CEO of ADT who received his MBA from the Harvard Business School in 1950, worked with union workers on employee share ownership. Like many corporate leaders before him, he developed a comprehensive analysis of the corporation and the modern economy based on his reading of economic and political philosophy that he describes in his book, *Democratic Capitalism*. He established models of profit and equity sharing that he personally implemented at ADT.[29]

As the U.S. entered a period of "normalcy" following the Depression, World War II, and the Korean War, there were firms that operated successfully with cash profit sharing. Kodak and Sears and members of the profit-sharing association provided large capital income and ownership stakes to workers above a fair fixed wage. Some companies continued to combine the profit-sharing and employee share ownership by funding the purchase of company stock with profit-sharing payments or stock dividends. This deferred profit sharing that combined short-term cash profit sharing and long-term employee stock ownership followed much along the lines that William Cooper Procter and George Perkins had envisioned. Other companies offered workers the opportunity to purchase company stock at a discount. Unions raised issues regarding the definition of profits, the firm's inclusion or exclusion of workers from various share plans, and the unilateral reduction of wages or wage increases for shares. Without some new policy initiative, it was "all quiet along the Potomac" in broad-based capital ownership. And then, influenced by the ideas of Louis O. Kelso and the political entrepreneurship of Senator Russell Long, Congress took action to establish a new vehicle for employee ownership—the Employee Stock Ownership Plan.

THE FIRST INDUSTRIAL HOMESTEAD LEGISLATION: LOUIS O. KELSO AND RUSSELL B. LONG

One person appeared with the ideas that led Congress to create a new vehicle, the Employee Stock Ownership Plan (ESOPs), specifically designed to advance significant employee ownership. Louis O. Kelso was a lawyer focused on corporate and municipal finance, who had many imaginative but practical ideas for broadening capital ownership. His law firm specialized in financing purchases of corporations by their workers and finding legal formats to make the ideas work. His first book, *The Capitalist Manifesto*, written with former University of Chicago philosopher Mortimer Adler synthesized his political philosophy and described creative ways to finance broad-based capitalism. He set up Kelso & Company, which early in its history assisted corporations in selling large stakes to their workers, and which then became a private equity firm after Kelso ceased to have a major operational role in the company. He continued to write books on broad-based capitalism with his collaborator and wife, Patricia Hetter Kelso. He died in 1991.

Kelso developed a straightforward way to provide lower-risk employee stock ownership not dependent on worker savings. Corporations often finance machinery, technology, and various kinds of infrastructure with either profits and retained earnings from operations or bank loans or bond issues. When existing owners use this financing, they extend and concentrate their own ownership. Kelso saw that it would be possible for worker or citizen trusts to take out loans and use the company's money to pay back the loans and buy shares in the corporations and then spread ownership more broadly. Kelso held that workers should not make risky investments in shares with their own wages or savings but should instead finance their stock ownership using the techniques other owners used to expand their own capital ownership—what he called self-liquidating finance—namely, assets can pay for themselves out of income and profits if the financing is properly designed. He redesigned the finance of capital formation in order to create more capitalists.

Kelso's ideas influenced a broad range of citizens across the political spectrum, and had a huge impact on Senator Russell Long, chairman of the Senate Finance Committee (and son of Huey Long, the 1930s populist governor of Louisiana famous for his Share Our Wealth program and motto "Every Man a King"). Long called for "policies to diffuse capital ownership broadly, so that many individuals, particularly productive workers, can participate as owners of industrial capital." Senator Hubert Humphrey asked the Joint Economic Committee to figure out how "to provide a realistic opportunity for more U.S. Citizens to become owners of capital." Then California governor Ronald Reagan said, "Ownership of land in most of the world had not been possible for the ordinary citizen. . . . The Homestead Act set the pattern for American capitalism. . . . Now we need an Industrial Homestead Act, and that isn't impossible." Later, as president, Reagan declared: "I've long believed one of the mainsprings of our own liberty has been the widespread ownership of property among our people and the expectation that anyone's child, even from the humblest of families, could grow up to own a business or a corporation. . . . I can't help but believe that in the future we will see in the United States and throughout the western world an increasing trend toward the next logical step, employee ownership." John D. Rockefeller 3rd, who in 1973 would return to the questions that so caught his family's attention in the 1920s, strongly endorsed Kelso's ideas as a way to address economic inequality.

Kelso collaborated with Senator Long to introduce the employee stock ownership plan as part of the Employee Retirement Security Act (ERISA) of 1974, which Congress enacted to protect the pension fund moneys of workers and to assure that the tax advantages of saving for retirement went to all workers. The ESOP law provides criteria for how an employee ownership plan distributes stocks to a range of workers in a corporation and for protecting the rights of employee shareholders and investors. The ERISA law was a bipartisan piece of legislation that grew out of retirement plan reforms initiated by President John F. Kennedy, was supported by President Richard Nixon, and was signed into law by President Gerald Ford. It passed the House and Senate unanimously. The federal government created an enforcement machinery in the U.S. Department of Labor to monitor ESOPs for fairness and in the U.S. Internal Revenue Service to monitor that firms were not abusing the tax incentive.

Under the law, any corporation can set up a trust called an employee stock ownership plan. The company contributes stock to the trust, or cash to purchase company stock that is distributed to workers. The trust can also borrow from a banking institution or other lender to buy company stock, so that large amounts of ownership can be purchased in single transactions. With an ESOP, a private banking institution or other lender makes the loan to the company. The ESOP grants stock to individual workers as the loan is repaid by the company out of its revenues. Workers' shares are held in a trust until workers retire and leave the company. When they leave or retire, workers can cash in the shares in a private company for a fair market price or sell them on a stock market in a public company. Because the company guarantees the loan and pays it back, workers do not have the risk of mortgaging their assets for the loan or using their wages or savings to pay for it.

Kelso and Long tackled the quandary that employee share plans based on individual workers buying small amounts had spread slowly and often did not amount to significant wealth stakes for workers. Kelso was firm in holding that workers' wages were for living and that the share idea should not be based in any way on the stock being paid for by workers themselves. He thus reversed a key failure of employee stock ownership thinking before the stock market crash of 1929 and created a principle around the alternative: workers would finance their ownership using the techniques other owners used to expand their own ownership. The ESOP gave substantial tax incentives to encourage employee ownership. When a corporation contributes to an ESOP or takes a loan to buy stock for workers, it receives a tax deduction similar to the deduction corporations receive for contributions to employee benefit plans in general.

In addition, with ESOPs, both the interest and principal on the loan and any dividends used to finance worker stock also became deductible. With a big loan, the ESOP worker trusts could create much larger amounts of worker wealth overnight compared to the more personally risky and slowly growing stock purchase plans of the 1920s. When the company wants to expand, it can finance additional loans through the ESOP so that the capital ownership for managers and workers continues to expand.

Later, the law introduced provisions for entrepreneurs with small family businesses to sell the company to an ESOP and be excused from capital gains tax under certain conditions. Proponents of the ESOP tax incentives argue that one of the chief threats to ongoing successful small businesses is that often there is no stable buyer for the business if a daughter or son does not want to take over. The alternative of selling the company to a competent team of existing managers and the workers as a group saves local jobs and creates a stable group of future taxpayers. Another tax incentive allows ESOPs to be set up as S corporations, a corporate form that pays no federal taxes itself because it passes the federal tax obligation to the individual worker shareholders, thus potentially broadening the tax base. Kelso and Long also recognized that worker shareholders would be coexisting with other shareholders in many corporations, and they tried to promote the idea among stock market companies.

The question of fairness to workers was addressed by federal rules that employee ownership plans had to include most employees in order to get the tax incentives. The plans had to grant ownership to individual workers at least according to their salaries. Detailed rules made clear that the highest-paid employees in an ESOP could not be the principal beneficiaries of the ownership plan, just as the highest-paid employee could not be the principal beneficiary of tax benefits for company-sponsored retirement or medical insurance plans. Later on, the law gave older workers the right to diversify their holdings in company stock well before retirement, which reduced their risk. The fact that private bankers or other lenders have to review and approve the loans to corporations that establish ESOPs presumably screens out some risk as well.

This effort has created the largest and, to date, the most durable pocket of meaningful employee share ownership in U.S. history. As we saw in Chapter 2, there are an estimated 10,300 corporations with ESOPs and similar plans, with about 10 million workers and almost a trillion dollars in total market value. In the first decade of the twenty-first century, about three thousand closely held companies are majority or 100 percent owned by their employees, about three thousand are 30 percent to 51 percent owned, and the rest have ownership ranging from about 5 percent to 30 percent. Researchers know a lot more about the companies with majority and 100 percent employee ownership because these companies form associations and often identify themselves to their customers and the public. Small- and medium-size closely held corporations tend to have majority and completely worker-owned ESOPs. Large public stock market companies like Procter & Gamble have more modest ESOPs with ownership ranging from 5 percent to 25 percent. Consistent with Francis Walker's and the American Economic Association experts' analysis a century earlier, most ESOPs are set up in ongoing corporations with professional management teams already in place. Most of the majority to 100 percent ESOPs result from the sales of an ongoing closely held family business to a new corporation whose managers and workers intend to operate the company after the founding entrepreneur or founding family members have retired.

There is a lively debate over the strengths and weaknesses of ESOPs, as there are for other activities or organizations that Congress seeks to encourage with tax deductions. Some critics see the ESOP tax incentives as a form of special-interest tax incentives from the Treasury. We see the ESOP as the continuation of the Founders' desire to reduce inequality and preserve democratic practices by extending property ownership to more Americans, as laid out in Chapter 1. The tax break given to persons who sell their business to their workers resonates with the primogeniture reform the Founders envisioned. Owners of small businesses are among the major groups of citizens advocating for the employee stock ownership idea, just as the widespread populist homestead movement got citizen support in the 1800s.

We also see the federal law that guarantees that individual workers in all closely held ESOP companies have a direct vote on all major corporate transactions such as the sale of the company, its merger, and so forth, as a force for increasing worker participation in the corporate cultures of ESOPs, especially in majority and completely employee-owned ESOP companies. One argument is that small business owners, especially owners of family businesses, would be less likely to sell a minority interest of a company to the workers, unless full voting rights on the stock were optional. The trend however is toward greater worker participation in the corporate cultures of ESOPs, especially in majority and completely employee-owned ESOP companies, and this needs to be strengthened by more training and benchmarking. Where nonexecutive worker board members have served on ESOP boards, the experience has been that they play a constructive role in the context of a diverse board.[30]

Seen through the perspective of the Founders' share and homestead ideas, the tax incentives for employee stock ownership are not just like any other tax deduction. They are putting our money behind the political and moral goal for broad-based ownership in American democracy. As a sidelight, a recent documentary film, *We the Owners: Employees Expanding the American Dream*, presents the story of managers and workers operating three corporations along the lines of these different share ideas and tells how they build a corporate culture that supports ownership.[31]

For over a hundred and fifty years, many citizens have worked to develop broad-based ownership models that can work inside the corporation and to study the impact of these ideas. Since the Revenue Act of 1921, the U.S. Congress and the administrations of successive presidents have responded to this citizen interest by encouraging the concepts. The original republican idea of a share in society and a homestead has always informed these efforts. What is the evidence that these ideas are good for companies, workers, and the nation as a whole? The next chapter looks at what we can learn when all the moving parts of profit sharing and employee stock ownership and the corporate cultures in which these ideas are situated are systematically studied using modern social science.

5 EVIDENCE

This chapter has a simple message: the cases of firms that succeed with various forms of broad-based capitalism in Chapter 2 generalize to business broadly.

To be sure, few firms succeed to the extent of Google, Procter & Gamble, or Southwest Airlines or do as well for their workers as some of the highlighted corporations of all sizes. The statistical evidence relates not to exemplars but to averages that reflect the experience of all firms in which employees have some property stake. The averages show that the key indicator of economic performance, namely productivity, and many other measures related to firm performance are higher for firms that operate with profit sharing and employee stock ownership than for otherwise comparable firms that do not follow those practices. The averages also show that workers in firms with shares and participatory work relations have higher compensation, stay on the job longer, and offer more suggestions for improvement than workers in other firms. In addition, workers in these businesses try to correct the behavior of fellow workers who are not working as hard as they should more than do workers without a property stake in their firm.

Studies that compare firms before and after they adopt profit sharing or employee stock ownership relative to firms that did not change policies also show that shares and participatory work practices improve performance. And in the few cases in which firms have experimented with different forms of shares or structures of work, or in which researchers have experimented with modes of pay and work in social science laboratories, the data show that workers also do better when they receive a share of output instead of solely being paid in fixed wages.[1] Beneath the averages, several studies find that success with broad-based capitalism and related work practices depends as much or more on the company building a supportive corporate culture as on pecuniary rewards.[2]

Does the superior performance of broad-based capitalist firms mean that extending profit sharing and employee stock ownership to more workers is "the solution" to America's economic problems and to the tension between inequality and democracy that exercised the Founders, or will the extension of broad-based ownership fail outside its current boundaries?

We are cautious to draw such a grand conclusion. Most of the evidence is from observational studies that compare outcomes between firms that have shares and participatory work relations because they believe this is the best choice for them, compared to firms that choose to operate differently because they believe that is their best choice. This type of evidence resembles medical studies where doctors analyze health outcomes between smokers and nonsmokers or between persons who take aspirin several times a week and those who do not take aspirin regularly, rather than from the scientific ideal where the scientist randomly assigns persons to smoking/not smoking, or to take/ not take aspirin. It is always possible that some unobserved genetic or other difference about people induced them to make those choices and also determined the outcomes. This muddies inferences about the causal impact of the choice and what would happen if the person (or firm) changed its choice.

Just as people differ from each other in ways that can produce different reactions to a medicine, companies differ in ways that make a particular share approach function well for one firm but not for another. In the medical case, differences in genetic makeup, medical history, environment, and age, among other factors, determine how a given medicine affects a person. In the company case, differences in organizational structure, history, economic environment, composition of the workforce, and age (think greenfield start-ups in Silicon Valley versus mature older companies) can influence how profit sharing, employee stock ownership, or granting stock options or restricted stock grants to all workers will affect performance. Statistical evidence that shows what works on average is no guarantee that it works for any particular patient or firm.

In the medical sciences, this is likely to change in the future. The frontier of medical science is personalized medicine, where doctors tailor medicines to individual patients. Building on the Human Genome Project, the National Institutes of Health is spending billions of dollars on basic research to create the knowledge base for personalized medicine. The biotechnology industry and large pharmaceutical firms are also spending large sums to move personalized medicine from lab research to patient care. The speed of scientific advance will, the experts tell us, create personalized medicine in the foreseeable future.

In the social and business sciences, the knowledge base for predicting how specific corporations or workers will respond to the introduction of profit sharing or employee stock ownership is not yet on the horizon. We do not have a Firm-Employee Genome Project to provide the scientific basis for developing share programs tailored to individual firms. What we have is a substantial body of evidence on the concomitants of employee stock ownership, profit sharing, and related work practices that can help guide judgments about the likely outcomes of increasing workers' stake in firms on average and in society broadly.

STARTING POINTS

When groups like the National Civic Federation, the Special Conference Committee, or the Industrial Relations Section at Princeton University tried to assess employee ownership and profit sharing in the 1920s, they spent a lot of time analyzing the detailed case histories of the companies. Today, with the advent of computerized data sets and statistical packages to analyze the data, many social scientists have estimated the effects of profit sharing and employee stock ownership on the productivity of firms using large samples of firms. The standard study of firm production relates the output of a firm to the inputs it deploys to create goods and services—capital, labor, and in some cases materials. Most studies use linear regression techniques to estimate the economists' workhorse "Cobb-Douglas" production function—a model that stretches back to U.S. Senator Paul Douglas's work in the 1920s.[3] Some studies add statistical bells and whistles to the model that improve standard errors of estimate or adjust for diverse statistical problems.[4]

To assess the effects on output of workers having a greater property stake, analysts expand the standard model with measures of the extent to which a firm has profit sharing, employee stock ownership, or related practices. The goal is to estimate the direction and magnitude of the coefficient of the measures of broad-based capitalism on output, conditional on all other inputs being the same. If the coefficient is positive and significant by standard statistical criterion, the analyst concludes that, on average, ownership or profit sharing is associated with greater productivity.

Researchers, including the authors of this book, have reviewed this work.[5] In 1995 Christopher Doucouliagos used a technique called meta-statistics to assess the magnitude and significance of coefficients from individual studies from different data scts, samples of different size, and subject to different biases or data imperfections, into a single estimate covering all studies. The notion is that the imperfections across studies are random, so that averaging gives a more accurate estimate of reality. These reviews find that firms with share arrangements average better outcomes than otherwise comparable firms without share arrangements.[6] The magnitude of effects is usually on the order of 2 percent to 5 percent. Profit sharing generally has larger effects on output than employee stock ownership, possibly because profit sharing is a more immediate reward than employee stock ownership, which is a more long-term reward. It may also reflect the fact that some companies are motivated by tax incentives to offer shares to their employees without changing their mode of operation to treat workers as owners or partners in the business. They talk the talk but do not walk the walk.

Combinations of programs—employee stock ownership and profit sharing, or a stock purchase plan and profit sharing—have larger effects on output than individual programs by themselves. Analyzing the pattern of programs at U.S. companies, Arin Dube and Richard Freeman found that companies tend to combine different kinds of share programs more than would occur if companies had selected programs independently.[7] Combining different kinds of shares makes a bigger difference. The higher return to combinations of programs than to single programs and disproportionate combinations suggests that share programs have substantial complementarity in their effects. A profit-sharing system gives fairly immediate rewards, while a stock ownership or employee stock option or restricted stock program focuses attention on actions that improve outcomes over the longer term. So it is better to combine them. We saw in Chapter 3 that a large number of citizens across the country have combinations of share programs, so managers appear to have figured this out. We saw in Chapter 2 that combining profit sharing and employee stock ownership quickly became common from the 1880s throughout the 1900s. Combining less risky approaches such as cash profit sharing and stock options and ESOPs and outright grants of company stock *with* more risky approaches such as employee stock purchase plans and buying company stock in 401(k) plans may be a way to design the share plan of the future.

To turn to specific studies, Appendix 5.1 summarizes five studies of the effects of share approaches on outcomes. The British government sponsored the first study, arguably the best existing study that uses standard production function methodology. The General Accounting Office (GAO; now the Government Accountability Office) of the U.S. Congress sponsored the second study. Both governments wanted to know whether policies that encouraged firms to introduce share approaches in their respective countries improved the productivity of firms, as proponents of the policies had predicted when the legislation was debated. Government sponsorship gave researchers access to financial and production information from within firms that was not in the public domain.

The 2007 United Kingdom Treasury commissioned study examined whether programs that gave firms tax incentives to introduce individual stock ownership, profit sharing, and employee stock options affected the economic performance of those firms. The analysis covered a sufficiently large proportion of the United Kingdom's economy to suggest that broad-based employee ownership improved performance.[8] A parallel study of publicly available information of corporations with broad-based capitalism in the UK by Alex Bryson of the London School of Economics and Richard Freeman gave comparable results and found that the effects were greatly influenced by management giving workers greater autonomy in decision making.[9]

The 1987 GAO study examined 414 firms that set up employee stock ownership plans in 1976–1979 when ESOPs were just getting off the ground. The research design matched each ESOP firm with a non-ESOP firm of similar size in the same industry. This study found that a combination of employee stock ownership with a supportive corporate culture raised productivity, whereas ESOPs by themselves had no statistically significant effect on output.[10]

The third study, by Joseph Blasi and Douglas Kruse in 2000, followed the design of the GAO study and looked at three hundred privately held firms that set up ESOPs between 1988 and 1994 and compared each ESOP firm to similar companies of the same size in the same industry but without an ESOP. It found that the ESOP firms had significantly higher sales growth and higher sales per worker and were more likely to have survived through 1999 than matching firms without ESOPs.[11]

The fourth study was a field experiment in which researchers randomly assigned profit sharing to several stores, helping overcome concerns that other factors could be responsible for any changes in performance. The stores where profit sharing was established had increases in productivity and profitability, and decreased turnover, relative to a group of stores that were not assigned profit sharing. The improvements for the profit-sharing firms were more immediate and long lasting than for the non-profit-sharing companies.[12]

The last study, summarized in Appendix 5.1, differs from the others by relying on management reports on quality of output, financial performance, and worker turnover rather than on financial and production data. It gives a similar picture: firms do better when they combine a participatory company culture with profit sharing and employee stock ownership.[13]

Finding a positive relation between broad-based capitalism approaches such as employee stock ownership and profit sharing and firm output across many studies shows that, consistent with the examples in Chapter 2 and the historical evidence in Chapter 4, something real is going on with corporations that adopt profit sharing or employee stock ownership. To get a better sense of what that real something was, in 2000 we initiated the Shared Capitalism Research Project at the National Bureau of Economic Research in Cambridge, Massachusetts.[14] In contrast to the studies just discussed, which obtained information from companies about their performance as firms, we sought information from workers about what was happening at their workplaces, what their responses were to having a property stake in the business, and what benefits flowed to them from employment in a corporation with broad-based capitalism.

THE NBER SHARED CAPITALISM STUDY

Our study surveyed over forty thousand employees in fourteen corporations. The companies included large multinationals traded on major U.S. stock markets, important high-technology innovators large and small, medium-size corporations and smaller factories with ESOPs, financial services firms and other service-oriented companies. One large multinational included over three hundred facilities spread across the country and in their foreign divisions. This meant that we have data on lots of workers but a small, almost case-study-size, sample of firms. Business school researchers call studies like this "insider econometrics," by which they mean a study that gathers sufficient quantitative data on performance to test hypotheses in a small number of companies (sometimes just one) but combines the quantitative analysis with discussions with the firm to help interpret the data.[15] Economists sometimes call this "pin factory" economics in honor of Adam Smith's famous pin factory: you go to a company, observe what goes on, talk with management and workers, and then generalize what you learned.[16] The difference between analysis today and in Smith's time is that analysts today gather enough data to test statistically their interpretation of what the firm does. In our study, we asked workers in each firm to fill out a detailed confidential survey. Over forty thousand did so, with a response rate averaging 53 percent. The survey measures can be found in our earlier book *Shared Capitalism at Work*.[17]

Our initial plan was to pair firms that had profit sharing and employee stock ownership with their closest competitors who paid workers solely with wages or salaries per unit of time, but this plan did not pan out. Fourteen firms with some form of broad-based capitalism agreed to participate in the study, but their competitors were unwilling to participate. We feared this would not give us enough contrast to reach firm conclusions about broad-based capitalism. To use the medical science analogy, we had firms that were trying the medicine but did not have evidence on the control firms without the medicine.

TROUBLE IN RIVER CITY, WITH A CAPITAL *T*

A few things rescued our study from trouble. We quickly learned that there was a wide variation in the share programs at the different corporations and in the extent to which workers had a property stake inside each corporation across all the businesses, among establishments within firms, and even among workers within establishments. The variation was sufficient to allow for detailed statistical analysis. We recognized that to the extent that broad-based capitalist arrangements improved outcomes, the absence of firms without such programs would likely bias downward estimates of those impacts.[18] While it is always desirable to have a representative sample, second best is to have a sample biased in a given direction, since that means that if the results are in that direction, they understate the effect and thus provide a lower bound in what the relevant policy accomplishes. Finally, in order to obtain a valid control group, we obtained information from the General Social Survey national survey described in Chapter 3 on workers in firms that had no employee stock ownership or profit sharing.

The first finding from the worker surveys was that shares and work practices varied widely inside and across these companies. We gave each worker an overall shared capitalism score based on how much ownership he or she had in the company and how much he or she shared in profits and stock options. The scores varied substantially among workers. Some had a large ownership stake. Some had little. Some were in establishments with strong gain-sharing or profit-sharing programs. Others were not. We then compared workers who had different overall shared capitalism scores but who were similar in their occupation, their fixed wages, supervisory responsibilities, tenure with the company, gender, age, disability, and so forth. Sometimes we analyzed how economic outcomes varied among workers within the same company. Sometimes we analyzed how economic outcomes varied among workplaces. While we had too few companies to compare companies, we used the General Social Survey sample of workers, who are chosen at random from the country as a whole and thus likely to represent single firms, to compare workers in companies with and without broad-based capitalism. Our goal was to estimate how workers responded to the different forms of shared equity and profits and to explore their views of these modes of sharing and work practices.

We found that workers with higher shared capitalism scores were more committed to their employer along a variety of dimensions than those with lower scores, and that these workers were better off in a host of important aspects of their work lives. In particular, workers with greater property in firms are more likely to stay with the company, are more loyal, are more willing to work harder, make more suggestions, and have better fixed pay and working conditions. This is quite similar to the characteristics that many of the Founders ascribed to the independent proprietor of land in early American history.

More Likely to Stay with Their Firm

Management in most firms seeks to lower the rate of turnover. The reason is that recruiting, training, and integrating new employees into a workforce costs money, time, and effort.[19] Our measure of turnover was whether workers intended to look for a new job—a strong predictor of actual future turnover behavior. In the National Bureau of Economic Research study, 9 percent of workers with high levels of profit sharing, employee stock ownership, or stock options reported that they were likely to look for a new job, compared to 15 percent of employees with low levels of broad-based capitalist compensation—a difference of 6 percentage points in the likelihood of staying. Among individual forms of shares, profit or gain sharing was associated with the lowest turnover. But the combination with employee stock ownership had an even greater impact in reducing turnover.[20] To see if this result fit the nation, we examined responses to a similar question on the General Social Survey and found that 15 percent of workers with profit sharing, stock options, or employee ownership were likely to leave their firm, compared to a fifth of workers without any form of broad-based capitalism—a difference of 5 percentage points.

Have Greater Loyalty and Pride Working for the Firm

In the National Bureau for Economic Research study, 58 percent of workers with a high level of broad-based capitalism reported great loyalty to the firm, compared to 46 percent of workers with low levels of such shares. The national General Social Survey asked a comparable question about whether workers were proud to work for an employer; 44 percent of workers with a high level of broad-based capitalism reported a high level of pride, compared to 29 percent of workers without employee stock ownership or profit or gain sharing. Workers with profit or gain sharing expressed the highest loyalty, while those with employee stock ownership and stock options had somewhat more modest increases in loyalty that nevertheless still exceeded that of workers without these forms of shares. Workers with the combination of the different forms, namely, employee stock ownership and profit shares, showed the greatest loyalty to their firm and greatest pride in working for it.

Express Greater Willingness to Work Hard

To obtain a measure of the work effort that employees give to their firm, we asked: To what extent do you agree or disagree with this statement: I am willing to work harder than I have to in order to help the company I work for succeed. Answers to a question like this offer potentially great insight into how workers feel about their firm and their effort at work. On a scale of 1 (strongly disagree) to 5 (strongly agree), the average response of workers in the fourteen broad-based capitalism firms was 4 (agree). The proportion who strongly agreed was 36 percent for workers with high levels of broad-based capitalism, compared to 30 percent for workers who did not participate in the firm's broad-based plans, either because they were too new to the job or for other reasons.[21] Workers with profit sharing and gain sharing were at the top of the willingness-to-work-hard ladder, whereas those who had only broad-based employee stock ownership and stock options did not differ from other workers.

Make More Suggestions

In 1832 Charles Babbage, famous as inventor of the concept of the computer, proposed two principles for spurring innovation: "1. That a considerable part of the wages received by each person should depend on the profits made by the establishment; and 2. That every person connected with it should derive more advantage from applying any improvement he might discover than he could by any other course."[22] We asked workers how often they made suggestions to their firm and found that among those with some form of broad-based capitalism, 26 percent made a suggestion at least once a month, compared to only 18 percent among workers without shares. Employee stock ownership had a larger impact than profit sharing on making suggestions, but the most effective practice was to combine employee stock ownership and profit sharing with supportive work practices.[23] Ownership gives workers a capital stake in the company. Profit sharing gives them short-term capital income. Employee involvement programs of diverse sorts, such as worker town meetings, open door policies, self-directed work teams, and worker problem-solving committees, encourage workers to participate in decisions. Workers in firms with employee stock ownership and profit sharing and supportive work practices not only made more suggestions than workers in other firms but also reported that management was more likely to heed their suggestions than workers in other non-share firms.[24]

One large company especially interested in innovation asked us to add questions to our survey of their corporation to find out whether their workers perceived a culture of innovation, or not, at their workplace. The responses to these questions showed that workers who had shares, a cooperative culture, and mutual monitoring were most likely to view the firm's culture as positively inclined toward innovation. One has to look beyond measurements of "effort" to understand broad-based capitalism in the new workplaces today because a lot of the success of work teams in the current economy has more to do with ingenuity and innovation than with sheer physical or mental effort. Workers do a lot less heavy lifting and pushing and pulling and shoveling and carrying and putting things on and taking things off than they did fifty years ago. Much of this effort is now done by machines, so what happens in teams and between workers and with workers and customers is far more important. In an examination of threshold effects, research by Dan Weltman indicates that the initial effect of employee share ownership on individual workers appears to kick in at very low thresholds in influencing a number of positive attitudes toward their job and toward the company. The effect on their overall company loyalty and their perception of company fairness appears to increase as cumulative grants of share ownership are larger.[25]

Have Better Wages and Work Conditions

Do workers gain from a property stake in their firm? The question may strike some readers as a clumsy setup to an obvious answer. However, some critics of employee shares believe that when workers have a stake in ownership, this stake comes at the cost of lower wages or other benefits so that, on a net basis, workers may not be better off with profit sharing or employee ownership than otherwise. It is entirely possible that this is how shares could end up. In fact, some managers believe in what they call "pay at risk" by putting the worker under the maximum possible pressure to earn even fair wages. Remember in the last chapter that Samuel Gompers harshly criticized some profit-sharing programs in the 1920s as being unfair for this reason. Other critics view the share systems as a bit of a sham, designed to elicit greater worker effort and to shift risk to workers without increasing their pay or the quality of their jobs or their overall take-home compensation. Some call such a system "management by stress," a method of sweating the workforce and curbing worker power and influence.[26] Our evidence dispels this criticism and supports the "obvious answer."

There is strong evidence that employee stock ownership and profit sharing have meaningful impacts on workers' wealth.

Workers with profit sharing or employee stock ownership are higher paid and have more benefits than other workers.[27] This means that the substantial profit sharing and gain sharing and ownership stakes for the typical worker in these plans (shown in Chapter 3) tend to come on top of, not in place of, fair fixed wages and benefits.[28] These workers also obtain more training and have greater job security than other workers, and enjoy better work conditions with greater participation in decisions, better treatment by the employer, and less supervision.[29] These better conditions are consistently linked to profit sharing, although some of the conditions are also better for workers with gain sharing, stock options, and employee stock ownership. Being eligible for profit sharing or being an employee-owner by itself is associated with better wages and work conditions. But the size of a profit or gain share, the value of the employer stock ownership stake, and the size of the potential stock option profit are also associated with much better conditions for workers. Having a stake in the firm is not manna from heaven to workers, but it brings American workers closer to the vision of the Founders for our democracy—as property owners with greater say in their working lives than hired hands.

What about Those Free Riders?

Imagine you are part of a team of one hundred workers that produces goods or services in a business that pays workers a share of profits beyond some level, so that by sharing with the other workers you get one-hundredth of the extra profits from better performance. You may be in a position to increase firm profits by $10 through your own extra effort, but because any extra profits are shared with all the other workers, you get only 10 cents of that extra $10 (with the rest going to the other ninety-nine workers). Let's say you value the personal cost of the time and energy you put into the extra effort at $1.00. Does it make sense for you to work hard? The arithmetic says no. The payoff of 10 cents is far short of the $1.00 cost of effort. But if *every* worker can increase profits by $10, does it make sense for all workers to work hard? Yes, because then the profits would rise by $1,000 (= 100 × $10), and the payoff to each worker would be $10, which far exceeds the $1.00 cost of effort. Everyone benefits if everyone works hard. But every individual has an incentive to shirk.

This example illustrates the classic free-rider objection to broad-based capitalism—that profit sharing or employee stock ownership in a large group cannot succeed because each individual has an incentive to shirk. Since all workers presumably know that everyone thinks this way, the gist of this criticism is that ownership stakes and profit shares will fail to motivate anyone to work hard. The free-rider objection is rooted in the self-interested rational behavior on which much of standard economics and game theory is built. The same analysis says no one should vote, that people should always defect in prisoner dilemma games, should never give to charity, and so on. In the free rider's world, altruism or cooperation for the good of all is as rare as hen's teeth.

For whatever reason or reasons, the world is not like that.[30] People vote, give to charity, cooperate with their neighbors, are willing to sacrifice some current consumption for the benefit of future generations, donate to charity, and so on. Bernard Madoff is the exception, not the rule.

What do actual corporations and actual workers in companies where workers share in profits or hold shares or stock options in the firm do to overcome the incentive to free ride and produce the positive outcomes that studies find enterprises with broad-based capitalism experience?

One potentially important channel for overcoming the free-rider problem is through worker co-monitoring—the process by which workers with an ownership stake and a profit share take on the responsibility of assuring that fellow workers do their part at workplaces. This can take the form of workers helping their peers learn the job and do it right or in some cases telling them to get their act together. While the notion that co-monitoring can reduce free-rider behavior is an old one in the analysis of team production, until the National Bureau of Economic Research's Shared Capitalism Project, no major survey had documented co-monitoring behavior, linked it to shares and the structure of work, and examined how it affected employee performance at workplaces.

The first step in our analysis was to find out if workers could observe fellow employees' work activity—a necessary precondition for trying to get their coworkers who were not doing a good job to improve their performance. We asked each of the workers in the study: "In your job how easy is it for you to see whether your coworkers are working well or poorly?" Using a scale of 0 (not easy at all to see) to 10 (very easy to see), the vast majority of workers reported that they could observe their coworkers' performance. On the General Social Survey of workers across the United States, 77 percent of workers gave answers in the 7–10 category, meaning that they too could observe their coworkers' performance, with nearly half giving the highest possible score (10). On the National Bureau of Economic Research's fourteen-firm survey, 62 percent of workers gave a response of 7 or more to this question. Thus, workers say that they can figure out what their fellow worker is doing.

Given that most workers could observe the effort of coworkers, we next asked how likely it was that they would take action involving "a fellow employee not working as hard or well as he or she should." Workers varied a lot in their answers to this question. Some said it was very likely they would talk directly to the employee. Some said they would speak to a supervisor or manager. And some said it was very likely they would do nothing. The size of a workplace was an important factor in these differences. In a workplace with fewer than ten employees, 44 percent of workers said they would definitely respond in some fashion to seeing a fellow employee shirk, whereas in a workplace with over one hundred workers, only 35 percent said they would respond. Since getting a worker who is not performing as well as they should to shape up has smaller benefits to other workers in a larger workplace, this is free-rider behavior at work in monitoring free riding!

Having an ownership stake or a profit share in the firm is another important determinant of worker co-monitoring. We discovered that workers with employee stock ownership or profit sharing or gain sharing are more likely to step forward to try to improve their fellow employees' work behavior than workers without shares. In the fourteen-firm survey of corporations with some form of broad-based capitalism, the intensity of profit sharing and gain sharing was the most important factor in whether workers seek to improve fellow workers' performance. In the General Social Survey, where some workers are in firms with no programs at all, the presence of profit sharing and gain sharing and employee stock ownership was the most important determinant of co-monitoring behavior. But it was the combination of the different share approaches with personnel practices that created an ownership culture that induced the most co-monitoring behavior: being part of a team, having a high participation in decisions, being treated with respect by supervisors, having formal training and job security, and being paid relatively well for a job. By contrast, when workers were paid large *individual* bonuses, they were less willing to try to improve the performance of a coworker who is not working well. If you and I are competing for a bonus, why should I help you perform better? The worse you do, the more likely I get the bonus. It is the team reward that generates cooperation and the willingness to take time and effort to press other workers to produce up to speed.

At one seminar where we presented these results, a critic complained that our question was a hypothetical one: "If you were to see someone not working as well . . . how likely would you be to (do X)?" Perhaps many of the workers who said they would take action were giving an answer they thought best fit social norms or that gave a positive impression of themselves. Because we surveyed companies on a rolling basis—first surveying company A, then company B, then C, and so on—we could improve the survey as we proceeded. Taking the concern about having asked a hypothetical question seriously, we added questions to the survey to find out if the workers had ever actually seen fellow employees not working as hard as they should, and what the employee had in fact done. The results from these questions about actual incidents correlated highly with those from the hypothetical incidents. Workers who had seen shirking and responded in a particular way reported that was what they would do in the hypothetical question, too. Workers with shares also work harder to support and monitor free riders, and better corporate cultures magnify this effect—that is what we found.

A Natural Experiment

Serendipity provided us with a "natural experiment" test of the impact of shares on co-monitoring behavior. As we were discussing our survey with one firm, the management told us that it intended to introduce a new profit-sharing plan a few months later. To measure workers' behavior before and after a firm changed policy was as close as we would get to the controlled before/after experiment that laboratory scientists regularly conduct in their labs. Management agreed to our administering the survey before and after the implementation of the cash profit sharing. This was already a generous company with broad-based employee stock ownership and stock options. The new cash profit-sharing plan that they were adding increased the number of workers who had cash profit sharing from 60 percent to 90 percent. After the profit sharing was introduced, we discovered a significant impact on worker responses. The percent of workers who said they were very likely to talk to a worker who was not performing his or her job properly increased from 42 percent to 55 percent. The percent who said they would take action in connection with the shirker because poor performance would hurt their share or stock value increased from 39 percent to 56 percent. The finding identifies the role of the monetary incentive of profit sharing on co-monitoring behavior about as well as one could do in a survey.[31]

Co-monitoring and Performance

The final step in our exploration of coworker monitoring was to see if co-monitoring improved company performance. We asked workers who had taken action to get their coworkers to improve their performance what happened as a result of their actions. Thirty-five percent of the workers said that the employee who was not working well resented it. But 45 percent said that the other employee appreciated the action, and 40 percent said the supervisor appreciated it. Over one-third said the employee's performance improved, but nearly the same proportion said the employee's performance did not improve, and one-third did not know. This could be viewed as a successful intervention if the employees who did not improve their performance did not worsen it, which we unfortunately did not ask.

Going beyond particular incidents, individual workers who report greater co-monitoring activity also report that their co-workers' effort levels are higher. They also report that workers encourage each other at their workplace more than do workers who say that they would not intervene with a worker who was not performing up to speed. They also report higher performance in their workplace in other areas of behavior that reflect higher productivity. One interpretation of this pattern is that having a stake in their firm leads these workers and their peers to develop a workplace norm for hard work that worker co-monitoring and support buttresses over time. To see if co-monitoring is more extensive at particular workplaces, we combined individual worker reports on their response to fellow workers not performing well into a co-monitoring score for each of the 323 work sites in the National Bureau for Economic Research survey. The score differed substantially among sites, indicating that co-monitoring is extensive in some workplaces and not in others. Measures of worker effort and better workplace behavior were higher in workplaces where a higher proportion of workers said they engaged in co-monitoring behavior. In short, co-monitoring improved group effort and workplace performance.[32]

THE NATION'S BEST EMPLOYERS

Every year the Great Place to Work Institute reviews the applications of major corporations who seek a place on the list of "100 Best Companies to Work for in America" that *Fortune* magazine presents with great fanfare. Because being named one of the hundred best is an honor that can attract additional and better job applicants and help retain and spur current employees, as well as bring companies acclaim and attention, every year about four hundred of the largest and most successful corporations apply for consideration and compete. The shares of half of the corporations applying are traded on the New York Stock Exchange and the NASDAQ, where they represent 20 percent of the market value of the U.S. public stock market and 10 percent of employment and sales of all stock market companies.

To determine the "100 Best Companies to Work For," the Great Place to Work Institute queries managements about their corporate culture and practices and obtains data on turnover and other aspects of work practices and corporate culture. The institute then surveys a random group of each company's workers and asks them how they are paid—including cash profit sharing, employee stock ownership, and broad-based stock options—and their attitude toward the company and behavior at work. Between 2006 and 2008 over 1,300 corporations applied for the "100 Best Companies to Work For in America" competition. Over three hundred thousand of their workers filled out the Great Place to Work Institute survey, which ultimately determines whether a corporation makes the "100 Best" list and where it places on the list. The Institute uses the survey responses to develop a comprehensive indicator of corporate culture, called the Trust Index©, which measures workers' views of the levels of credibility, respect, fairness, pride, and camaraderie that exist in their company.

The Great Place to Work Institute gave us limited access to its data under strict confidentiality procedures to examine the relation between employee stock ownership and profit sharing and work practices and the performance of applicant firms. We sought to determine whether firms that gave their workers some property stake were disproportionately represented among applicants and whether firms with greater degrees of shares and work practices performed better than their peer firms with weaker or no such programs.

Since firms with exceptional human resource policies and corporate cultures self-select into the applicant pool, comparisons of outcomes within this group are likely biased against finding any effects for broad-based capitalism approaches such as employee stock ownership and profit sharing. A firm that believed its practices merited recognition as among the "100 Best" and that did not have profit sharing or employee ownership presumably had other policies to reward and motivate workers (an especially well-designed promotion system? Generous, worker-friendly benefits?) that would compensate for the absence of those programs. One can presume that many applicants were trying very hard to be "the best" corporations.

A large proportion of the applicants in the competition had some form of employee stock ownership or profit sharing for their workers. Eighteen percent had ESOPs. Eighteen percent had cash profit- or gain-sharing plans. Twenty-two percent had deferred profit-sharing plans. The average ESOP in the sample owned about 17 percent of company stock. One-tenth of the companies were even majority worker-owned. One in six companies granted stock options to a majority of their workers. Another 17 percent of the companies granted stock options to between a quarter and half of all the corporation's workers. The average profit-sharing or gain-sharing plan provided workers a 7 percent bonus on top of their pay.

Corporations with more extensive employee ownership and profit sharing had higher scores on the Trust Index©. The workers in these corporations rated their company as more credible, respectful of workers' interests, fairer, and as providing greater participation in decisions than did workers in other firms. ESOPs and profit-sharing plans where profits added a lot to annual salary topped the list in the Trust Index©. Workers with stock options did not differ much on the Trust Index© from workers without those options. Corporations with more extensive broad-based capitalism had reduced voluntary turnover, increased employees' intentions to stay with the firm, and had higher return on equity for the firm. Corporations that combined shares with participative work practices and a supportive corporate culture had the biggest payoff in reduced turnover and higher return on equity. Finding these effects in the nonrepresentative "100 Best Companies to Work For" sample strengthens the likelihood that the policies have a causal impact on employee well-being and firm performance.[33]

The statistical evidence that firms in which workers have a property stake are more productive, induce more worker effort and responsibility, spur workers to innovate more, and produce diverse other benefits for workers and the corporation shows that a broad-based capitalist organizational form of capitalism can work. It pays off, at least for those firms and workers that choose it. The impacts are larger when the programs are larger, as in many closely held ESOP companies and some model publicly traded companies. But the share idea is not simply about workers getting more money in the pocket. It is also about the firm and its employees developing a culture that supports employee participation and cooperation between management and employees over the long term. The corporations and workers that do best combine shares and workplace practices in the context of a participative ownership culture. Our analysis found that giving workers more responsibility, having more teams and problem-solving groups, having a less hierarchical workplace where supervision involved more coaching than control, paying workers at or above the market rate for their fixed wages, and providing workers with greater training were important parts of this culture.[34]

Extending these practices to more workers and firms and strengthening the practices in the workplaces where they exist offer a road for normal workers to tap into the wealth embodied in corporate property. Extending these practices can help resolve the Founders' problem of creating a more equitable wealth distribution while protecting property rights. If the evidence has convinced you—as we believe it would have convinced Jefferson, Adams, Madison, and their fellow leaders and citizens who created the United States—that this is a viable better model of capitalism for the United States, the key question is how to get from here to there.

APPENDIX 5.1. FIVE STUDIES OF THE RELATION BETWEEN BROAD-BASED CAPITALISM AND FIRM OUTPUTS

Study 1: UK Treasury-sponsored study of British firms (2007). This study obtained data from confidential tax records that identified firms that had approved profit-sharing plans, "Save as You Earn" plans, and company share option plans for 16,844 firms. It linked this data to company value added, employment, profits, and capital for 7,633 businesses. The study covered enough firms and years to permit the analysts to conduct a panel study of firms that entered or left the programs, as well as to compare firms with and without the programs at a point in time, and to examine whether the effects differed among industries. The conclusion: "on average, across the whole sample, the effect of tax-advantaged share schemes is significant and increases productivity by 2.5% in the long run."

Study 2: General Accounting Office of the U.S. Congress (1987). This study examined 414 corporations with employee stock ownership plans that were set up between 1976 and 1979, when ESOPs were just getting off the ground in the United States. The companies were mostly small- and medium-size businesses whose stock was not traded on a public stock market. The worker ownership share of the average company was just under 10 percent. The study matched the ESOP firms with non-ESOP firms in the same industry and of the same size and compared outcomes three years after employee ownership started to two years before. The conclusion: by itself employee stock ownership did not change performance, but the combination of employee stock ownership with a change in corporate culture was associated with an increase in productivity "fifty two percentage points higher than the change for firms that did not have such employee involvement."

Study 3: Blasi-Kruse study of ESOPs set up between 1988 and 1994. These were small businesses with about four hundred workers each. The study compared ESOPs to businesses of similar size without broad-based employee ownership in the same industry a decade into the future. Workers in the ESOPs had a capital ownership stake of about $15,000, were five times more likely to have a traditional pension plan, were five times more likely to have a 401(k) plan, were four times more likely to have a profit-sharing plan, and seven times more likely to have another retirement plan than workers in the non-ESOP companies. The ESOPs had significantly higher sales growth and higher sales per worker than the companies without employee ownership. The ESOP corporations survived longer and had fewer bankruptcies. By 1999 almost 70 percent of the employee ownership businesses were still in existence, compared to only 55 percent of the non-employee-ownership companies. A 2002 follow-up on all ESOPs found similar results.

Study 4: This was a field experiment based on twenty-one fast-food franchises owned by one firm, where researchers were allowed to randomly assign profit sharing to three franchises and nonfinancial incentives (social recognition and performance feedback) to six franchises, with the remaining twelve as the control group. A pre/post comparison using monthly data found increased profitability and productivity and decreased employee turnover in the profit-sharing franchises relative to the control group. In addition, profit sharing had a more immediate positive effect on profitability and productivity, as well as a greater long-lasting effect on reducing employee turnover relative to the nonfinancial incentives.

Study 5: A 2003 survey of just over a thousand establishments in the state of California done at the Institute of Industrial Relations at the University of California-Berkeley came to conclusions similar to those of the above studies. Managers' assessments of quality, financial performance, and the turnover of workers were best when a participatory company culture was combined with profit sharing and employee stock ownership.

6 THE ROAD TO INCREASING THE CITIZEN'S SHARE

As the holders of property have at stake all the other rights
common to those without property, they may be the more
restrained from infringing, as well as the less tempted to infringe,
the rights of the latter. It is nevertheless certain that there are
various ways in which the rich may oppress the poor; in which
property may oppress liberty; and that the world is filled with
examples. It is necessary that the poor should have a defense
against the danger.

James Madison, August 1797[1]

Stipulate that the findings in this book are correct and that extending broad-based capitalism to more workers and increasing
the citizen's shares of business property and capital income offers a way to help cure our economic ills and resolve the tension
between inequality and democracy that concerned the Founding Fathers.

What can citizens—employees, employers, political leaders,
business leaders, you, and we, the authors of this book—do to
advance a broad-based capitalist economic agenda? What policies

can move our economy along the road of broad-based property ownership?

This chapter offers a set of guiding policy ideas and suggestions to address the how-to-get-there-from-here question in a world in which, as Madison stressed, property may oppress liberty and the poor should have a defense against the danger. Some of the ideas and policies may appeal to readers with a conservative bent. Some may appeal to readers with a progressive or liberal bent. Many have a chance of appealing across the political spectrum. Some suggestions may strike persons who believe that the country is going in the wrong direction as too modest. Others may find the policies too radical. But hopefully everyone will find one or more policy suggestions as providing a way to expand the citizen's share. Our goal is to begin a policy discussion that will create broad-based property ownership and profit sharing that is private-sector-led but helped with modest tax incentives. An important factor in looking forward toward new policies is understanding the policy mistakes of the past. (Appendix 6.1 reviews recent policy missteps regarding shares.)

Policy analysts often direct recommendations to top political decision makers, the president and sitting Congress, or a state governor and legislator, a mayor and city council. Follow the analysts' advice and do X, and the country, state, or city will benefit, and the politician will get more votes. Our suggestions are directed to citizens more widely because broadening capital ownership and having more workers enjoy the capital income from the fruits of their labor starts with the individual citizen. If every reader who agrees that a healthy, sustainable democracy requires an economy with more broad-based ownership of property and income streams from property would speak up for policies that would increase his or her share of capital ownership and capital income and move the economy along the road to increasing the citizen's share broadly, the United States would start moving from here to there. Change can be inspired or sparked by leadership, but it depends fundamentally on the attitudes and activities of citizens. This is what we mean by relying on the civic virtue of citizens.

FROM AN IDEA TO A NATIONAL COMMITMENT

The first step to increasing the citizen's share is for the United States to make increasing the property ownership and capital income of citizens a national goal. By this we mean more than someone saying a few perfunctory nice words about broad-based capitalism. Many world figures, from presidents to popes, have endorsed some form of broad-based capitalism, with little or no impact on the economic world.[2] A national commitment requires specificity in the form of benchmarks or goals. For employee stock ownership, this means setting a target for the fraction of the shares that employees beyond top managers own in corporations and for empowering workers to act as owners; a target for the proportion of citizens' income that comes from capital ownership, high enough to provide meaningful income but not structured so as to create great risk; a target for the proportion of privately held family firms that sell the firm to workers when the founders of the firm retire; and so on.

To move from idea to commitment requires more—from leadership and grassroots citizens. Given the "bully pulpit" of the White House, a president who declared that increasing the citizen's share was a priority for the administration would put broad-based capitalism front and center in the national economic discourse. Congress could hold hearings about ways to increase the citizen's share that would similarly galvanize attention. The president and/or Congress could establish an expert commission to assess different inclusive capitalist initiatives and evaluate ways to improve and promote them in American society. The United States has used commissions to take a longer-term perspective on economic policies in many areas, some of whose ideas and recommendations succeed in moving national debate and policy.[3] Successive British governments have pushed employee share ownership and profit-sharing initiatives and reviewed the success or lack thereof of their policies in pushing this form of capitalism. Shortly after the Conservatives won the 2010 election in the United Kingdom, the government commissioned a report on the state of broad-based capitalism, the Nuttall Report, which gives the idea some presence in current British economic policy.[4]

But commissions, while valuable, are a step removed from the functioning of government. Another route for committing the United States to increasing the citizen's share would be for a president to establish a White House Office of Broad-Based Capitalism to coordinate federal policies dealing with broad-based capitalism and to work with the private sector to publicize and encourage best practices.[5] The office could work with statistical agencies to improve our measures of broad-based capitalism by adding questions to the country's major surveys of individuals: the Current Population Survey, which measures employment and unemployment every month, to the American Community Survey, which has become a mini yearly census; and to update the Survey of Consumer Finance, which is the major survey of finances in the U.S. population. Other executive agencies might also consider establishing point persons or groups to find ways in which they can modernize regulations and assist firms seeking to improve employee ownership and profit sharing. Congress could regularly review legislation and its implementation relating to the national goal of increasing the citizen's share.

In the private sector, institutions of higher education and the media can affect national discussion and decisions. Colleges and universities, particularly schools of management, and social science disciplines can increase our understanding of how broad-based capitalism works and how it can be improved through their research, following in the footsteps of the nineteenth- and twentieth-century scholars at Johns Hopkins, Princeton, the American Economic Association and elsewhere described in Chapter 4. Through teaching students, they can further improve practice.

But in the Internet world of blogs, social media, and YouTube videos, citizens can initiate discussion and change outside the terrain of traditional media giants. In the fall of 2011, a twenty-two-year-old college graduate working as a part-time nanny got upset at the Bank of America levying a five-dollar debit card fee on customers and wrote an Internet petition that drew over three hundred thousand signatures almost immediately and enough national media attention that BofA backed down and withdrew the charge.[6] The hosts of talk radio and TV could spark debate over citizen's share initiatives and introduce listeners and viewers to employers and workers in firms operating with broad-based capitalist principles.

FROM COMMITMENT TO POLICIES AND PROGRAMS

To turn a commitment to expanding broad-based capitalism into reality requires action by government and firms.

In a world of uncertainty, the most sensible way to develop policies and programs is through trial and error—experimentation with an array of policies from which the decision maker chooses the most efficacious on the basis of the evidence. The U.S. federalist system offers the opportunity for the states (and localities in some situations) to develop their own policies to stimulate broad-based capitalist solutions from which other states and ultimately the federal government can choose the most efficacious to apply elsewhere. The decentralized nature of U.S. capitalism offers thousands of large firms and millions of small- and medium-size firms and tens of millions of workers to choose what works best in their workplaces, from which others can learn. We have seen that private-sector initiative by citizens, firms, managers, and workers created the existing formats and policies of employee stock ownership and profit sharing so far.

Here are our suggestions for moving along the road to increasing the citizen's share. There are eleven policies organized into three broad categories: policies to disseminate information widely about broad-based capitalist solutions and to provide benchmarks for the country to judge where it stands; tax and expenditure policies to encourage broad-based capitalism; and policies to reduce capital constraints on broad-based capitalist firms (Box 6.1). If you have better policy suggestions, we are eager to hear them. Indeed, if *The Citizen's Share* can stimulate readers to do better than we have, we would view our job as being well done. The book's website offers ways to express yourself and to suggest additional policy ideas and react to those of others along with additional learning materials such as books, articles, and films that you may find useful. The website is www.thecitizensshare.com. It also contains expanded notes and commentary.

BOX 6.1. POLICIES TO MOVE US FROM HERE TO THERE

Information and Benchmarking Policies:
1. Establish local institutions for disseminating information and technical expertise on broad-based capitalism.
2. Have the Small Business Administration establish programs to aid small- and medium-size firms to increase the sales to employee trusts and other forms of inclusive capitalism.
3. Create a scorecard of broad-based capitalism for firms as a benchmark and as an objective measure for qualifying for programs designed to help such firms.

Tax and Expenditure Policies to Encourage Broad-Based Capitalism:
4. Pass progressive capital gains taxation.
5. Create "baby bonds" for newborn citizens that give them a small capital stake at age twenty-one.
6. Allow publicly traded firms to treat incentive pay for top executives and highly paid individuals as a cost of business only if an incentive plan covers all workers.
7. Include firms with broad-based capital ownership in government procurement and tax abatement programs to extend business opportunities to more Americans.
8. Predicate "tax expenditures for business" on the business having some minimal program for employee ownership and profit sharing.

(continued)

Policies to Reduce Capital Constraints on Broad-Based Capitalism Firms:

9. Expansion of state policies to allow new forms of companies/cooperatives that can more easily operate with a goal of expanding broad-based capitalism.

10. Induce financial firms to invest/loan money to corporations with broad-based employee stock ownership or profit sharing.

11. Lower the estate tax for a retiring founder/owner of a family firm on the part of a firm sold to workers— encourage the continuance of small successful business.

Information and Benchmarking

1. Establish local institutions for disseminating information and technical expertise on broad-based capitalism.

To spread information and provide technical assistance to businesses and citizens about ways to increase employee stakes in firms and develop supportive corporate cultures requires more than the White House Office of Broad-Based Capitalism proposed earlier or any other Washington-based program. To bring the goal to states, cities, and firms requires activity by state and local development agencies in conjunction with state departments of commerce and labor and tax authorities, business associations, and firms. We therefore propose that different jurisdictions create offices for broadening capital ownership in their area, for advising state and local government officials on what works and does not, for developing information and training on employee stock ownership and profit sharing in businesses of every size, and for communicating regularly with corporations with employee ownership and meaningful profit sharing so they can meet and exchange ideas and lessons learned.

This would be like the agricultural extension agencies that helped U.S. farmers become the most productive and successful in the world by providing advice and technical information: state and local development agencies would assist local businesses in developing and benefiting from operating with greater employee stakes. Ohio has created the Ohio Employee Ownership Center, which has helped develop an extensive network of stable employee-owned firms that provides a useful model for what state centers could look like. Vermont has a similar center. California has a center. Several cities around the country are developing worker cooperatives as a response to poverty and are having encouraging success.

One modest idea would be for the federal government to consider a seed grant of several million dollars to each state to help initially establish fifty state centers of employee ownership and profit sharing that would be expected to become self-sufficient after the preliminary grant was spent. The state centers would advise state and local government officials on policies to encourage a variety of formats of broad-based capitalism in their regions. They could also develop community college courses, including online courses, on the subject. These centers would develop information and training on businesses of every size. We have no doubt that some useful policy ideas for the federal government would emerge from these efforts.

2. Have the Small Business Administration establish programs to aid small- and medium-size firms to increase the sales to employee trusts and other forms of inclusive capitalism.

Small businesses are the modern equivalent to the independent farmers and artisans of Revolutionary America. They offer an important frontier to extend capital ownership and income to more citizens. A key survey indicates that business succession is the top urgent challenge to small businesses. About half of small business owners expect to retire within five years, and fewer than a third have selected a successor. Many do not have a son or daughter or family member to take over the business, so a sale to employees and managers can help the owner cash out of the business and broaden capital ownership at the same time. Many would be open to having shares for employees.[7] The natural agency to take a lead in developing programs for small- and medium-size businesses consistent with a national commitment to moving along the road to an increased citizens' share is the Small Business Administration (SBA). It could inform small business owners about employee stock ownership as a solution to business succession and also educate business owners about broad-based capitalism plans of all kinds. It could ask businesses that receive SBA loans to agree to provide managers and employees a right of first refusal to make a competitive offer to purchase the firm over a certain period.

Small businesses are started by millions of entrepreneurs who eventually need to sell their businesses to gain wealth. Like family farms, they are a source of future wealth. If they cannot be passed on to family members, as many business founders intend, passing them to single concentrated owners is one possibility, but offering incentives to sell them to broad groups of managers and employees addresses "the new primogeniture."

3. Create a scorecard of broad-based capitalism for firms as a benchmark and as an objective measure for qualifying for programs designed to help such firms.

To judge how particular firms and the country as a whole are advancing along the road to increasing citizens' ownership stakes in the firms that employ them, we need measures of ownership stakes, profit-sharing arrangements, and the like. Government agencies most suitable to efficiently provide the relevant statistics need to be identified, such as the Census Bureau, which conducts surveys of establishments and firms across the economy. The objective should be data gathering done by professionals protected from political pressures. Indicators should be publicly available.

Tax and Expenditure Policies to Encourage Broad-Based Capitalism

4. Pass progressive capital gains taxation.

Capital income is concentrated among a small number of extremely wealthy persons, who benefit disproportionately from the tax advantages given to capital income. In 2009 the Internal Revenue Service reported that the four hundred taxpayers with the highest adjusted gross income paid 16 percent of all capital gains taxes and thus earned about 16 percent of capital gains.[8] Taxing capital gains at a progressive rate would encourage middle- and lower-income citizens to accumulate capital, including but not limited to capital in their own firms, would boost their share of capital and capital gains, and redress at least some of the disproportionate advantage that lower capital gains tax rates gives to the superwealthy. As many workers have access to purchasing shares in their firm through employee share purchase plans, this would likely lead to greater employee ownership as well. The more citizens who have ownership and profit shares, the larger the tax base would be, and potentially there could be an increase in tax revenues. We suggest in addition that the capital gains rate of taxation fall for lower- and middle-income persons the longer they hold an asset, thereby helping create a pool of "patient capital" interest in broad-based employee stock ownership. Currently, the United States taxes capital gains on assets held more than a year at a lower rate than capital gains on capital held for less than a year.[9]

The notion that middle-class persons should get a tax break on capital income to encourage them to become owners is within the mainstream of discussion of tax reform. The Obama administration's Economic Recovery Advisory Board Report on Tax Reform Options questioned whether the middle class should even pay capital gains taxes and recommended reduced capital gains for them. In his presidential campaign, Governor Mitt Romney recommended that the capital gains and the dividend tax rate be zero for citizens with incomes under $200,000. Without endorsing any particular progressive schedule (a critical detail for the tax specialists to evaluate), we believe that it makes sense to apply a progressive rate to citizens with "unearned income" so that small business owners with unearned income also receive the benefit of the progressive rates.[10]

5. Create "baby bonds" for newborn citizens that give them a small capital stake accessible at age twenty-one.

In 2005 the Labour Party in the United Kingdom instituted the Child Trust Fund, popularly known as the baby bond program, with the aim of accumulating money so that every child had capital ownership and income when he or she left school at age eighteen. The government committed to assuring every child born in the period covered by the law with £250 capital at eighteen but allowed for family and friends to top up trust funds, so that the amount for many would be much higher. The Cameron government abolished the baby bond program in 2010 on the grounds of fiscal austerity, while later lowering taxes on the wealthy to promote growth.[11]

The idea for guaranteeing that all citizens have some property income actually comes from the founding days of the United States when Thomas Paine proposed that every twenty-one-year-old man and woman receive £15 financed from a tax on inheritance and land.[12] The Alaska Permanent Fund, which pays every state resident a dividend from the state's ownership rights on oil assets, with support from both political parties, is the most recent example to come closest to Paine's 1795 proposal. "Individual development accounts" that supplement the savings of low-income households with matching funds are another mechanism through which the government or private parties can try to help poor persons accumulate assets that provide property income. In 2007, campaigning for the Democratic nomination for president, Hillary Clinton proposed a $5,000 baby bond.[13]

Without getting into details, the notion that all newborns should have an individual trust account set up for them at birth seems a reasonable way to provide low-income citizens with property ownership and an income stream. Viewing capital assets as the new land, the baby bond idea addresses what we have called "the new primogeniture," namely, the modern phenomenon that the successor assets to land—capital, knowledge, corporations, financial assets—do not end up being broadly owned.[14]

6. Allow publicly traded firms to treat incentive pay for top executives and highly paid individuals as a cost of business only if an incentive plan covers all workers.

In 1993, seeking to rein in executive pay in a weak economy, the Clinton administration proposed to allow firms to deduct as a cost of business the salary for the top five executives only up to $1 million. Corporations could pay higher salaries, but could not claim the higher deductions in figuring their corporate profits tax. Congress enacted the limitation of $1 million of salary as deductible from corporate profits but, in Section 162(m) of the tax bill, allowed firms to deduct as a cost of business unlimited amounts of certain "performance-based pay." This included various employee stock ownership and profit-sharing plans—namely, stock options, grants of stock, or bonuses paid for nonequity incentive plans—for the top five executives of all public corporations, without requiring any evidence that the performance pay reflected performance. The result was an unintended system of tax-subsidized "unshared capitalism," in which firms get tax savings by paying the top five executives with ownership stakes and profit shares in the firm. We estimate that the exemption may have cost taxpayers $5 billion to $10 billion per year since 1993. In addition, many publicly traded corporations offer various narrow employee stock ownership or profit-sharing plans to the top 5 percent of their employees, which cost taxpayers from 2001 to 2007 many more billions per year.[15] As a result, most of the tax incentives for broad-based capitalism are for narrow employee stock ownership and profit-sharing plans.

Since studies show that broad-based capitalism is associated with better economic performance, while the evidence that performance pay that goes only to executives leads to better performance for shareholders is mixed at best, it is hard to justify the distinction between salary and performance pay in the tax code.[16] Giving a huge tax break to firms that give an ownership stake to a small number of top executives or a few percent of the highest-paid employees is inconsistent with the goal of extending ownership to all workers. The tax expenditure for this huge tax break far exceeds—by many multiples—the annual tax expenditure for employee stock ownership plan (ESOP) firms that give ownership to all workers.[17]

Our proposal is simple: if a corporation traded on a stock market offers any type of profit sharing, gain sharing, employee stock ownership, restricted stock, stock option, or equity plan to its top five executives, the business can deduct this equity and profit sharing beyond the $1 million limit only if it offers the same plan to all workers.[18] If corporations do not provide the same plan for all, they have to pay normal corporate profits tax on compensation beyond the $1 million amount. Under the Employee Retirement Income Security Act (ERISA), companies can only receive tax deductions and tax incentives for such plans if they cover most employees. Under this principle, nearly all firms that have retirement and insurance programs include all employees. We say, treat incentive plans that create ownership stakes for workers the same way.[19]

7. Include firms with broad-based capital ownership in government procurement and tax abatement programs to extend business opportunities to more Americans.

Federal, state, and local governments spend huge sums procuring goods and services from other companies. Under current law, procurement often takes account of the social desirability of the ownership of firms through programs that give advantages to small- and medium-size firms and to firms headed by women or underrepresented minorities. The goal is to extend the range of Americans in business ownership and leadership roles. We propose that federal and state procurement policy include businesses that have broad-based equity ownership or profit sharing in these programs. State and local economic development authorities that award tax abatements to businesses for socially desired reasons should give special attention to firms with broad-based equity and profit-sharing plans.

8. Predicate "tax expenditures for business" on the business having some minimal program for employee ownership and profit sharing.

The U.S. corporate tax contains numerous provisions that reduce corporate tax liability by huge sums. From 2008 to 2014 accelerated depreciation, deductions for U.S. production and manufacturing activities, and research and experimentation tax credits by themselves were estimated to lower corporate taxes by about a trillion dollars. Some of these expenditures are socially desirable because the activity they encourage has positive spillovers to society, but some are simply payoffs to particular firms or sectors for successful lobbying. Without judging any particular expenditures, we suggest that these tax deductions be allowed only to businesses that offer a profit-sharing plan or a broad-based employee stock ownership plan that meets some threshold. In its assessment of the corporate tax system, the National Commission on Fiscal Responsibility and Reform (the Deficit Commission) recommended: "Eliminate all tax expenditures for businesses" and reduce the corporate tax rate commensurately. Following the principle that corporate tax policy should encourage broad-based capitalism, we suggest that any deductions should be greater for businesses that offer a broad-based cash or deferred profit-sharing plan or a broad-based employee stock ownership plan.[20]

Policies to Reduce Capital Constraints on Broad-Based-Capitalism Firms

9. Expansion of state policies to allow new forms of companies/cooperatives that can more easily operate with a goal of expanding broad-based capitalism.

Because firms incorporate at the state level, states can amend their laws on corporations to create legal forms that make it easier for firms to make decisions consistent with the national goal of extending broad-based capitalism. Six states have passed laws creating a new type of corporation, called the B corporation, that makes it easier for businesses to take employee, community, and environmental interests into consideration when making decisions. The B corporation can refuse to sell itself to the highest bidder, can operate with a longer-term financial horizon and/or value interests beyond maximizing shareholder wealth, in ways that other corporations cannot easily do. A firm with broad-based capitalism incorporated as a B corporation would have greater options to maintain its programs than a firm incorporated under different provisions.

Similarly, states can make it easier for worker cooperatives to raise new capital without selling control of the cooperative to outside investors. Several states, Iowa, Minnesota, and Wisconsin among them, have passed laws to allow cooperatives to have investor members who have forms of nonvoting stock. One city-based initiative in Cleveland, the Evergreen Cooperatives, has the Cleveland Clinic and the Cleveland Foundation teaming up to help low-income workers develop green worker cooperatives that receive procurement contracts from local businesses like the Cleveland Clinic. There are many networks of worker cooperatives around the country along with consulting and training groups to help workers set up sustainable cooperatives.

The United Steelworkers Union has an initiative to develop worker cooperatives. Worker cooperatives are emerging in both high-tech and less capital intensive industries and may be increasingly relevant to emerging knowledge-based businesses. The University of Wisconsin Center for Cooperatives estimates that there are around 7,500 worker cooperative employees in more than 223 cooperatives nationally. A group in San Francisco is founding a credit union bank that will finance worker-owned businesses with deposits. The Ohio Employee Ownership Center has reported that thirty-eight states have used federal funding under the Workforce Investment Act to explore employee buyouts. Iowa has passed a law providing state-level tax incentives to small business owners who sell their companies to employees, and New Jersey has considered legislation that excuses small business owners from capital gains taxes for sales to ESOPs and worker co-ops. We recommend that other states examine these experiences as part of their effort to extend capital ownership to workers in their jurisdiction.[21]

10. Induce financial firms to invest/loan money to corporations with broad-based employee stock ownership or profit sharing.

There are two ways to incentivize financial institutions to allot more of their portfolio of loans or investments to further a national goal of broadening capital ownership. Financial institutions that lend money to businesses that establish or expand broad-based employee ownership could be allowed to deduct a proportion of interest income on the loan from corporate taxes, as was the case during the administrations of President Ronald Reagan, President George H. W. Bush, and President Bill Clinton before these incentives were cut back. The second is to require those institutions to invest a given percentage of their assets in companies with significant profit sharing or employee stock ownership. Had policies like these been followed in the aftermath to the 2008 financial crisis, we might have had a seminal moment for moving the ownership structure toward employees. When the incentives are right, financial institutions have helped broad-based employee ownership and they can do so in the future. Here more than anywhere else, however, we note James Madison's concern about "the sagacious, the enterprising, and the monied few" taking advantage of insiders' knowledge to exploit the rest of the country.[22]

11. Lower the estate tax for a retiring founder/owner of a family firm on the part of a firm sold to workers—encourage the continuance of small successful business.

A substantial proportion of the closures of family businesses result from poor planning of the transfer to new owners rather than the inherent failure of the business. This often results in loss of local jobs and temporary increases in unemployment.[23] Employee stock ownership plans are common among small businesses in part because they offer the founders of small businesses a federal capital gains tax break for cashing out their value from the business by selling it to the workers. The federal government established a tax incentive program in the 1980s that is largely responsible for creating this sector of employee ownership. Under this program, a small business owner who sells 30 percent or more of his or her firm to a broad group of workers is excluded from capital gains taxes on the sale if the proceeds are invested in other securities after the sale. Given this program's success in stimulating employee ownership, the government should consider expanding coverage to a wider range of corporations, such as S corporations.[24]

As the primogeniture debate in early American history illustrated, the shifting of ownership of estates creates an opportunity to encourage broader ownership. This was a classic method favored by the Founders almost without any dissent. We recommend giving the estates that often hold family businesses an incentive to sell to a broad-based group of managers and employees in the form of some modest discount on taxation of the proceeds of the sale.[25]

The policies in this chapter suggest ways in which the government can help move the United States along the road to increasing the citizen's share and reducing inequality. They cover a lot of terrain, some of which we know well, and some of which we know less well. We selected those where there is some evidence on how they would work and some policy analysis of their strengths and weaknesses. There may be other ideas that work as well or better than those we have considered. Weaknesses may turn up in the policies we believe are most likely to succeed. What is essential is to commit the country to broadening the base of capital ownership and to try different ways to accomplish this goal.

APPENDIX 6.1. RECENT POLICY MISTAKES

Here are some examples of recent policy mistakes that undermined broad-based capitalism, incentivized approaches that shifted more risk to workers, pushed middle-class workers out of employee ownership plans, and subsidized the concentration of wealth with taxpayer money.

Financing Employee Ownership Mainly with Wages

Building employee stock ownership mainly around the idea that workers should buy stock for cash with their savings and wages was a policy error in the 1920s. When the 1929 stock market collapse hit, the difficulty with this highly risky strategy was clear to everyone. The lesson that should have been learned was not to base employee stock ownership solely or mainly on investment of workers' savings based on their fixed wages. This policy misstep was made during the Republican administrations of Presidents Warren Harding, Calvin Coolidge, and Herbert Hoover.

The recent relevant version of this error involves encouraging or allowing workers to use too much of their wages to purchase excessive amounts of company stock in 401(k) plans. Briefly, the 401(k) plan is a trust to which workers and companies contribute funds for workers' retirement. Assets in the trust grow tax free, and they are invested in stocks, bonds, and various mutual funds. In 1978, when Congress added Section 401(k) to the Internal Revenue Code (to allow workers to place some of their income in a trust and invest those assets, without the gain creating taxes until the worker retired), Congress believed it was doing something modest in order to encourage retirement savings plans that workers could use to supplement their traditional pension plans. As traditional pension plan coverage proceeded to disappear for many American workers, 401(k) plans became the predominant retirement plan and many corporations began to offer company stock as an investment choice in these 401(k) retirement plans. In some cases, workers were not properly educated about acceptable levels of portfolio diversification; some companies even encouraged workers to take buying company stock with their wages in these plans to extremes; and some workers made very ill-advised personal investment decisions, in spite of education, by buying too much company stock with cash from their wages or savings in spite of company cautions and investment education. There are a number of empirical studies examining excessive worker investment in company stock 401(k) plans and the thought processes that lead workers to overinvest.[26]

However, there is one aspect of employee stock ownership in 401(k) plans that actually can build long-term employee stock ownership in the nation while minimizing the risk of excessive worker purchases of company stock with their wages. Some large publicly traded companies match employees' contributions to their 401(k) plans with company stock. Obviously, individual workers do not have to pay for this company stock match with their wages or savings. It is a grant of stock. In some cases this is based on a use of the ESOP idea because some companies will set up ESOPs, finance the purchase of a large amount of company stock that can be used for these stock matches over many years in the future, receive tax incentives for doing this, and then use the shares to match workers' contributions to their 401(k) plan. This is a potentially workable idea because the employees do not have to purchase company stock with their own contributions to the 401(k) plan. Those contributions can be diversified while the employee ownership stock grants that workers receive as company matching contributions can constitute an employee ownership stake in the company. Workers would be unlikely to get this benefit otherwise. There is research suggesting what might be appropriate levels of diversification in such plans.[27]

Excessive worker purchases of company stock with their wages or savings came back to bite workers in the 1987, 2000, and 2007–2009 stock market crashes. The mistake of funding excessively risky worker ownership with wages and savings was made basically three more times in this century after 1929. This fact underlines how little serious thought has gone into a coordinated federal policy on broad-based capitalism. The law that led to what was certainly unintended consequences was made during the Democratic administration of President Jimmy Carter, when the 401(k) plan was established, and it has continued through every Republican and Democratic administration and Congress since that time. This constitutes an avoidable policy mistake because the government has had at its disposal several alternative policy options to encourage forms of broad-based employee stock ownership—such as various kinds of stock grants including restricted stock and ESOPs and stock options and even Employee Stock Purchase Plans with less risky features—that are not financed principally by worker wages and savings and are less risky.

Subsidizing Exclusive Equity and Profit-Sharing Plans for the Few

In the first Clinton-Gore presidential campaign, the candidates wrote and distributed a campaign paperback book called *Putting People First*. One idea presented in their book in order to address public concern over executive compensation was to cap at $1 million corporate deductions when figuring corporate income taxes for the salaries of the top five executives in a publicly traded corporation. The unintended consequence was that when this idea wound its way through the legislative process and then passed the Congress and became law, Congress allowed publicly traded corporations to get virtually unlimited deductions from corporate income tax for giving various performance-based employee stock ownership, stock option, and profit-sharing plans to the top five executives. The law involves Section 162(m) of the Internal Revenue Code. The result was that corporations paid fixed salaries just below $1 million and received that deduction but then received unlimited deductions for offering executives various large employee stock ownership, stock option, profit-sharing, and gain-sharing packages. This is ironic since the tax deductions for broad-based plans such as employee stock ownership plans and even employee stock purchase plans are strictly limited by the federal government to various modest amounts. For example, an average middle-class worker can only buy a very modest amount of company stock per year through an Employee Stock Purchase Plan with the employee share being capped. Company deductions for Employee Stock Ownership Plans are also capped, as are deductions for broad-based profit-sharing plans.

Certainly, in a private market economy, the boards of directors of corporations have the right to pay their executives what they wish to pay them. The policy question is whether unlimited employee stock ownership and profit-sharing payments for the top five executives of public corporations should be subsidized with tax deductions paid for by a broad group of citizens when broad-based employee ownership and profit-sharing plans are very limited. The unintended consequence of 162(m) ended up having the opposite effect that the Clinton-Gore book initially intended since the new law ended up subsidizing some executive compensation at unlimited levels and oddly enough created a major tax incentive for just the opposite of broadened stock ownership and profit sharing in the nation. Successor administrations and Congresses since this law passed in the early 1990s, both Republican and Democrat, have never changed this policy and Congress has never debated such a change. The size of tax expenditures for 162(m) by various estimates suggests that the federal government has thrown most of its weight behind narrowly based equity and profit-sharing plans in complete contradiction to the broad-based share idea in American history. Corporations also receive substantial tax deductions for equity plans offered to the top 5 percent of their employees and the tax expenditures for these plans put more of the weight of the federal government principally behind narrow plans. It is hard to imagine that this is the kind of ownership policy the Founders would have supported. This and other policy errors suggest a lack of policy coordination in presidential administrations after Clinton and within Congress on broad-based capitalism. The policy issue is whether the top five executive plans favored by 162(m) and all of these narrow-based equity and profit-sharing plans should be the major goal of U.S. tax policy and citizen tax expenditures. Meanwhile, whenever the federal government is looking for deficit reduction, officials typically target what is left of the encouragement for broad-based employee ownership plans.[28]

Eliminating Public Company ESOP Tax Incentives

Another constructive capital ownership and capital incomes policy took place during the first Bush administration and the Clinton administration. During the administration of President George H. W. Bush, a number of financial services firms discovered that the employee stock ownership plan (ESOP) could be used to spread ownership in publicly traded companies. Many investment banks set up employee stock ownership departments to approach large corporations about setting up employee stock ownership trusts by having the trusts borrow money to purchase company stock paid for out of company profits that could be granted to workers. Because these plans were not based on workers purchasing the stock with their savings, they were potentially less risky. Sometimes these ESOPs were for the purpose of buying stock for the company stock match to worker contributions in 401(k) plans. The investment banks even packaged corporate bonds to fund these ESOPs for the workers of corporations. Congress had provided a tax incentive that dividends used to repay these loans would be deductible from corporate income. In addition, banks and other lenders were able to deduct half of their own interest income on loans to establish these ESOPs with the result that lenders passed on some of the saving by making loans to the employee trusts at lower interest rates. A number of corporations established large ESOPs that bought 5–10 percent of a large corporation's stock. For the first time in American history, many of the major Wall Street firms were actually marketing financial products based on building broad-based equity and profit sharing in the largest American corporations. When the tax incentives were eliminated, broad-based employee stock ownership plans in stock market companies slowed down enormously. This entire result was caused by unexamined federal policy that then continued for over two decades to the present day since the 1990s.

While the deductions required fine-tuning, the first Bush administration simply cut this interest deduction incentive as part of deficit reduction without considering the overall policy considerations. What was left was the interest deduction for cases where workers would buy 51 percent of an entire company, a policy that effectively ended the incentive for large public corporations. Then, as the Clinton administration went through its deficit reduction cuts, this last tax incentive was eliminated. Both administrations lost an important opportunity to encourage broad-based employee ownership through stock grants in publicly traded corporations. Meanwhile, as we have seen, with the passage of Section 162(m) of the Internal Revenue Code, billions and billions of dollars of tax incentives were established under the Clinton administration to benefit narrowly based equity and profit-sharing plans. The Financial Accounting Standards Board changed some of the accounting on employee stock ownership that made the large, broad-based employee ownership transactions less doable. The result of these actions was the collapse of transactions to finance employee stock ownership in large publicly traded corporations on the NYSE and the NASDAQ that were based on grants of stock to workers rather than the riskier pattern of workers buying stock in 401(k) plans. The broader policy mistake involved the irrationality of cutting this form of broad-based employee ownership in the Bush and Clinton administrations for deficit reduction and then legislating 162(m) in the Clinton administration that led to billions of tax expenditures for narrowly based plans apparently without much awareness of the contradiction or policy coordination.[29]

Changing the Rules of Stock Options so that Middle-Class Workers Got Kicked Out of Company Stock Option Plans

The most recent policy misstep was again caught up with the executive compensation debate that has swept the country in the last two decades, with another ironic outcome. It took place during the recent President George W. Bush administration. After Enron, WorldCom, Tyco, and other scandals, Congress and the Securities and Exchange Commission advanced the policy of changing the way that corporations did their accounting for employee stock options. Some defenders of "stock option expensing," as the reform is called, hoped that the policy would create more transparency in financial statements, limit excessive executive compensation using options, and thus reduce risky behavior by top executives. The hope of some of the regulators was that boards of directors would reduce the number of stock options that they granted to top executives if the companies had to account for them more clearly to shareholders. Stock options have certainly been abused at times, and some business leaders and economists such as Warren Buffett, Bill Gates, and

Paul Volcker have articulated reasons to reform the entire stock option mechanism. Regulators ordered stock options expensed in 2005.

This particular reform did not have the intended consequence that was predicted by the reformers. The impact was largely felt by the middle class. Thirteen percent of all U.S. adults were getting stock options in 2002 before the stock option expensing was implemented. This was way more than the top five executives of the major stock market companies who constituted less than the 100,000 individuals who received options at the time. The 2002 General Social Survey found that 57 percent of all the workers in the computer services industry, many of them in Silicon Valley, arguably America's innovation nursery, received stock options, and 58 percent of all the workers in this industry were employee owners. After the implementation of stock option expensing, an analysis of the 2006 General Social Survey by Blasi and Kruse found that the number of nonexecutive workers with stock options and employee stock ownership in the computer services industry went down by over a third. This happened in many other industries across the country, including manufacturing where innovative plans were using worker shares.[30]

What was going on here? Many companies, as was widely predicted by compensation consultants and academics in the press, simply reduced the number of employee stock options that they gave to middle-income and professional and mid-level managers and supervisory workers and regular employees (in order to reduce their "expense" for accounting purposes) while maintaining employee stock programs for top executives and highly paid workers. In the end, the companies did manage to reduce the expensed cost of their stock option programs, but the main group of citizens who received the brunt of the "reform" was the middle class. Many corporations then started giving top executives grants of entire shares of stock (restricted stock or performance shares) rather than stock options so that remaining with the company rather than an increase in the price of the stock was the main requirement for securing the ownership. The percent of the U.S. citizens receiving stock options fell to 8.7 percent in 2006—a huge drop of 36 percent from the 13 percent who had options before stock option expensing—and the percent of employee stock ownership in the U.S. population also fell significantly. Stock option expensing was a very controversial subject with arguments on both sides of the question. However, despite the disagreements over expensing, the federal government and Congress could have potentially avoided the unintended consequence of a policy that resulted in pushing the middle class out of broad-based stock option programs, for example, by supporting the regulator, the Financial Accounting Standards Board's (FASB) effort to impose stock option expensing and then providing a modest tax incentive for corporations that had broad-based stock option and employee ownership plans. Instead, the policy error was for the government and the Congress to allow a policy that favored the form of employee ownership that benefited the smallest number of citizens as it has in many previous employee ownership policy debates, while making the choice to ignore examining the larger implications. The main result has been that scores of companies exited from offering broad-based stock options and many companies cut middle-class workers from the plans.

EPILOGUE

The idea of *The Citizen's Share*—that the economic and political success of the United States depends on citizens sharing in the ownership and profits of the economic system as well as in the electoral process of the political system—is both traditional and radical.

It is traditional because, as this book has shown, many of the Founders of the country and their successors throughout U.S. history believed that a thriving middle class with capital ownership is necessary for political liberty and economic independence. Generation after generation, Americans with diverse views in other domains have favored policies to strengthen a "property-owning democracy" as essential to the American dream.[1] The debate on the cod fishery; the policies against primogeniture; the sale of public land to as many citizens as possible; the Louisiana Purchase to obtain more land for independent farmers; the Homestead Act; the expansion of the economic and political rights to all groups and enactment of laws to protect them against discrimination; programs and policies to expand small business ownership; and the development of different forms of profit-sharing and employee stock ownership plans—all are variations on the same theme: that the United States does better when more of us participate as owners as well as workers in the economy and voters in our democracy.

The research in this book shows that the economic case for greater sharing of ownership and employee participation in improving business results is a valid one. A greater locus of ownership and participation works, on average, in the businesses that do it. The historical evidence has brought home to us, and hopefully to readers, that the goal of greater citizen ownership is traditional Americana.

The idea behind *The Citizen's Share* is radical because it stands against several ongoing trends in the U.S. economy and the way a few in policy circles think about our society. Massive inequality in income and wealth and "crony capitalism" arrangements in which some corporations and a small coterie of the super-wealthy extract special privileges from the government through lobbying, political donations, and the revolving door between high political office and high-paid corporate jobs are often the economic and political reality. The elites who work the system see the vision of an economy with expanded ownership as a radical departure from the current reality under which they prosper. The share idea has played no meaningful role in discussions on restructuring the tax system, broadening the tax base, reducing the deficit by pruning corporate welfare and tax expenditures that favor concentrating wealth, or expanding the middle class. It needs to play that role. There is a road to a broader prosperity. Many of the current approaches in our economic system are not the only ways to operate a market democracy.

Some critics will invariably dismiss the idea of broad-based capitalism as a blue-sky pipe dream that the United States cannot implement. They are wrong. Our vision of an economy that operates on these principles is not some idealistic picture of an economy based on altruism and a perfectly functioning government, nor, alternatively, of an economy where self-employed artisans exchange products in a perfectly functioning competitive market. The ways in which many of our best operating firms reward workers through stock grants and other equity and profit sharing such as employee stock ownership plans in high-technology firms, in independent closely held businesses of all sizes, in entrepreneurial start-ups, and in some stock market corporations, provide concrete examples of businesses prospering for themselves and their workers.

The Citizen's Share vision offers a direction in which citizens and policy makers can seek to move the economy in ways that fit with the share heritage in American history and the experiences of many firms and workers today. We citizens can press our elected officials and business leaders to adopt concrete policies to implement broad-based capitalism more widely—from changes in the tax system on equity and profit-sharing plans to encourage firms to spread ownership widely, to compensation and personnel practices within companies that offer ownership stakes to all regular employees. Such a policy direction fits with the general sense of the American people. Most citizens say that they favor broad-based employee stock ownership and that profit sharing would improve the condition of the economy.[2] It is the way many of the Founders of the United States would reduce inequality.

Increasing the citizen's ownership stake in our society is not a panacea for all our economic problems, but it offers a heritage-rich starting point for practical policies that will improve the functioning of our economy and lower income inequality. It will expand the positive outcomes that we see in pockets across the

American economy to more workers and firms. Whatever objections you may have about broad-based capitalism, consider the alternative policies that the major political parties have tried. Important efforts to expand manufacturing jobs, to improve education and training, to contain health care costs, and to cut middle-class taxes have not reversed the trend toward increased concentrated capital ownership and capital income among citizens nor restored the historic pattern in which the benefits of improved productivity showed up in the paychecks of ordinary workers widely. Nor have those policies reduced inequality.[3] *The Citizen's Share* requires a special emphasis in each of these policy areas to move the economy in a direction that benefits more citizens.

In sum, the research for the book has convinced us, and hopefully convinces you, that we citizens should put a single short question to every policy proposal before our government and our companies: what does it do for the citizen's share? Policies that advance a citizen's share agenda will improve our well-being, the well-being of the firms where we work, and the well-being of the country. There is a road to a broader prosperity. Let's get moving on it in the traditional radical American way, with citizens taking the lead.

NOTES

For an expanded version of the notes with additional commentary, see www.thecitizensshare.com.

INTRODUCTION

1. George Washington, *The Papers of George Washington Digital Edition*, ed. Theodore J. Crackel (Charlottesville: University of Virginia Press, Rotunda, 2008), 6:339, Original source: Confederation Series (January 1, 1784–September 23, 1788) letter to Richard Henderson, Mount Vernon, June 19, 1788. This quote does not represent an isolated observation by Washington. On May 28 of the same year Washington wrote a similar letter to a Dutch Mennonite minister, Rev. Francis Adrian Van der Kemp, who was considering immigrating with his family after being imprisoned in Holland for political reasons. The minister later settled in Esopus Creek, north of Kingston, New York, and later near Oneida Lake. Washington wrote: "Under a good government (which I have no doubt we shall establish) this Country certainly promises greater advantages, than almost any other, to persons of moderate property, who are determined to be sober, industrious and virtuous members of Society. And it must not be concealed, that a knowledge that these are the general characteristics of your compatriots would be a principal reason to consider their advent as a valuable acquisition to our infant settlements." See Washington, *Papers . . . Digital Edition*, 6:301, Original source: Confederation Series, vol. 6 (January 1, 1788–September 23, 1788). On June 18, 1788, Washington wrote to former Revolutionary War general the Marquis de Lafayette: "I really believe that there was never so much labor and economy to be found before in the country as at the present moment . . . when the burdens of war shall be in a manner done away by

the sale of . . . Western lands . . . and when every one (under his own vine and fig tree) shall begin to taste the fruits of freedom." See Washington, *Papers . . . Digital Edition*, 6:335–339, Original source: Confederation Series (January 1, 1784–September 23, 1788), vol. 6 (January 1, 1788–September 23, 1788).

2. James Madison, *Debates on the Adoption of the Federal Constitution in the Convention Held at Philadelphia in 1787, with a Diary of the Debates of the Congress of the Confederation as Reported by James Madison, Revised and Newly Arranged by Jonathan Elliot; Complete in One Volume*, vol. 5. *Supplement to Elliot's Debates* (Philadelphia: J. B. Lippincott & Co., 1836), 580–581. This edition contains the Appendix to the Debates in the Federal Convention, 577–588. See the chapter "Appendix to the Debates in the Federal Convention, No. 4, Second Note to Speech of Mr. Madison of August 7, 1787."

3. See Joseph R. Blasi, *George Washington, Thomas Jefferson, and Alexander Hamilton and an Early Case of Shared Capitalism in American History: The Cod Fishery* (New Brunswick, NJ: Rutgers University School of Management and Labor Relations working paper, April 15, 2012) and Christopher Magra, *The Fisherman's Cause: Atlantic Commerce and the Maritime Dimensions of the American Revolution* (Cambridge: Cambridge University Press, 2009).

4. Alex Roland, W. Jeffrey Bolster, and Alexander Keyssar, *The Way of the Ship: America's Maritime History Re-envisioned, 1600–2000* (Hoboken, NJ: John Wiley & Sons, 2008), 12, 31–36, 65, 82–98. See also Mark Kurlansky, *Cod: A Biography of the Fish That Changed the World* (New York: Penguin Books, 1997), 82–83, and Benjamin W. Labaree, William M. Fowler Jr., John B. Hattendorf, Jeffrey J. Safford, Edward W. Sloan, and Andrew W. German, *America and the Sea: A Maritime History* (Mystic, CT: Museum of America and the Sea, 1998), 24, 33–34, and 179 on the allowance system.

5. United States Department of State, *The Revolutionary Diplomatic Correspondence of the United States Edited under the Direction of Congress*, ed. Francis Wharton, 2 vols. (Washington, DC: Department of State, 1889), 2:743, letter of John Adams to R. Izard, September 25, 1778.

6. Washington, *Papers . . . Digital Edition*, 4:270–272, Original source: Presidential Series (September 24, 1788–April 30, 1794), vol. 4 (September 8, 1789–January 15, 1790), letter to the citizens of Marblehead, November 2, 1789, and note 1 by the editors following.

7. Thomas Jefferson, *The Papers of Thomas Jefferson Digital Edition*, ed. Barbara B. Oberg and J. Jefferson Looney (Charlottesville: University of Virginia Press, Rotunda, 2008), 19:206–234, Original source: Main

Series, vol. 19 (January 24–March 31, 1791). Washington presented an "emphatic positive recommendation" on the fisheries to the third session of Congress (159).

8. Letter of February 1, 1790, from Marblehead, Massachusetts, signed by thirteen owners of ships, and insert no. 5 to the report. Jefferson, *Papers . . . Digital Edition*, 19:225–226, Original source: Main Series, vol. 19 (January 24–March 31, 1791).

9. Jefferson, *Papers . . . Digital Edition*, 19:196, Original source: Main Series, vol. 19 (January 24–March 31, 1791).

10. Jefferson, *Papers . . . Digital Edition*, 19:195–197, Original source: Main Series, vol. 19 (January 24–March 31, 1791).

11. Blasi, *George Washington, Thomas Jefferson*, 30.

12. Ron Chernow, *George Washington: A Life* (New York: Penguin Press, 2010), 277.

13. Chernow, *George Washington*, 256. See note 62 for original source.

14. For the entire act see William Graydon, *An Abridgement of the Laws of the United States* (Harrisburg, VA: Printed by John Wyeth, 1803), 215–218. The division of the profit share between the owners and the crew is on 215, Section I.

15. See Blasi, *George Washington, Thomas Jefferson*, 37–39. The implementation of the law by the Treasury Department has been confirmed by studying Alexander Hamilton's original record books of letters received from customs officials at ports, at the National Archives and Records Administration in College Park, MD.

16. Graydon, *Abridgement*, 215–218. The allowance in the law had a seven-year term and was increased by 20 percent on May 2, 1792, and by 30 percent on July 8, 1797. On April 12, 1800, it was extended for ten years from March 3, 1800.

17. See No. 71, Seventh Congress, 2nd Session, in Walter Lowrie and Matthew St. Clair Clark, *American State Papers: Documents, Legislative and Executive of the Congress of the United States* (Washington, DC: U.S. Congress, 1832), 7:511.

18. Gordon S. Wood, *Empire of Liberty: A History of the Early Republic, 1789–1815* (Oxford: Oxford University Press, 2009), 7–8. For a discussion of the early conflicts between elites and the middle classes over the yeoman farmer idea, see Sean Wilentz, *The Rise of American Democracy: Jefferson to Lincoln* (New York: W.W. Norton & Company, 2010), 15–20, 36–37, 47–48, 83. The book also addresses the relationship between the yeoman farmer idea and the politics of the slaveholding elite in the south as well as its connection to the politics of Indian land.

19. The general theme of broad-based ownership should not paper over disagreements between major figures in the founding generation on the radical enlightenment regarding slavery and the Indians; see "The American Revolution," in Jonathan I. Israel, *Democratic Enlightenment: Philosophy, Revolution, and Human Rights, 1750–1790* (New York: Oxford University Press, 2011), 443–479.

20. On the share from 1789 to 1790 see table no. 3 in Jefferson, *Papers . . . Digital Edition*, 19:225, Original source: Main Series, vol. 19 (January 24–March 31, 1791).

21. Roland, Bolster, and Keyssar, *Way of the Ship*, 65. See also Eric Williams, *Capitalism and Slavery* (Chapel Hill: University of North Carolina Press, 1944), 51–84, esp. 59, 108, 116, and 118.

22. See Emmanuel Saez, "Striking It Richer: The Evolution of Top Incomes in the United States," *Pathways Magazine*, Winter 2008, 1–8, esp. table 1, 8.

23. Pew Center for the People and the Press, *A Political Rhetoric Test*, May 4, 2010, Pew Research Center, Washington, DC.

24. See G. E. Mingay, *English Landed Society in the Eighteenth Century* (London: Taylor and Francis, 1963), 26, with special attention to estimates for 1790 in table 1; F. M. L. Thompson, "The Social Distribution of Landed Property in England since the Sixteenth Century," *Economic History Review* 19, no. 3 (1966): 565–517.

25. While many historians recognize the Founders' appreciation of broad distribution of wealth as a political idea, concentration of wealth did exist.

26. For evidence on the top 10 percent having three-quarters of wealth see Linda Levine, *An Analysis of the Distribution of Wealth across Households, 1989–2010* (Washington, DC: Congressional Research Service, Report for Congress RL 33433, 7–570, July 17, 2012), 35. For evidence on 90 percent of 1982–2008 income growth going to the top 10 percent, see Thomas Piketty and Emmanuel Saez, "Income Inequality in the United States, 1913–1998," *Quarterly Journal of Economics* 118, no. 1 (2003): 1–39. These data have been updated to 2008 at http://www.econ.berkeley.edu /~saez/TabFig2008.xls. For evidence on more than 80 percent of capital income going to the top 10 percent, see Lawrence Mishel, Jared Bernstein, and Heidi Shierholz, *The State of Working America, 2008–2009* (Ithaca, NY: Cornell University Press, 2009), 85.

27. Lee Soltow, *The Distribution of Wealth and Income in the United States in 1798* (Pittsburgh, PA: University of Pittsburgh Press, 1989), 9.

28. Alexander Hamilton, *Report of the Secretary of the Treasury of the United States on the Subject of Manufactures Made in His Capacity of Secretary of the Treasury on the Fifth of December 1791. . . . ,* ed. Matthew Carey (Philadel-

phia: William Brown, 1827), 28, 47. See also Alexander Hamilton, *The Papers of Alexander Hamilton Digital Edition*, ed. Harold C. Syrett; Mary-Jo Kline consulting editor for the Digital Edition (Charlottesville: University of Virginia Press, Rotunda, 2011), 10:292. Hamilton mentioned the broad-based property ownership viewpoint several times as the larger agricultural framework for a move into manufacturing, but he had his own unique perspective. He wrote that European emigration was attractive because of "the facility with which the less independent condition of the artisan can be exchanged for the more independent condition of a farmer" (233); that "the cultivation of the earth" was "most favorable to the freedom and independence of the human mind" (236) and that he expected foreign immigrants to be more drawn to this agricultural vision; that a nation of proprietors "would insure a continually increasing domestic demand" (273). See Hamilton, *Papers . . . Digital Edition*, 10:230–240, Original source: vol. 10 (December 1791–January 1792). Several scholars provide evidence against Hamilton's interest in expanding manufacturing. See John R. Nelson, "Alexander Hamilton and American Manufacturing: A Reexamination," *Journal of American History* 65, no. 4 (March 1979): 971–995, claiming Hamilton failed "to formulate any adequate means of reaching out to the small property holders—the majority of the people" (973) and providing evidence that Hamilton's Society for Establishing Useful Manufactures was mainly an endeavor to support Hamilton's government bond program and benefit monied interests (974–977, 980–981). See also Jacob E. Cooke, "Tenche Coxe, Alexander Hamilton, and the Encouragement of American Manufactures," *William and Mary Quarterly*, Third Series, 32, no. 3: 369–392. For more on his views see the expanded notes.

29. See Mishel, Bernstein, and Shierholz, *State of Working America*. See also Sylvia Allegretto, The *State of Working America's Wealth* (Washington, DC: Economic Policy Institute briefing Paper #292, 2011). For recent data on the concentration of capital income and capital ownership see Lawrence Mishel, Josh Bivens, Elise Gould, and Heidi Shierholz, *The State of Working America*, 12th ed. (Ithaca, NY: Cornell University Press, 2012), 63–65, 94–102, 105, 109–111, 115, 286–291.

30. See Mishel, Bernstein, and Shierholz, *State of Working America*, 81–85.

CHAPTER 1. THE AMERICAN VISION

1. George Washington, *George Washington: A Collection*, ed. William Barclay Allen (Indianapolis: Liberty Classics, 1988), chap. 167 (fragments of the discarded first inaugural address).

2. Jefferson, *Papers of Thomas Jefferson*, 8:681–683, Original source: February 25–October 31, 1785.

3. General Assembly of Pennsylvania, *Debates and Proceedings of the General Assembly of Pennsylvania on the Memorials Praying a Repeal or Suspension of the Law Annulling the Charter of the Bank*, ed. Matthew Carey (Philadelphia: Seddon and Pritchard, 1786), 123–124. The bank's charter had been repealed in 1785, and the debate was about reversing this repeal.

4. On the history of the bank see Lawrence Lewis, *A History of the Bank of North America, the First Bank Chartered in the United States* (Philadelphia: J. B. Lippincott & Co., 1882). After the Revolution, the bank directors were fully personally liable for the bank's debts. See Robert E. Wright, *Origins of Commercial Banking in America, 1750–1800* (Lanham, MD: Rowman & Littlefield, 2011), 77.

5. Adam Smith, *An Inquiry into the Nature and Causes of the Wealth of Nations* (Hollywood, FL: Simon & Brown, 2012), 439.

6. For Findley's speech see General Assembly, *Debates and Proceedings*, 122–125.

7. For more detail on his intellectual background and his ideas see Hans Louis Eicholz, *The Bank of North America and the Transformation of Political Ideology in Early National Pennsylvania* (PhD dissertation, University of California–Los Angeles, 1992), 32–33, 155–157, 238–269, and 254–256 on farmer interest in loans, banks, and credit, especially 245 on his reading of "philosophical and scientific works." See also Terry Bouton, "William Findley, David Bradford, and the Pennsylvania Regulation of 1794," in *Revolutionary Founders: Rebels, Radicals, and Reformers in the Making of the Nation*, ed. Alfred F. Young, Gary B. Nash, and Ray Raphael (New York: Alfred A. Knopf, 2011), 233–251, 132.

8. See Gary B. Nash, "Philadelphia's Radical Caucus That Propelled Pennsylvania to Independence and Democracy," in Young, Nash, and Raphael, *Revolutionary Founders*, 67–86, esp. 80.

9. See William B. Scott, *In Pursuit of Happiness: American Conceptions of Property from the Seventeenth to the Twentieth Century* (Bloomington: Indiana University Press, 1978), 6, 12, 13.

10. See George David Rappaport, "The First Description of the Bank of North America," *William and Mary Quarterly*, 3rd Series, 33, no. 4 (October 1976): 661–667, esp. 662.

11. Drew R. McCoy, *The Elusive Republic: Political Economy in Jeffersonian America* (Chapel Hill: University of North Carolina Press, 1996), 68.

12. General Assembly, *Debates and Proceedings,* 15. On Lollar see State of Pennsylvania, *Minutes of the Supreme Executive Council of Pennsylvania from Its Organization to the Termination of the Revolution* (Harrisburg, PA: J. Severns & Co., 1852), 11:488.

13. United States Congress, *Biographical Directory,* entry for John Smilie (1741–1812) at http://bioguide.congress.gov/biosearch/biosearch.asp. For Smiley's speech see General Assembly, *Debates and Proceedings,* 21.

14. United States Congress, *Biographical Directory,* entry for Robert Whitehill (1738–1813) at http://bioguide.congress.gov/biosearch/biosearch.asp. For Whitehill's speech see General Assembly, *Debates and Proceedings,* 62–66.

15. Coxe's essays are discussed in Eicholz, *The Bank of North America and the Transformation of Political Ideology in Early National Pennsylvania,* 165–237.

16. On the vote see General Assembly, *Debates and Proceedings,* 132.

17. See Eric Foner, *Tom Paine and Revolutionary America* (New York: Oxford University Press, 2004), 183–210.

18. See Wright, *Origins of Commercial Banking,* 191. In 1787, 10 percent of account holders were artisans (151).

19. See Janet Wilson, "The Bank of North America and Pennsylvania Politics: 1781–1787," *Pennsylvania Magazine of History and Biography* 66, no. 1 (January 1942): 3–28.

20. See Alexander Hamilton, James Madison, and John Jay, *The Federalist Papers,* ed. Charles R. Kesler and Clinton Rossiter (New York: Penguin Group, 2003), 79 (Federalist No. 10), 163–164 (No. 26), 521 (No. 85), 72–78 (No. 10), 391 (No. 51), and 382–384 (No. 63).

21. See Samuel Eliot Morison, *The Oxford History of the American People* (New York: Oxford University Press, 1965), 317.

22. On Franklin see McCoy, *Elusive Republic,* 52–84, 121–122. Paine largely agreed with the various elements of their vision of the republican political economy. See Foner, *Tom Paine,* 71–106.

23. See C. Bradley Thompson, *John Adams: The Spirit of Liberty* (Lawrence: University Press of Kansas, 1998), 165.

24. On colonial Massachusetts property distribution see Scott, *In Pursuit of Happiness,* 10, 13–20; Thompson, *John Adams,* 211, 238–239.

25. See John Adams, *Adams Papers Digital Edition,* ed. C. James Taylor (Charlottesville: University of Virginia Press, Rotunda, 2008), 3, dairy entry of March 3, 1761, Original source: John Adams, *Diary and Autobiography of John Adams,* vol. 3, Diary 1782–1804, Autobiography, Part 1, to October 1776. See Thompson, *John Adams,* 123, 143–146, esp. 145, 196–198, and 192–193.

26. Thompson, *John Adams,* 170–173, 175, 180–181.

27. Ibid., 200.

28. This analysis is based on a review of Adams's writings on property. Adams's "share in government" formulation is in his extensive discussion of the definition and true meaning of "republic." See John Adams, *A Defense of the Constitutions of Government of the United States, History of the Principal Republics of the World,* vol. 3 (London: Printed for John Stockdale, Piccadilly, 1794), 160. In 1765, Adams saw a lack of property under Europe's system and believed that "the feudal system is inconsistent with liberty and the rights of mankind" and he saw concentration of property holdings in the church as an example of an entrenched aristocracy. See John Adams, *Adams Papers Digital Edition,* 1:115–117, Original source: *Papers of John Adams,* vol. 1, September 1775–October 1773, *A Dissertation on Canon and Feudal Law,* reprinted from the *Boston Gazette,* August 19, 1765. In 1775, Adams stressed to his wife that after the war, "People reduced to Poverty, may acquire fresh property" [1:241, Original source: *Adams Family Correspondence,* vol. 1, December 1761–May 1776, letter to Abigail Adams of July 7, 1775, Philadelphia)]. In 1776, writing Abigail, he praised "the old Project of an equal division of conquered Lands as "a genuine republican Measure" of the Roman Gracchi brothers [2:110, Original source: *Adams Family Correspondence,* vol. 2, June 1776–March 1778]. In 1780, he wrote the Comte de Vergennes that "America is a Nation of Husbandman, planted on a vast Continent of wild uncultivated Land. And there is and will be for centuries no way in which these people can get a living and advance their interests so much as by Agriculture" [10:46, Original source: *Papers of John Adams,* vol. 10, July 1780–December 1780, July 26, 1780, Paris]. In 1782, he argued for the wealth benefit of capital ownership and income, writing "as long as wild land is to be had cheap and it will be for centuries . . . [farmers] will find that they can advance themselves and their children faster by it" and "a days labor worth two shillings in manufacture, produces but two shillings, whereas a day's labor on wild land, produces the two shillings in immediate production, and makes the land itself worth two shillings more" (showing his appreciation of the capital gains possible on ownership of assets) [9:575, Original source: *Papers of John Adams,* vol. 9, March 1780–July 1780, *Letters from a Distinguished American,* Paris, January 30, 1782, and *Parkers General Advertiser & Morning Intelligencer,* September 3, 1782]. The analysis in this chapter has benefited from Thompson's comprehensive study of Adams, whose interpretation it largely echoes. See esp. chaps. 6–11, esp. 210–211, on Adams's support of public policies to broaden ownership, where Thompson argues that Adams was indeed a republican but disagreed with the idealistic classic republican notion that one could create a perfect republic principally by instilling homogeneity and virtue in the population.

29. Adams looked to constitutional design and government to correct for the lust for power and self-deceit of human beings.

30. See "Westward Expansion: The Northwest Ordinance of 1787 and the Louisiana Purchase Ratification of 1803," in Dennis E. Johnson, *The Laws That Shaped America: Fifteen Acts of Congress and Their Lasting Impact* (New York: Routledge, 2009), 1–34.

31. See Scott J. Hammond, Kevin R. Hardwick, and Howard Leslie Lubert, *Classics of American Political and Constitutional Thought, vol. 1, Origins through the Civil War* (Indianapolis: Hackett Publishing, 2007), 295–296 (June 12, 1776).

32. On Jefferson's bills against primogeniture and entail in the Virginia Assembly in October 1776 see *Itinerary and Chronology of Thomas Jefferson, 1771–1779*, in Thomas Jefferson, *The Works of Thomas Jefferson*, vol. 2 (in 12 vols.), collected and ed. Paul Leicester Ford (New York: Cosimo, 2009), xviii, 268, 270. Jefferson did not favor redistributing existing wealth and wrote Pierre Samuel du Pont de Nemours, the French writer and father of the founder of the DuPont Corporation, that "the equal partition of intestate estates, constitute the best agrarian law." See Jefferson, *Papers . . . Digital Edition*, 3:559–560, Original source: Retirement Series, vol. 3 (August 12, 1810–June 17, 1811), letter to Pierre Samuel du Pont de Nemours, April 15, 1811, Monticello. See Jefferson, *Papers . . . Digital Edition*, on his 1779 correspondence with George Washington about land for officers and soldiers [3:227–229, Original source: Main Series, vol. 3 (June 18, 1779–September 30, 1780), letter of December 16, 1779, Williamsburg; on the 1779 promise of one hundred acres of unimproved land to recruit Virginia infantry [3:204, Original source: Main Series, vol. 3 (June 18, 1779–September 30, 1780), form of recruiting commission], on 1781 bounties and land grants to British mercenary troops [4:505–506, Original source: Main Series, vol. 4 (October 1, 1780–February 24, 1781)], on his 1780 conveyance of three hundred land warrants for 560 acres each to raise a battalion to fortify the mouth of the Ohio River [3:273–278 , Original source: Main Series, vol. 3 (June 18, 1779–September 30, 1780), letters to George Rodgers Clark]. On the Louisiana Purchase see McCoy, *Elusive Republic*, 193–301. On the Report on Public Lands, completed in 1791 see Jefferson, *Papers . . . Digital Edition*, 22:274–288, Original source: Main Series, vol. 22 (August 6, 1791–December 31, 1791), with an informative note. Jefferson went so far as to say regarding the theories of political economy and demography that the extensive territory of the United States meant that the "greatest part of his book is inapplicable to us" in reference to Malthus's arguments that population would outpace the ability of a country to support itself and lead to declining incomes (194). See also Julian P. Boyd, "Thomas Jefferson's 'Empire of Liberty,' " *Virginia Quarterly Review* 29 (1948): 538–554. On his planned social engineering see Jefferson, *Papers . . . Digital Edition*, 14:492–493, Original source: Main Series, vol. 14 (October 8, 1788–March 26, 1789), letter to Edward Bancroft, January 26, 1788, Paris. Jefferson also wrote about some comparable experiments by Quakers in Virginia who wished to end slavery, efforts in which he was very interested. Bancroft was a physician who served as a spy for Benjamin Franklin in London and at the American Commission in Paris. However, Jefferson tried to dissuade Edward Coles, Madison's private secretary and a former Virginia slaveholder, from his own plan to eliminate his personal involvement in slavery. Coles visited Illinois, bought land, freed the slaves working for him, and gave each family 160 acres in the reform effort. He was later elected governor of Illinois in a fight with pro-slavery forces. His efforts helped keep Illinois a free state in the Civil War. On this story see Jefferson, *Papers . . . Digital Edition*, 2:225, Original source: Retirement Series, vol. 2 (November 16, 1809–August 11, 1810) and the note to the letter to Edward Coles, February 16, 1810, Monticello.

33. On manufactures see McCoy, *Elusive Republic*, 227–233. On his 1785 financing idea to have investors buy land with certificates of Revolutionary War debt (bonds) using 50 million acres "purchased" from Indians see Jefferson, *Papers . . . Digital Edition*, 8:401–402, Original source: Main Series, vol. 8 (February 25–October 31, 1785), letter to William Carmichael, August 18, 1785, Paris (Carmichael was a U.S. diplomatic envoy for Spain who had represented Maryland in the Continental Congress in 1778 and 1779). Jefferson was also involved in a 1786 endorsement of a financing idea for European investors to buy up Revolutionary War bonds cheaply in Europe in order to buy land or for France to issue bearer bonds to land speculators in Europe representing U.S. debts to France, which these investors could use to buy uncultivated lands for settlement. See [10:519–523, Original source: Main Series, vol. 10 (June 22–December 31, 1786), letter to John Jay, November 12, 1786, Paris]. On Jeffersonian ends and Hamiltonian means see Herbert D. Croly, *The Promise of American Life* (New York: Macmillan Co., 1914) and *Progressive Democracy* (New York: Macmillan Co., 1915). Croly supported the idea of workplace democracy and worker ownership. The other founding coeditors of the *New Republic* were Walter Lippmann, a journalist who was an adviser to President Woodrow Wilson, and Walter Weyl, an intellectual leader of the Progressive movement. On the notion that Jefferson's ideas were more market oriented than commonly conceded (as the above examples illustrate) see the literature contrasting republicanism and liberalism during the period, especially Joyce Appleby, *Liberalism and Republicanism in the Historical Imagination* (Cambridge, MA: Harvard University Press, 1992).

34. Robert A. Dahl, *A Preface to Economic Democracy* (Berkeley: University of California Press, 1985), 70–71. On the first inaugural address see Jefferson, *Papers . . . Digital Edition*, 33:148, Original source: Main Series, vol. 33 (February 17–April 30, 1801). On "real wealth," see Jefferson, *Papers . . . Digital Edition*, 12:36–38, Original source: Main Series, vol. 12 (August 7, 1787–March 31, 1788), letter to George Washington, August 14, 1787, Paris. Jefferson emphasized again to Tench Coxe that mixing the capital of the soil with the labor of the farmer built more prosperity. See Jefferson, *Papers . . . Digital Edition*, 23:617–618, Original source: Main Series, vol. 23 (January–May 31, 1792), letter to Tench Coxe, May 21, 1792, Philadelphia. On Jefferson's vision see McCoy, *Elusive Republic*, 166–269. Jefferson wrote effusively to John Adams, "Never was a finer canvas presented to work on than our countrymen. All of them engaged in agriculture or the pursuits of honest industry, independent in their circumstances, enlightened as to their rights, and firm in their habits of order and obedience to the laws." See Jefferson, *Papers . . . Digital Edition*, 28:618–619, Original source: Main Series, vol. 28 (January 1, 1794–February 29, 1796), letter to John Adams, February 28, 1796, Monticello.

35. Wood, *Empire of Liberty*, chap. 10, "The Jeffersonian West," 357–399, esp. 357, 363, and 369. On "enlarging the empire of liberty" see note 2 for the original source, Merrill D. Peterson, *Thomas Jefferson and the New Nation: A Biography* (Oxford: Oxford University Press, 1970), 773.

36. See Federalist No. 10, in Hamilton, Madison, and Jay, *Federalist Papers*, 71–79, esp. 72–73 on removing the cause of factions or controlling their effects, and 78 on "extending the sphere." Madison states about redistribution, "Theoretic politicians, who have patronized this species of government [pure democracy versus a representative republic] have erroneously supposed that by reducing mankind to a perfect equality in their political rights, they would at the same time be perfectly equalized and assimilated in their possessions, their opinions, and their passions" (76). See James Conniff, "The Enlightenment and American Political Thought: A Study of the Origins of Madison's Federalist Number 10," *Political Theory* 8, no. 3 (August 1980): 381–402, esp. 394. On the Senate see Madison's comments on June 26, 1787, on "Terms of the Senate."

The entire quote is "A necessary fence against this danger would be to select a portion of enlightened citizens, whose limited number, and firmness might seasonably interpose against impetuous counsels. It ought finally to occur to a people deliberating on a Govt. for themselves, that as different interests necessarily result from the liberty meant to be secured, the major interest might, under sudden impulses be tempted to commit injustice on the minority." See Madison, *Debates*, 242.

37. For a discussion of this dilemma at the Constitutional Convention and Madison's approach see Jennifer Nedelsky, *Private Property and the Limits of American Constitutionalism* (Chicago: University of Chicago Press, 1990), 4–15, with a long discussion of Madison's dilemmas in "The Madisonian Vision: The Republican Solution to the Republican Problem" (16–37). Nedelsky says that despite Madison's serious concerns about the connection between protecting property rights and liberty, he "never said the security of property was more important" than the rights of persons (19) and that he believed that both the rights of property and the rights of persons "cannot well be separated" (20). Nedelsky notes that Madison "always presented the predicament as a troubling one, and he was never entirely satisfied with the solutions he arrived at" (20). This is consistent with our presentation of Madison's point of view.

38. For Madison's amendments to the Constitution on June 8, 1789, see James Madison, *The Papers of James Madison Digital Edition*, ed. J. C. A. Stagg (Charlottesville: University of Virginia Press, Rotunda, 2010), 12:196–210, esp. 200, Original source: Congressional Series, vol. 12 (March 2, 1789–January 20, 1790, and supplement 1775–1789). Indeed, Madison said the "personal right to acquire property" was a "natural right" and the "right to protection" of property "once acquired" was "a social right." See "Speech to the Virginia Constitutional Convention" (1829), in Hammond, Hardwick, and Lubert, *Classics of American Political and Constitutional Thought*, 757–758. On primogeniture see his letter to George Washington on the subject [10:196–198, esp. 196, Original source: Congressional Series, vol. 10 (May 27, 1787–March 3, 1788), October 18, 1787, New York], his strong condemnation of the practice with the evaluation that "in Countries where there is a rapid increase of population as the U.S. these provisions are evidently sufficient" [1:610, Original source: Retirement Series, vol. 1 (March 4, 1817–January 31, 1820), detached memoranda, ca. January 31, 1820], and Conniff, "Enlightenment," 388.

39. For Madison's land table see "Speech to the Virginia Constitutional Convention" (1829), in Hammond, Hardwick, and Lubert, *Classics of American Political and Constitutional Thought*, 757–758. Madison's letter of June 19, 1786, to Jefferson went over these worries in more detail.

Madison estimated that if one divided up all the lands in Europe there would still be a surplus of inhabitants without property. He wrote: "What is to be done with this surplus? Hitherto we have seen them distributed into manufactures of superfluities, idle proprietors of productive lands, domestics, soldiers, merchants, mariners, and a few other less numerous classes. All these classes notwithstanding have been found insufficient to absorb the redundant members of a populous society; and yet a reduction of most of those classes enters into the very reform which appears so necessary & desirable." He goes on to say that he expects that "from a juster Government must result less need of soldiers either for defence agst dangers from without, or disturbances from within," but he provides no further solution, at least, for Europe. See Madison, *Papers . . . Digital Edition*, 9:76–81, Original Source: Congressional Series (April 9, 1786–May 24, 1787), letter to Thomas Jefferson of June 19, 1786, Orange.

40. On Madison's conviction that broad-based property ownership was needed for the viability of a republic see James H. Read, who says, "Rights for Madison always meant more than property rights alone [although that is what he concentrates on in Federalist 10]. And it is worth pointing out that he favored whatever measures could maintain a broad equality of property without violating property rights." See James H. Read, "Our Complicated System: James Madison on Power and Liberty," *Political Theory* 23, no. 3 (August 1995): 452–475, esp. 469. See also David Ingersoll, "Machiavelli and Madison: Perspectives on Political Stability," *Political Science Quarterly* 85, no. 2 (June 1790): 259–280, esp. 268 and 273, and Neal Riemer, "James Madison's Theory of the Self-Destructive Features of Republican Government," *Ethics* 65, no. 1 (October 1954): 34–43, esp. 42. Madison praised the United States as the opposite of Europe in this respect. On this see Roy Branson, "James Madison and the Scottish Enlightenment," *Journal of the History of Ideas* 40, no. 2 (April–June 1979): 235–250, esp. 244. He had also read James Harrington's work as a student of John Witherspoon at Princeton University. On this see also Jeff Broadwater, *James Madison: A Son of Virginia and a Founder of the Nation* (Chapel Hill: University of North Carolina Press, 2012), 96.

41. See "Speech to the Virginia Constitutional Convention" (1829) in Hammond, Hardwick, and Lubert, *Classics of American Political and Constitutional Thought*, 757–758.

42. Abraham Lincoln, *Speeches of Abraham Lincoln Including Inaugurals and Proclamations*, ed. G. Mercer Adam (New York: A. L. Burt Co., 1906), 373–392, esp. 385.

43. See Charles Judah Bayard, *The Development of the Public Land Policy, 1783–1820, with Special Reference to Indiana* (New York: Arno Press, 1979), 91, 141, 204, 212–213, 216–217, 265–270, 281–289. On Gallatin see 285.

44. See William Montgomery Meigs, *The Life of Thomas Hart Benton* (Philadelphia: J. B. Lippincott & Co.), 57–59, 164–178.

45. See Mark A. Lause, *Young America: Land, Labor and the Republican Community* (Champaign: University of Illinois Press, 2005), 121, and Jamie L. Bronstein, *Land Reform and Working-Class Experience in Britain and the United States* (Palo Alto, CA: Stanford University Press, 1999), 169–171. On the Republican Party and Frémont see William E. Gienapp, *The Origins of the Republican Party, 1852–1856* (New York: Oxford University Press, 1987).

46. On the Free Soil Party see Eric Foner, *Free Soil, Free Labor, Free Man: The Ideology of the Republican Party before the Civil War* (Oxford: Oxford University Press, 1995), and Frederick J. Blue, *The Free Soilers: Third Party Politics, 1848–1854* (Champaign: University of Illinois Press, 1974).

47. For the veto message see http://www.presidency.ucsb.edu/ws/index.php ?pid=68441. See also "The Promise of Land," in Johnson, *Laws That Shaped America*, 75–104, esp. 82–83.

48. See Republican National Committee, *The Republican Campaign Text Book for 1882* (New York: Republican Congressional Committee), 188 (part 11, "Public Land"), providing both Democratic and Republican platforms from 1856 to 1884.

49. On the overall impact see Dahl, *Preface to Economic Democracy*, 71, although estimates differ. For an overall acreage estimate see Johnson, *Laws That Shaped America*, 94, and Trina Williams Shanks, "The Homestead Act: A Major Asset-Building Policy in American History," in *Inclusion in the American Dream: Assets, Poverty, and Public Policy*, ed. Michael Sherraden (New York: Oxford University Press, 2005), 20–41.

50. See Claude F. Oubre, *Forty Acres and a Mule: The Freedmen's Bureau and Black Land Ownership* (Baton Rouge: Louisina State University Press, 1978).

51. See Wood, *Empire of Liberty*, 44.

52. See Naomi Lamereaux, *The Great Merger Movement in American Business, 1895–1904* (Cambridge: Cambridge University Press, 1988), 210.

53. See Dahl, *Preface to Economic Democracy*, 71.

54. See "Mr. Grow's Farewell: Venerable Ex-Speaker Makes His Last Address to the House," *New York Times*, December 11, 1902.

55. John Adams, *A Defense of the Constitutions of Government of the United States of America in Three Volumes,* vol. 1, *The Third Edition* (Philadelphia: Budd and Bartram for W. Corbett, 1797), 216–217. The current edition is Clark, NJ: Lawbook Exchange, 2007.

56. Robert Yates, *Secret Proceedings and Debates of the Convention Assembled at Philadelphia, in the Year 1787, for the Purposes of Forming the Constitution of the United States of America* (Richmond, VA: Wilbur Curtiss, 1839), 182–183.

57. Ibid., 144–145.

58. Adams, *Defense of the Constitutions . . . Third Edition*, 108–110, 183, letter 25, Dr. Franklin, Ancient Republics and Opinions of Philosophers.

59. Madison, *Papers . . . Digital Edition*, 9:76–77, Original: Congressional Series, vol. 9 (April 9, 1786–May 24, 1787, and supplement, 1781–1784).

60. See Alexander Hamilton, *The Papers of Alexander Hamilton Digital Edition*, ed. Harold C. Syrett; Mary-Jo Kline consulting editor for the Digital Edition (Charlottesville: University of Virginia Press, Rotunda, 2011), 3:104, Original source: vol. 3, 1782–1786, *The Continentalist* no. 6, July 4, 1782, Fishkill, NY.

61. See Adams, *Adams Papers Digital Edition*, 1:106–107, Original source: *Papers of John Adams*, vol. 1 (September 1755–October 1773), "Fragmentary Notes for a 'Dissertation on the Canon and the Feudal Law,'" May–August 1765.

62. Ibid., 1:318, Original source: *Adams Family Correspondence*, vol. 1 (December 1761–May 1776), letter to Abigail Adams, October 29, 1775.

63. Ibid., 4:208–212, Original source: *Papers of John Adams*, vol. 4 (February–August 1776).

64. Ibid., 4:210, 201 and footnote 6, Original source: *Papers of John Adams*, vol. 4 (February–August 1776).

65. See John Adams, *The Works of John Adams, Second President of the United States with a Life of the Author, Notes and Illustrations by His Grandson Charles Francis Adams*, ed. Charles Francis Adams, 10 vols. (Boston: Little, Brown, 1856), 1:320, chapter B, extract from the *Boston Patriot*, May 15, 1811.

66. John Adams, *The Portable John Adams*, ed. John Patrick Duggins (New York: Penguin Classics, 2004), 414.

67. See Jefferson, *Papers . . . Digital Edition*, 1:193, Original source: Main Series, vol. 1 [1760–1776]), Jefferson's composition draft of the Declaration of Independence, June 26–July 6, 1775.

68. See "Proposed Constitution for Virginia, A Bill for New Modeling the Form of Government and for Establishing the Fundamental Principles Thereof in Future," in Ford, *Works of Thomas Jefferson*, 2:158–183, esp. part 4, Rights, Public and Private, on 178.

69. Thomas Jefferson, *Notes on the State of Virginia* (London: John Stockdale, 1787), 274–275.

70. See Jefferson, *Papers . . . Digital Edition*, 8:681–683, Original source: February 25– October 31, 1785.

71. Ibid., 8:426, Original source: Main Series, vol. 8 (February 25–October 31, 1785), letter to John Jay, August 23, 1785, Paris.

72. Ibid., 12:475–478, Original source: Main Series, vol. 12 (August 7, 1787–March 31, 1788), letter to Uriah Forrest with enclosure, December 31, 1787, Paris.

73. Ibid., 33:150–151, Original source: Main Series, vol. 33 (February 17–April 30, 1801).

74. Ibid., 2:275, Original source: Retirement Series, vol. 2 (November 16, 1809–August 11, 1810), letter to John Langdon, March 5, 1810, Monticello.

75. Madison, *Papers . . . Digital Edition*, 9:76–81, Original source: Congressional Series (April 9, 1786–May 24, 1787), letter to Thomas Jefferson, June 19, 1786, Orange.

76. Ibid., 10:212–213, Original source: Congressional Series, vol. 10 (May 27, 1787–March 3, 1788), letter to Thomas Jefferson, October 24, 1787, New York.

77. Ibid., 10:138, Original source: Congressional Series, vol. 10 (May 27, 1787–March 3, 1788), Suffrage Qualifications for Electing the House of Representatives, August 7, 1787.

78. Ibid., 14:132, Original source: Congressional Series, vol. 14 (April 6, 1791–March 16, 1793), Note on the Influence of Extent of Territory on Government, ca. December 1791.

79. Ibid., 14:267, Original source: Congressional Series, vol. 14 (April 6, 1791–March 16, 1793), *National Gazette*, March 29, 1792.

80. See Madison, *Debates*, 583 (Third Note on the Same Subject, during the Virginia Convention for Amending the Constitution of the State, 1829–30), Appendix to the Debates of the Federal Convention.

81. Madison, *Papers . . . Digital Edition*, 14:197–198, Original source: Congressional Series, vol. 14 (April 6, 1791–March 16, 1793), *National Gazette*, ca. January 23, 1792. The article is entitled "Parties." Nedelsky explains Madison's greater concern for "the many" that is clearly reflected in the *National Gazette* essays in this way: "By the 1790s, Madison was shocked and frightened by the direction governmental policy was taking under the influence of Alexander Hamilton. Madison thought Hamilton's plans for the redemption of public securities and for the national bank would favor the wealthy few. Worse still, these policies reflected the power of the 'monied interests' and their unholy collusion with government. Now the many were the victims of the few. Under these circumstances, Madison shifted the emphasis of his arguments. Property now seemed the dominant

interest, and the rights of persons in need of special emphasis" (21). She also adds: "I have argued that Madison opposed laws with redistributive consequences. But we know that he did not envision a government that simply took a hands-off attitude toward property." See Nedelsky, *Private Property*, 30.

82. For the Free Soil Party's August 11, 1852 Pittsburgh Platform, see Thomas Valentine Cooper and Hector Tyndale Fenton, *Campaign of '84: Biographies of James G. Blaine, the Republican Candidate for President, and John A. Logan, the Republican Candidate for Vice-President, with a Description of the Leading Issues and the Proceedings of the National Convention. Together with a History of the Political Parties of the United States: Comparisons of Platforms on All Important Questions, and Political Tables for Ready Reference* (Chicago: Baird & Dillon, 1884), 34–35. For Speaker Galusha Grow in the Homestead debate, see Marion Mills Miller, *Great Debates in American History: Economic and Social Questions, Part 1 (1913), From the Debates in the British Parliament on the Colonial Stamp Act (1764–1765) to the Debates in Congress at the Close of the Taft Administration (1912–1913)*, (New York: Current Literature Publications Company, 1913), 36–39. For the Republican Platform, see Republican National Committee, *The Republican*, Part XI, Public Lands, 1860, Plank 18, 188. Updates on the positions to 1876 are also provided. On Greeley, see John Rodgers Commons, *Horace Greeley and the Working Class Origins of the Republican Party* (Boston: Ginn & Company, 1909; reprinted from *Political Science Quarterly* 24 (1909): 468–488, see note 1 for the source, which is the *Weekly Tribune* of May 2, 1846. On Lincoln, see Abraham Lincoln, *Abraham Lincoln: Complete Works, Comprising His Speeches, Letters, State Papers, and Miscellaneous Writings*, ed. John Nicolay and John Hay (New York: The Century Company, 1894), 1:676. On Johnson, see Thomas Donaldson, *The Public Domain: Its History with Statistics* (Washington, DC: U.S. Government Printing Office, 1880), 349. On Boutwell, see George Sewall Boutwell, *Why I Am a Republican: History of the Republican Party, a Defense of Its Policy, and the Reasons Which Justify Its Continuance in Power, with Biographical Sketches of the Republican Candidates* (Tecumseh, Mich.: W. J. Betts & Company, 1884), 86. On Hale, see James T. DuBois and Gertrude S. Mathews, *Galusha A. Grow: Father of the Homestead Law* (New York: Houghton Mifflin Company, 1917), 198.

CHAPTER 2. EXAMPLES

1. Based on an interview with Arthur Rock by Joseph Blasi, in San Francisco, 2009.

2. See Larry Page and Sergei Brin, "2004 Founders IPO Letter: An Owners' Manual for Google Shareholders," in Google Inc., *Form S-1 Registration Statement*, U.S. Securities and Exchange Commission, August 18, 2004.

3. See "The Hundred Best Companies to Work For," *Fortune*, February 6, 2012, 165. See also Bo Cowgill and Eric Zitzewitz, *Incentive Effects of Equity Compensation: Employee-Level Evidence from Google*, June 2009. Available at http://faculty.haas.berkeley.edu/bo_cowgill/papers /StockOptionIncentives.pdf and http://www.dartmouth.edu/~ericz /incentives.pdf. On Gallatin's profit sharing see Jerry W. Markham, *A Financial History of the United States* (Armonk, NY: M. E. Sharpe, 2002), 326. For a detailed account dating the beginning of the profit sharing partnership agreement to September 20, 1797, see Raymond Walters, *Albert Gallatin: Jeffersonian Financier and Diplomat* (Pittsburgh, PA: University of Pittsburgh Press, 1957), 136–137.

4. For the history of the idea in Silicon Valley see Joseph Blasi, Douglas Kruse, and Aaron Bernstein, *In the Company of Owners* (New York: Basic Books, 2003), 3–29. On one of the earliest introductions of profit sharing and later employee stock ownership in Silicon Valley, Hewlett Packard, see David Packard, *The HP Way: How Bill Hewlett and I Built Our Company* (New York: HarperCollins, 1995).

5. Google Inc., *Google December 31 2009 Annual Report*, U.S. Securities and Exchange Commission, February 12, 2009 (date filed), 18.

6. Google Inc., *Google 2011 Proxy Statement*, U.S. Securities and Exchange Commission, April 20, 2011, 23.

7. Google Inc., *2009 Annual Report*, 18.

8. Ibid., 90–91, and Google Inc., *Google 2009 Proxy Statement*, U.S. Securities and Exchange Commission, March 24, 2009, 37, 55–58.

9. See Cowgill and Zitzewitz, *Incentive Effects*, 2009.

10. On the GEO (Global Equity Organization) Prize for Google in 2012 and 2010 see http://globalequity.org/geo/geoawardrecipients.

11. For P&G's statement on PhDs and innovation see https://www.facebook .com/DoctoralRecruiting. See also Procter & Gamble Inc., *Procter & Gamble Proxy Statement*, U.S. Securities and Exchange Commission, August 24, 2012, 26, 38–39, 40, and Procter & Gamble Inc., *Procter & Gamble Annual Report*, U.S. Securities and Exchange Commission, August 8, 2012, 52–53. Glassdoor.com is a web-based firm that provides "an inside look at jobs and companies."

12. See Richard Redwood Deupree, *William Cooper Procter (1862–1934), Industrial Statesman* (New York: Newcomen Society, American Branch,

1951). The observations on Professor Atwater and William Cooper Procter at Princeton are based on Joseph Blasi's research at the Princeton University Archives from 2007 to 2010.

13. Merle Crowell, *An Interview: William Cooper Procter, a Man Who Thinks Fast and Straight* (Cincinnati, Procter & Gamble Co., 1919). Procter's comments were compiled from the late 1880s and early 1900s.

14. Ida M. Tarbell, *The History of the Standard Oil Company*, 2 vols. (Gloucester, MA: Peter Smith, 1903); Ida M. Tarbell, *New Ideals in Business: An Account of Their Practice and Their Effects upon Men and Profits* (New York: Macmillan, 1916), 238–249; Ida M. Tarbell, *All in the Day's Work: An Autobiography* (New York: Macmillan, 1939).

15. Based on Joseph Blasi's research at the Procter & Gamble Archives, Cincinnati, 2007–2010.

16. In 2012, J. D. Power and Associates made Southwest one of fifty companies earning a Customer Service Champions award. Southwest is 82 percent unionized, with eighteen separate collective-bargaining agreements. On the awards see Southwest Airlines, *Southwest Airlines Proxy Statement*, U.S. Securities and Exchange Commission, April 5, 2012, 18. See also Southwest Airlines, *Southwest Airlines Annual Report*, U.S. Securities and Exchange Commission, February 9, 2012, 18, 20.

17. See Southwest Airlines, *Proxy Statement*, April 5, 2012, 19.

18. Nobles and Staley, retired senior executives, worked to define the concept, although some of their early examples have ceased to practice these ideas as a result of management changes. See http://freedom-basedmanagement.com/.

19. See Jeff Bailey, "On Some Flights Millionaires Serve the Drinks," *New York Times*, May 15, 2006, A1; Jody Hoffer Gittell, *The Southwest Airlines Way* (New York: McGraw-Hill, 2005).

20. The estimate for the Fortune 500 is based on our analysis of the U.S. Department of Labor's Form 5500, which is the form used to report retirement and savings plans under the Employee Retirement Income and Security Act of 1974 (ERISA).

21. See J. Robert Beyster with Peter Economy, *The SAIC Solution: How We Build an $8 Billion Employee-Owned Technology Company* (Seattle: Amazon.com Books, forthcoming 2013).

22. See National Center for Employee Ownership, "Employee Ownership Again Dominates the List," *Employee Ownership* 32, no. 3 (May–June 2012): 8, at http://www.nceo.org/members/pdf/newsletter_05_2012.pdf. For the Great Place to Work Institute that develops the *Fortune* list each year see http://www.greatplacetowork.com/. For the Global Equity

Organization and its annual peer-judged competition see http://www.
globalequity.org/geo/geoawards.

23. See the ESOP Association, at http://www.esopassociation.org/, which
represents about 1,500 ESOP companies, sponsors educational programs
for all employees, and has the *ESOP Report Newsletter*; the National Center
for Employee Ownership, a nonprofit research organization, at http://
www.nceo.org/, which has *The Employee Ownership Report*; and a smaller
group, the Employee-Owned S Corporations of America, at http://www
.esca.us/, which mainly does lobbying.

24. The ComSonics case study is based on public sources. See Vic Bradshaw,
"Childhood Gadgets Led to Creation of Innovative Business," *Daily
News-Record*, August 29, 2002; Dan Wright, "The Boys from the Base-
ment: More than Three Decades after Helping Launch Company, Six Still
There," *Daily News-Record*, March 6, 2006; "Self-Control: Employees in
Charge at ComSonics," *Daily News-Record*, October 31, 1994; "ComSonics:
Manufacturing Begins Work at Weyers Cave Location," *Daily News-
Record*, February 11, 2004; "Working for Yourself: At Three Area Compa-
nies, Employees Are Their Own Bosses," *Daily News-Record*, September 30,
2008; "Entrepreneur a Pioneer in Employee Ownership: Warren Braun
Also Key in Nascent Cable TV Industry," *Daily News-Record*, May 22, 2009;
"10 Elected to ComSonics Council," *Valley Business*, July 10, 2006; The
ESOP Association, *ComSonics Named 2010 ESOP Company of the Year by the
ESOP Association*, Press Release, May 12, 2010; Jean Buchanan, "ESOPS:
Want Employees to Think and Act Like Owners? Then Give Them Stock
and Make Them Owners," *Office Systems*, December 1, 1998; John Case,
"It's a Great Place to Work," *Inc. Magazine*, September 1, 1988; Warren T.
Brookes, "ESOPS: A New Declaration of Independence," *San Francisco
Chronicle*, July 8, 1987. As in ComSonics, combinations of citizens' shares
using both employee stock ownership and forms of profit sharing are
quite common. See Chapters 3 and 4, and note 5 from Chapter 3, noting
that 21 percent of adult citizens have employee stock ownership, with
many having cash profit or gain sharing, stock options together with it,
or having all three share practices.

25. See http://www.nceo.org/articles/statistical-profile-employee-owner
ship, based on their review of U.S. Department of Labor Forms 5500s,
which contain reports to the U.S. government about ESOPs. About 83
percent of the corporations in the ESOP Association are majority
employee owned, with 41 percent having 41–99 percent employee
ownership and 42 percent having 100 percent employee ownership. See
ESOP Association, *ESOP Survey* (Washington, DC: ESOP Association,
2010), 18.

26. On winners of peer awards see http://www.esopassociation.org/about
-the-association/esop-awards/aace-awards/winners.

27. For a searchable database of ESOPs by state based on the publicly
available federal records see http://www.nceo.org/US-ESOP-Company
-Database/m/262/. For a searchable map of ESOPs see www.ownershi
passociates.com/EO. On the Evergreen Cooperatives see http://evergre
encooperatives.com/.

28. See Blasi, Kruse, and Bernstein, *In the Company of Owners*, 20–21.

29. See also Martin Ruef, *The Entrepreneurial Group* (Princeton, NJ: Princeton
University Press, 2010), 113–137.

30. The paper is W. Gates and C. Papadimitriou, "Bounds for Sorting by
Prefix Reversal," *Discrete Mathematics* 27 (1979): 47–57.

31. See Microsoft Corp., *Microsoft Corporation Proxy Statement*, U.S. Securities
and Exchange Commission, March 10, 2011, 6, 13.

32. On VentureOne see http://www.dowjones.com/privateequityventure
capital/. See also John R. N. Hand, "Give Everyone a Prize: Employee
Stock Options in Private Venture-Backed Firms," *Journal of Business
Venturing* 23, no. 4 (2008): 385–404.

33. See Blasi, Kruse, and Bernstein, *In the Company of Owners*, 84, 87, 91.

34. Randall Smith, Suzanne Craig, and Annalena Loeb, "The Lehman Stock
Slide Hits Home: Employees Face More than $10 Billion in Losses," *Wall
Street Journal*, September 12, 2008. On Enron, WorldCom, and Lehman
see the expanded notes.

35. Even when employee ownership works to the benefit of the firm and
workers, this does not necessarily mean that what the firm does benefits
society broadly. For centuries, pirates have operated with a "share the
booty" operation and a participatory employee culture. The pirate code
specified that each member of the crew shared in the treasure that they
seized. The code for Captain Roberts's pirate crew that operated in the
1700s included the following: I. Every Man has a Vote in the Affairs of
the Moment; has equal Title to the fresh Provisions, or strong Liquors, at
any time seized . . . IX. No Man to talk of breaking up their Way of
Living till each shared one thousand pounds. If in order to do this any
Man would lose a Limb, or become a Cripple in their service, he was to
have eight hundred Dollars, out of publick Stock, and for lesser hurts
proportionately . . . X. The Captain and Quarter-Master to receive two
shares of a Prize, the Master, Boatswain, and Gunner, one share and a
half, and other Officers one and a quarter [everyone else to receive one
share]. The expert on pirate economics, Peter Leeson, notes in his book,
The Invisible Hook: The Hidden Economics of Pirates, that "this contrasts
sharply with merchant vessels' pay scales where captains earned four or

five times as much as regular sailors during peacetime." More or less equal splitting of the booty on pirate ships varied with economic opportunities. The famous buccaneer Henry Morgan divided booty more in line with that on merchant vessels' scales: I. The fund of all payments under the articles is the stock of what is gotten by the expedition, following the same law as other pirates, that is, No prey, no pay. II. Compensation is provided the Captain for the use of his ship, and the salary of the carpenter, or shipwright, who mended, careened, and rigged the vessel (the latter usually about one hundred and fifty pieces of eight). A sum for provisions and victuals is specified, usually two hundred pieces of eight. A salary and compensation is specified for the surgeon and his medicine chest, usually two hundred and fifty pieces of eight. III. A standard compensation is provided for maimed and mutilated buccaneers. "Thus they order for the loss of a right arm, six hundred pieces of eight, or six slaves; for the loss of a left arm, five hundred pieces of eight, or five slaves; for a right leg five hundred pieces of eight, or five slaves; for the left leg, four hundred pieces of eight, or four slaves; for an eye, one hundred pieces of eight, or one slave; for a finger of the hand, the same reward as for the eye. IV. Shares of booty are provided as follows: "the Captain, or chief Commander, is allotted five or six portions to what the ordinary seamen have; the Master's Mate only two; and Officers proportionate to their employment. After whom they draw equal parts from the highest even to the lowest mariner, the boys not being omitted. For even these draw half a share, by reason that, when they happen to take a better vessel than their own, it is the duty of the boys to set fire to the ship or boat wherein they are, and then retire to the prize which they have taken." See Daniel Defoe, *A General History of the Pyrates*, ed. Manuel Schonhorn (Mineola, NY: Dover Publications, 1999), 211–212 and Leeson, 62–63, 68.

36. On United Airlines see Jeffrey Gordon, "Employee Ownership in Economic Transitions: The Case of United Airlines," *Bank of America Journal of Applied Corporate Finance* 62, no. 3 (1998): 39–62, and Adam Bryant, "Labor Rifts Return to Employee-Owned United Airlines," *New York Times*, January 16, 1997, n.p.

CHAPTER 3. CITIZEN SHARES IN THE UNITED STATES

1. See Henry Hansmann, *The Ownership of Enterprise* (Cambridge, MA: Harvard University Press, 2000). Hansmann noticed this trend early and observed where employee ownership was prominent.

2. For information on the General Social Survey (GSS) see the website of the University of Chicago National Opinion Research Center at http://www3.norc.org/gss+website/.

3. Stock options can give employees the right to buy the stock for other periods than ten years.
4. The General Social Survey questionnaires are available at http://www3 .norc.org/GSS+Website/Publications/GSS+Questionnaires/.
5. For detail on each individual practice and combination, see Kruse, Freeman, and Blasi, *Shared Capitalism at Work*, 47, table 1.1 and the expanded notes for updates from successive samples of the General Social Survey.
6. Because of budget limitations the 2010 survey focused on ownership and options and did not include the profit- and gain-sharing questions.
7. Table 3.1 is based on the 2006 General Social Survey.
8. This formula takes into account the variability of the stock price in estimating the likely gain from exercising the option when the stock price is high.
9. Obtaining the value of all options, vested or not, if exercised the day of the survey, is not an ideal way to value them. But we deemed it more sensible to ask this question than to ask workers to calculate the mathematical formula to value options, which is itself an approximation. On the National Bureau for Economic Research data set see Douglas L. Kruse, Richard B. Freeman, and Joseph R. Blasi, eds., *Shared Capitalism at Work: Employee Ownership, Profit and Gain Sharing and Broad-Based Stock Options* (Chicago: IL: University of Chicago Press, 2010).
10. Ibid., 52–54, table 1.3, "Shared Capitalism Types and Intensities in GSS and NBER Data Sets."
11. The chart is based on our analysis of the 2006 General Social Survey.
12. See Kruse, Freeman, and Blasi, *Shared Capitalism at Work*, 56, table 1.4.
13. For the "typical employee ownership" group of workers the numbers are the minimum that at least half the workers with employee stock ownership in their company possess. This is the median—namely, the value separating the higher half from the lower half of the distribution. Obviously, many workers above the median have more than this dollar value, although the typical number establishes a good rough estimate of what is common. For the "high employee ownership" group of workers the numbers are the seventy-fifth percentile, namely, the dollar value of employee stock ownership for the workers who have more than the bottom 75 percent of workers have and for whom the next 25 percent have more. For example, this chart means that 25 percent of workers making less than $50,000 per year had employee stock ownership valued at *more than* $40,000, 25 percent of workers making $50,000–$99,000 per year had employee ownership valued at *more than* about $45,000, and finally, that 25 percent of workers making $90,000–

$149,000 per year had employee ownership valued at *more than* about $60,000 in total at the time of the survey.

CHAPTER 4. HOW IT EVOLVED

1. Selected sentence excerpts from John H. Gray, "Economics and the Law: Annual Address of the President," *American Economic Review* 5, no. 1, Supplement, "Papers and Proceedings of the Twenty-Seventh Annual Meeting of the American Economic Association" (March 1915): 3–23.

2. See Page Smith, *The Rise of Industrial America: A Peoples' History of the Post-Reconstruction Era* (New York: McGraw-Hill, 1984), 140–163.

3. See Richard Scott, "Artisans and Capitalist Development," in *Wages of Independence: Capitalism in the Early American Republic*, ed. Paul A. Gilje (Madison, WI: Madison House Publishers, 1997), 101–116. On how the hypocrisy of slavery clashed with the Revolutionary legacy of wealth distribution see James L. Huston, *Securing the Fruits of Labor: The American Concept of Wealth Distribution, 1765–1900* (Baton Rouge: Louisiana State University Press, 1998), 296–336.

4. See John R. Commons, David J. Saposs, Helen L. Sumner, E. B. Mittelman, H. E. Hoagland, John B. Andrews, and Selig Perlman, *History of Labor in the United States*, vol. 1 (New York: Macmillan, 1918), 56–87 and 95–100, 104, 106–107, 127, 235, 436, 466–467, 378, 493–521, 564–574. On the concept of "slavery" applied to wage earners see Michael Sandel, *Democracy's Discontent: In Search of a Public Philosophy* (Cambridge, MA: Harvard University Press, 1996), 183, 168–200. See Fred A. Shannon, "The Homestead Act and the Labor Surplus," *American Historical Review* 41, no. 4 (July 1936): 637–651.

5. See Charles Perrow, *Organizing America: Wealth, Power, and the Origins of Corporate Capitalism* (Princeton: Princeton University Press, 2002), 97–228, esp. 180, 182–184, 196–201.

6. Lyman Hotchkiss Atwater, "The Labor Question in Its Economic and Christian Aspects," in *Presbyterian Quarterly and Princeton Review*, New Series, vol. 1, ed. Lyman H. Atwater and Henry B. Smith (New York: J. M. Sherwood, 1872), 468–496.

7. See Charles Babbage, *On the Economy of Machinery and Manufactures* (London: C. Knight, 1832), 250–259, esp. 253–254 and 257, outlining the system of profit sharing in detail in chap. 26, "On a New System of Manufacturing." Babbage discussed profit sharing among whaling fishermen. See also John Stuart Mill, *Principles of Political Economy: With Some of Their Applications to Social Philosophy* (London: J. W. Parker, 1848), bk. 4, chap. 7, section 5–6.

8. Joseph Blasi evaluated the Waltham story using the Harvard Business School's extensive Waltham Watch Company Collection, Baker Business Historical Collections, Business Manuscripts MSS 598, 1854–1929. See also, H. M. Gitelman, "The Labor Force at Waltham Watch during the Civil War," *Journal of Economic History* 25, no. 2 (June 1965): 214–242. Baldwin used a form of partnership for managers and efficiency wages for mechanics. See John K. Brown, *The Baldwin Locomotive Works, 1831–1915: A Study in American Industrial Practice*, Studies in Industry and Society Series (Baltimore: Johns Hopkins University Press, 1995); and *Baldwin Locomotive Works, History of the Baldwin Locomotive Works from 1831 to 1897* (Philadelphia: J. B. Lippincott Company, 1897).

9. For an assessment, see John R. Commons, David J. Saposs, Helen L. Sumner, E.B. Mittelman, H.E. Hoagland, John B. Andrews, and Selig Perlman, *History of Labor in the United States*, vol. 2 (New York: Macmillan, 1918), 41, 53–54, 76, 79, 111, 124, 171, 340, 347–348, 351, 430–437. There are two empirical assessments, using more systematic data from both primary and secondary sources. See Derek Jones, "U.S. Producer Cooperatives: The Record to Date," *Industrial Relations*, col. 18, no. 3 (Fall, 1979): 342–357, and Howard Aldrich and Robert N. Stern, *"Resource Mobilization and the Creation of US Producer's Cooperatives, 1835–1935,"* vol. 4, no. 3, 371–406. For detail, see the expanded notes.

10. See Drew R. McCoy, *The Last of the Fathers: James Madison and the Republican Legacy* (New York: Cambridge University Press, 1989), 204–206. On this and Owen's speeches before Congress see the expanded notes.

11. These scholars knew about British experiments in profit sharing and worker ownership from Charles Babbage and John Stuart Mill. See "Labor and Capital," in Washington Gladden, *Working People and Their Employers* (Boston: Lockwood, Brooks, and Co., 1876), 30–51, esp. 30, 40–45, and 46 on English cases of cooperation that he was following. For the Churches of Christ statement see Washington Gladden, *The Labor Question* (New York: Pilgrim Press, 1911), 167–169. From 1871 to 1875 Gladden worked in New York City and served as editor of the *Independent*, a religious newspaper of the stature of today's *Time* or *Newsweek*, with a far-reaching circulation across the entire country. The *Independent* played a dominant role in educating clergy, their business parishioners, and thinking citizens about profit sharing and employee stock ownership. William Cooper Procter and his father were seeing regular articles on the topics in the issues of the *Independent* where they bought the first advertising for their Ivory Soap; their ads regularly

featured the large, artist-inspired pictures of mothers and babies and workmen using Ivory Soap. Procter invited Gladden to speak at the "Dividend Days" he organized at Procter & Gamble to distribute profit-sharing checks.

12. Atwater frequently mentions the work of John Stuart Mill in his early writings on these subjects. On Atwater's class notes see Lyman H. Atwater, *Ethics and Political Economy from Notes Taken in the Lecture Room of Lyman H. Atwater, D.D., L.L.D* (Trenton, NJ, 1878), 117–118. For William Cooper Procter's name on Atwater's grade sheet see "1883 Grading Sheet: Political Economy: Seniors," folder 1, Atwater Papers, box 4, C0792, Lyman H. Atwater Collection, Department of Rare Books and Special Collections, Princeton University Library. On Atwater's exam questions see the expanded notes. See also Walter Rauschenbush, *Christianity and the Social Crisis in the 21st Century*, ed. Paul Rauschenbush (New York: Harper One, HarperCollins, 2007): 184, 186, 191, 194, 203.

13. See Herbert B. Adams, ed., *History of Cooperation in the United States* (Baltimore: N. Murray, Publication Agent, under the auspices of Johns Hopkins University, 1988), 5 (on the debt of American scholarship to John Stuart Mill), and especially for its conclusions, 124–125, 165, 230–242, 260–262, 298–301, 387–391, 400, 423–426, 477–478. One of the Johns Hopkins doctoral students, Richard T. Ely, later of the University of Wisconsin, became the American Economics Association's third president. Pastors-turned-social-scientists Gladden and Gilman were on the economic association's executive council for years. See the expanded notes for the early history of the American Economic Association group. See Nicolas Paine Gilman, *Profit Sharing between Employer and Employee: A Study of the Evolution of the Wages System* (Boston: Houghton, Mifflin, 1891). See also John Bates Clark, *The Philosophy of Wealth: Economic Principles Newly Formulated* (Boston: Ginn & Co., 1886), 183–190 and 196–199 on his share design, iv–vii, 107, 127–128, 131–133, 147–148, 177–178, 204–206, and 216.

14. On Walker see his later work, Francis A. Walker, *Political Economy* (New York: Henry Holt and Co., 1887), 341–351, and Francis A. Walker, *First Lessons in Political Economy* (New York: Henry Holt & Co., 1889; later Macmillan and Co., 1890), 225–236.

15. See http://hollis.harvard.edu/?q=employer%20and%20employed (accessed October 19, 2012).

16. On Charles A. Pillsbury see H. B. Adams, *History of Cooperation*, 255–262, esp. 256, 258, and 259 on his motives for introducing profit sharing. On Charles Sturgis Pillsbury see Lori Sturdevant with George S. Pillsbury,

The Pillsburys of Minnesota (Minneapolis: Nodin Press, 2011), 348–355, esp. 352–354 on work on employee stock ownership.

17. On Nelson O. Nelson see Kim McQuaid, *A Response to Industrialism: Liberal Businessmen and the Evolving Spectrum of Capitalist Reform* (Washington, DC: Beard Books, 2003), 24–49.

18. This account closely follows David Nasaw, *Andrew Carnegie* (New York: Penguin Press, 2006), 256–258, 278–279, 318–320, 452–453. Nasaw presents evidence that Carnegie knew about all the details and was personally involved in managing the conflict. On Carnegie's book on profit sharing and worker ownership, Nasaw cites a cable from Andrew Carnegie to Henry Clay Frick of July 12, 1892 from the Harvey Folder, Helen Clay Frick Foundation Archives, Frick Collection, New York. The book is Andrew Carnegie, *The Problems of To-day* (Garden City, NY: Doubleday, Page & Co., 1908), 63–82, esp. 73 (on tax breaks), 73–75 (on the Filenes), 75 (on the "proprietor" idea and sharing in the fishery), and 76 (on Nicholas Paine Gilman). He opens the chapter by discussing how he learned the value of employee stock ownership by granting it to managers and extensively quotes John Stuart Mill on these ideas. See Andrew Carnegie, "How Labor Will Absorb Capital: The Final Relation between Them Which the Continuous Upward Progress of Labor Fore-shadows," *The World's Work: A History of Our Time*, vol. 17, 11124–11128.

19. On the details of the first profit-sharing plan see Kodak's 1916 letter to the National Civic Federation for its profit-sharing study in National Civic Federation, *Profit Sharing by American Employers* (New York: E. D. Dutton & Co., 1921), 42–43. For a study of Kodak's corporate culture see Sanford Jacoby, *Modern Manors* (Princeton, NJ: Princeton University Press, 1998), 57–94. Eastman was personally engaging. He built the famed Eastman School of Music in Rochester because he never wanted another artist like the young beautiful dancer with whom he had fallen in love—his only true love—to leave Rochester for greener pastures, as she did when she skipped town and broke his heart. Years later, before his tragic suicide as he gave up on a life of illness, she returned to visit him, still unmarried! During Kodak's phenomenal expansion just after the Bolshevik Revolution in Russia, a group of highly trained workers in the lens and optical workshop approached Eastman one day and said that they were so central to the company's money-making that they wanted to take over their little workshop and own and manage it themselves. To everyone's surprise, Eastman gave them the small factory with a contract to supply Kodak, and he put it on the front page of the newspapers. The workers did not take into account the important role of

management, so they tried to elect inexperienced managers among themselves and soon drove the factory into the ground through bickering and inefficiency. Eastman took the factory back under Kodak's wing and then continued to aggressively promote employee ownership. These highly trained professionals got the point across to Eastman that was so central to Francis Amasa Walker's analysis: management mattered, but workers should and could own and participate, and top management did not require all the rewards. Eastman also had ideas about shirkers; he believed, for example, that since much of the company's sensitive work was done in the dark and that an unhappy employee could easily mess up a chemical mixture and cost the company a lot, it would be better to have share partners on the job. On Eastman's life, see Elizabeth Brayer, *George Eastman: A Biography* (Rochester, NY: University of Rochester Press, 2006). The story of Eastman's agreement to worker ownership of an entire factory is from an undated newspaper article in the files of the George Eastman Archives at the George Eastman House in Rochester, NY. Unfortunately, Kodak, in its recent bankruptcy, also demonstrated that missing a strategic call—in this case the impact of the digital age and the Internet on the future of photography—will undermine a corporation with broad-based capitalism or without broad-based capitalism every time.

20. For the Himrod quote see Francis Russell, *The Shadow of Blooming Grove: Warren G. Harding and His Times* (New York: McGraw-Hill, 1986), 384.

21. The statements on Procter's efforts to slowly build profit sharing over several decades are based on Joseph Blasi's review of the William Cooper Procter and profit-sharing files in the Procter & Gamble Archives in Cincinnati. On the Procter-Wilson relationship and the Wood campaign see August Heckscher, *Woodrow Wilson: A Biography* (Newtown, CT: American Political Biography Press, 2010). For the Roosevelt quote see Theodore Roosevelt IV, *State of the Union Addresses of Theodore Roosevelt* (Middlesex, England: The Echo Library), 207, 255. On the Wood interview see Evan J. David, "Leonard Wood on Labor Problems: An Interview by Evan J. David," *Outlook*, February 25, 1920, 326–328, and "Wood's Labor Plan Is Golden Rule: With Profit Sharing It Would End Most Industrial Disputes Says General," *New York Times*, February 23, 1920. On the testimony of Procter see U.S. Congress, *Presidential Campaign Expenses, Hearings before a Subcommittee of the Committee on Privileges and Elections, U.S. Senate, 66th Congress, Second Session Pursuant to S. Res. 357, Part I* (Washington, DC: Government Printing Office, 1920), 174–202, esp. 196, where Procter says his reason for taking on the chairmanship was "idealism." For a complete account see Karen Miller, *Populist Nationalism: Republican Insurgency and American Foreign Policy, 1918–1925* (Westport,

CT: Greenwood Press, 1999), 73–96, and 81 on Procter's total contribution of $745,433. For the Penrose quote, see Roberta Ann Johnson, *The Struggle against Corruption: A Comparative Study* (New York: Macmillian, 2004), 26. On General Wood's refusal to give certain Republicans control of three cabinet seats in return for the presidential nomination see U.S. Congress, *Leases upon Naval Oil Reserves, Hearings, U.S. Senate Committee on Public Lands and Surveys* (Washington, DC: Government Printing Office, 1924), 3212. The hearings were reported widely in the press, for example, "Says Wood Refused Deal with Penrose for Help in 1920: Witness Tells Oil Committee Senator Wanted Three Cabinet Places in Return," *New York Times*, April 19, 1924, 1. See the expanded notes.

22. See U.S. Commission on Industrial Relations, *Final Report of the Commission on Industrial Relations* (Washington, DC: U.S. Government Printing Office, 1916). Several firms with a history of profit sharing or worker ownership testified including Wanamaker's and the Philadelphia Rapid Transit Company. See also, Joseph A. McCartin, *Labor's Great War: The Struggle for Industrial Democracy and the Origins of Modern American Labor* (Chapel Hill: University of North Carolina Press, 1998), 12–13; Bruce E. Kaufman, *The Origins and Evolution of Industrial Relations in the United States* (Ithaca, NY: Cornell University Press, 1992), 3; "Labor Offers to Operate Railroads for U.S. on Profit Sharing Basis," *Washington Post*, February 7, 1919, 1; and, "Hines for Five Year Plan," *Washington Post*, February 4, 1919, 2. John R. Commons was a commissioner and part of the report advocated impartial arbitration bodies. The chair was labor lawyer Francis P. Walsh. For the U.S. Labor Department report, see Boris Emmet, *Profit Sharing in the United States* (Washington, DC: U.S. Government Printing Office, Bulletin of the U.S. Department of Labor, Bureau of Labor Statistics, Bulletin 208, Missl. Series No. 13, 1916), 169–171 on company outcomes, 129–157 on employee ownership plans, and a complete bibliography to date at 173–188. Three other industrial commissions, the Hewitt hearings of 1878–1879, the Blair committee that lasted to 1886, and the 1898–1902 United States Industrial Commission appointed by President William McKinley did not significantly deal with the share idea.

23. See Profit Sharing Department of the National Civic Federation, *Profit Sharing by American Employers, Examples from England, Types in France* (New York: E. P. Dutton & Co., 1920), 8–21, 365.

24. See National Industrial Conference Board, *Practical Experience with Profit Sharing in Industrial Establishments* (Boston: National Industrial Conference Board, Research Report no. 19, June 1920), 29–30, 48, 75, 78, with a list of firms on 81–86 and one of the first analyses of employee ownership plans on 61–69. See Sanford Jacoby, *Employing Bureaucracy:*

Managers, Unions, and the Transformation of Work in the 20th Century (New York: Psychology Press, 2004), 198.

25. On the development of welfare capitalism see Jacoby, *Modern Manors*, 11–34. On Rockefeller's initiatives see the expanded notes. On Princeton see http://www.irs.princeton.edu/about-us and http://www.irs.princeton.edu/history.

26. On the Wharton Industrial Research Department see "Carnegie, Rockefeller, and Economic Research," in Malcolm Rutherford, *The Institutionalist Movement in American Economics, 1918–1947* (New York: Cambridge University Press, 1911), 263; Steven A. Sass, *The Pragmatic Imagination: A History of the Wharton School, 1881–1981* (Philadelphia: University of Pennsylvania Press, 1982), 209–213; and Joseph H. Willits, "An Industrial Personnel Research Program," *Journal of Personnel Research* 5, no. 3 (1924): 125–128.

27. Robert F. Foerster and Elise H. Dietel, *Employee Stock Ownership in the United States* (Princeton, NJ: Princeton University Industrial Relations Section, 1926), 5–8, 23, 33, and 162–163; on Standard Oil 67–68, 91–97; 99–174. See, for summaries of plans, 29–30 and 85–86 on corporate governance. On the Depression see Eleanor Davis, *Employee Stock Ownership and the Depression* (Princeton, NJ: Princeton University Industrial Relations Section, 1933). See Jacoby, *Modern Manors*, 1998.

28. See Council on Profit Sharing Industries, *Proceedings, First Annual Conference* (Akron: Council on Profit Sharing Industries, 1948), 2–9; Council on Profit Sharing Industries, *Revised Profit Sharing Manual, Containing a Digest and Analysis of Ninety-One Representative Profit Sharing Plans* (Akron: Council on Profit Sharing Industries, 1951); Philip A. Knowlton, *Profit Sharing Patterns; A Comparative Analysis of the Formulas and Results of the Plans of 300 Companies with 730,000 Employees* (Evanston, IL.: Profit Sharing Research Foundation, 1954); Bert L. Metzger, *Profit Sharing in Perspective, in American Medium-Sized and Small Business* (Evanston, IL.: Profit Sharing Research Foundation, 1966), containing the Dun and Bradstreet and the Opinion Research Corporation study and the new data on unions on 109–119; Profit Sharing Council of America, *Guide to Modern Profit Sharing* (Chicago: Profit Sharing Council of America, 1973); Bert L. Metzger and Jerome A. Colletti, *Does Profit Sharing Pay? A Comparative Study of the Financial Performance of Retailers with and without Profit Sharing Programs* (Evanston, IL.: Profit Sharing Research Foundation, 1971); Bert L. Metzger, *Profit Sharing in 38 Large Companies: Piece of the Action for 1,000,000 Participants* (Evanston, IL.: Profit Sharing Research Foundation, 1975–1978). The Profit Sharing Council of

America, founded in 1947, later the Profit Sharing/401 Council of
America, is now called the Plan Sponsor Council of America at
http://www.psca.org/ and continues to have leading profit sharing
corporations as members and sponsor conferences and an Annual Survey
on Profit Sharing at http://www.psca.org/55th_survey. Many profit-
sharing plans today are deferred profit-sharing plans where company
profit sharing is integrated with the company match in 401(k) plans.

29. See Ray Carey, *Democratic Capitalism* (Bloomington, IN: Author House,
2004), 15–48 on the evolution of his designs. See the expanded notes.

30. See Louis O. Kelso and Mortimer J. Adler, *The Capitalist Manifesto* (New
York: Random House, 1958). On Kelso's biography, policy activities, and
writings see: http://www.kelsoinstitute.org/index.html. Kelso was
featured on the television program *60 Minutes* by journalist Mike Wallace
in 1975 and by journalist Bill Moyers in his TV special *A World of Ideas* on
the Pubic Broadcasting System. On ESOP statistics, see http://www.nceo
.org/articles/comprehensive-overview-employee-ownership
/printable. For more background on the policy statements, see the
expanded notes.

31. See www.wetheowners.com.

CHAPTER 5. EVIDENCE

1. Adam Smith wrote that the craftsman had "what are usually two
distinct revenues, belonging to two distinct persons, the profits of stock,
and the wages of labour," in *The Wealth of Nations*. In a discussion
contrasting feudalism to workers who had shares in agriculture, Smith
long ago recognized that a worker could be interested in owning a piece
of the rock and having capital income in addition to wage income. See
Adam Smith, *An Inquiry into the Nature and Causes of the Wealth of Nations*
(Hollywood, FL: Simon & Brown, 2012), 488–503 (bk. 3), 93 (bk. 1).

2. See Chris Doucouliagos, "Worker Participation and Productivity in
Labor-Managed and Participatory Capitalist Firms: A Meta-analysis,"
Industrial and Labor Relations Review 40, no. 1 (1995): 58–77, esp. 67–72,
which uses a method called a meta-analysis to reanalyze the statistical
findings of multiple systematic studies; Douglas Kruse and Joseph Blasi,
Employee Ownership, Employee Attitudes and Firm Performance, National
Bureau for Economic Research, working paper 5277 (Cambridge:
National Bureau for Economic Research, 1995), 1–52, esp. 24 and 26,
summarizing twenty-six studies of employee attitudes and twenty-nine
studies of firm performance, and examining over 128 studies; Eric
Kaarsemaker, "Employee Ownership and Human Resource Manage-

ment" (PhD dissertation, Radboud University, Nijmegen, Netherlands, 2006), 29–37 (table 2.2), 37–44 (table 2.3), which finds "by far the majority . . . of the studies found a clearly favorable result" (35–36, 44) on both employee attitudes and behaviors and firm performance, while underlining the importance of supportive people practices.

3. C. W. Cobb and P. H. Douglas, "A Theory of Production," *American Economic Review* 18 (Supplement, 1928): 139–165. As a University of Chicago professor, Douglas sought to estimate the marginal product of additional workers and capital on output.

4. For example, there may be time-varying unobservable variables that affect the firm's choice of when to adopt a plan, and which may be responsible for any performance changes. To address this, many of the studies have used selectivity corrections (e.g., instrumental variables, two-stage least squares, Heckman corrections) and continued to find generally positive results. While it is possible that worker self-selection helps account for the higher performance of broad-based capitalism firms, pre/post evidence from two studies indicates that average worker quality did not change as compensation was changed from individual to group incentives (initially high- and low-productivity workers were equally likely to leave), while average worker performance improved under the group incentives. See Daniel G. Hansen, "Worker Performance and Group Incentives," *Industrial and Labor Relations Review* 51, no. 1 (October 1997): 37–49, and Andrew Weiss, "Incentives and Worker Behavior," in *Information, Incentives, and Risk Sharing*, ed. Haig Nalbantian (Totowa, NJ: Rowman & Littlefield, 1987), 137–150.

5. See Martin L. Weitzman and Douglas L. Kruse, "Profit Sharing and Productivity," in *Paying for Productivity*, ed. Alan S. Blinder (Washington, DC: Brookings Institution, 1990), 95–141. Kruse and Blasi, *Employee Ownership*, 1995; Alex Bryson and Richard Freeman, *Doing the Right Thing? Does Fair Share Capitalism Improve Workplace Performance?* (London: UK Department of Trade and Industry, Employment Relations Research Series, no. 81, 2007). The following studies reviewed research for the United Kingdom: Oxera Economic Consultancy, *Tax Advantaged Employee Share Schemes: Analysis of Productivity Effects, Report 1, Productivity Measured Using Turnover*. Prepared for Her Majesty's Revenue And Customs (London: Her Majesty's Revenue and Customs, HMRC, Report 33, August 2007a); Oxera Economic Consultancy, *Tax Advantaged Employee Share Schemes: Analysis of Productivity Effects, Report 2, Productivity Measured Using Gross Value Added*. Prepared for Her Majesty's Revenue And Customs (London: Her Majesty's Revenue and Customs, HMRC, Report 33, August

2007b); Oxera Economic Consultancy, *Tax Advantaged Employee Share Schemes: Analysis of Productivity Effects, Overview,* Prepared for Her Majesty's Revenue and Customs (London: Her Majesty's Revenue and Customs, HMRC, Report 33, August 2007c); and Oxera Economic Consultancy, *Tax Advantaged Employee Share Schemes: Analysis of Productivity Effects, Appendices to Report 1,* Prepared for Her Majesty's Revenue and Customs (London: Her Majesty's Revenue and Customs, HMRC, Report 33, August 2007d).

6. These studies are listed in a document at the website of this book.

7. See Arindrajit Dube and Richard Freeman, "Complementarity of Shared Compensation and Decision-Making Systems: Evidence from the American Labor Market," in *Shared Capitalism at Work,* ed. Douglas L. Kruse, Richard B. Freeman, and Joseph R. Blasi, 167–200.

8. See Oxera, *Tax Advantaged Employee Share Schemes*: 2007a, b, c, d. In 2010 the UK commissioned another economic consultancy to review the evidence that supported these conclusions in the Matrix report. See Matrix Knowledge Group, *The Employee Ownership Effect: A Review of the Evidence* (London: Matrix Evidence, 2010).

9. See Alex Bryson and Richard Freeman, "How Does Shared Capitalism Affect Economic Performance in the United Kingdom?" in Kruse, Freeman, and Blasi, *Shared Capitalism at Work,* 201–224.

10. See U.S. General Accounting Office, *Employee Stock Ownership Plans: Report to the Chairman, Committee on Finance, U.S. Senate* (Washington, DC: GAO, October 1987), Report Number GAO-PEMD-88-1.

11. See Joseph Blasi, Douglas Kruse, and Daniel Weltmann, "Firm Survival, Performance, and Employee Ownership: Comparing Privately-Held ESOP and non-ESOP Firms," in *Advances in Economic Analysis of Participatory and Self-Managed Firms* (Greenwich, CT: JAI Press, forthcoming 2013). In 2002 Douglas Kruse replicated some of the findings of the commissioned study with the conclusion that ESOPs were four times more likely to offer defined benefit plans to their employees, in an analysis of the entire research file of the U.S. Department of Labor's Form 5500 records on ESOPs using the Department of Labor's 1998 research file.

12. Suzanne J. Peterson and Fred Luthans, "The Impact of Financial and Nonfinancial Incentives on Business-Unit Outcomes over Time," *Journal of Applied Psychology* 91, no. 1 (2006): 156–165.

13. This survey was designed by the University of California–Berkeley Institute of Industrial Relations and conducted between May and October 2003 covering 2,806 establishments. On this California Establishment Survey see Kruse, Freeman, and Blasi, *Shared Capitalism at Work,* 187–191.

14. The National Bureau of Economic Research is the world's leading nonprofit, nonpartisan economic research center, sufficiently trusted that it determines business cycles for the U.S. economy. It was set up in the 1920s. It does extensive economic analysis and makes no policy recommendations. The study is Kruse, Freeman, and Blasi, *Shared Capitalism at Work*. The book can be found at http://www.nber.org/books /krus08-1/ and is available in print and online at the University of Chicago Press and online at Google Books.

15. Ann Bartel, Casey Ichniowski, and Kathryn Shaw, "Using 'Insider Econometrics' to Study Productivity," *American Economic Review* 94, no. 2, Papers and Proceedings of the One Hundred Sixteenth Annual Meeting of the American Economic Association San Diego, California, January 3–5, 2004 (May 2004), 217–223.

16. Severin Borenstein and Joseph Farrell, "Inside the Pin-Factory: Empirical Studies Augmented by Manager Interviews," *Journal of Industrial Economics* 46, no. 2 (June 1998): 123–124.

17. See Kruse, Freeman, and Blasi, *Shared Capitalism at Work*, 10–11, 24–34, and the survey measures in Appendix A, 387–401.

18. This assumes that the arrangements have a reasonably monotonic linear relation to outcomes.

19. See turnover cost calculator at http://www.cepr.net/calculators/turnover _calc.html.

20. See Kruse, Freeman, and Blasi, *Shared Capitalism at Work*, 152–157.

21. This comparison adjusts for differences in demographic and job characteristics (e.g., age, sex, tenure, occupation). The numbers represent the estimated likelihood of strong agreement for an average worker in the sample.

22. See Jean-Jacques Laffont and David Martimort, *The Theory of Incentives: The Principal-Agent Model* (Princeton, NJ: Princeton University Press, 2001), 11 (quoting Babbage 1989, 8:177).

23. See Erika E. Harden, Douglas Kruse, and Joseph Blasi, "Who Has a Better Idea? Innovation, Shared Capitalism, and Human Resources Policies," in Kruse, Freeman, and Blasi, *Shared Capitalism at Work*, 225–256.

24. See Arindrajit Dube and Richard Freeman, "Complementarity of Shared Compensation and Decision-Making Systems: Evidence from the American Labor Market," in Kruse, Freeman, and Blasi, *Shared Capitalism at Work*, 167–200.

25. See Dan Weltmann, Joseph Blasi, and Douglas Kruse, *At What Threshhold Do Employee Shares Have a Meaningful Effect?* (New Brunswick, NJ: Rutgers University School of Management and Labor Relations, 2013).

26. David Handel and David Levine, "The Effect of New Work Practices on Workers," *Industrial Relations* 43, no. 1 (January 2004): 1–41, esp. 6.

27. See Douglas Kruse, Richard Freeman, and Joseph Blasi, "Do Workers Gain by Sharing?" in Kruse, Freeman, and Blasi, *Shared Capitalism at Work*, 257–289.

28. The most recent evidence is from the 2006 General Social Survey, where 70–80 percent of a random sample of adult workers reported that they were paid at or above the market rate for their jobs if covered by profit sharing, gain sharing, employee stock ownership, or if they were holding employee stock options in their firm. See Douglas Kruse and Joseph Blasi, *Report on the 2006 General Social Survey on Shared Capitalism* (New Brunswick, NJ: Rutgers University School of Management and Labor Relations, 2007), table 3. The higher pay and benefits under these plans would appear to go against the economic theory of compensating wage differentials, which predicts that workers receiving employee ownership or profit sharing will have lower regular pay, fewer benefits, and/or worse working conditions to compensate for the benefits of these plans. There were some publicized cases of workers making wage or benefit concessions in exchange for employee ownership or profit sharing in the 1980s, but these constituted a very small fraction of plan adoptions (between 4 percent and 7 percent, according to a GAO survey). On this, see U.S. General Accounting Office, *Employee Stock Ownership Plans: Benefits and Costs of ESOP Tax Incentives for Broadening Stock Ownership* (Washington, DC: GAO, 1986). On concession bargaining with employee stock ownership see Joseph Blasi and Douglas Kruse, *The New Owners: The Mass Emergence of Employee Ownership in Public Companies and What It Means to American Business* (New York: HarperCollins, 1991), 325–328. Apart from these few concessionary situations, over twenty studies find employee ownership and profit sharing are not linked to generally lower fixed pay or benefits, and are often found to exist along with higher base pay and benefits. This is found both in comparisons of matched ESOP and non-ESOP firms. On this see P. Kardas, A. L. Scharf, and J. Keogh, "Wealth and Income Consequences of ESOPs and Employee Ownership: A Comparative Study from Washington State," *Journal of Employee Ownership Law and Finance* 10, no. 4 (1998): 3–52, and A. Scharf and C. M. Mackin, *Census of Massachusetts Companies with Employee Stock Ownership Plans (ESOPs)* (Boston: Commonwealth Corp., 2000). It is also found in pre/post comparisons of plan adoption controlling for state-level and industry-level wage changes and other company characteristics. See E. H. Kim and P. Ouimet, *Employee Capitalism or*

Corporate Socialism: Broad-Based Employee Stock Ownership (Washington, DC: U.S. Census Bureau Center for Economic Studies, Paper Number CES-WP-09-44, 2009). ESOP companies are four times more likely than non-ESOP companies to have traditional pensions, as noted in Douglas Kruse, *Research Evidence on Prevalence and Effects of Employee Ownership* (Washington, DC: Testimony presented before the Subcommittee on Employer-Employer Relations, Committee on Education of the Workforce, U.S. House of Representatives, February 13, 2002). Available at: http://esop.com/pdf/esopHistoryAndResearch/researchEvidence.pdf. The pension assets per employee of ESOP companies are substantially higher than in non-ESOP companies with other types of defined contribution plans. On this see Loren Rodgers, "Are ESOPs Good for Employees?" Bloomberg BNA, *Pensions & Benefits Daily*, November 1, 2010, 1–5. For detailed reports on the original data see Loren Rodgers and Michael Keeling, *ESOPs as Retirement Benefits* (Oakland, CA, and Washington, DC: National Center for Employee Ownership and Employee Ownership Foundation, September 20, 2010), and National Center for Employee Ownership, *ESOPs as Retirement Benefits—Supplemental Tables* (Oakland, CA, and Washington, DC: National Center for Employee Ownership and Employee Ownership Foundation, September 15, 2010). Going against the idea that the higher pay levels simply reflect higher worker quality, average base pay of individuals goes up as workers join profit-sharing companies, and down as they leave them. See Douglas Kruse, "Profit-Sharing and the Demand for Low-Skill Workers," in *Generating Jobs*, ed. Peter Gottschalk and Richard Freeman (New York: Russell Sage Foundation, 1998), 105–153. Workers appear to be sharing in the average higher productivity of broad-based capitalism firms. As such, their higher total compensation may represent a compensating differential for their higher quantity and quality of work, and/or an efficiency wage that motivates and sustains high performance. See George Akerlof, "Gift Exchange and Efficiency-Wage Theory: Four Views," *American Economic Review* 74, no. 2 (May 1984): 79–83. For a listing of studies on this topic see the website of this book.

29. See Kruse, Freeman, and Blasi, "Do Workers Gain by Sharing?" 257–289.

30. A massive scientific literature that stretches from genetics to game theory to psychology and neuroscience seeks to explain the prevalence of cooperative behavior in the face of the incentive to free ride; see for example Robert Axelrod, *The Evolution of Cooperation* (New York: Basic Books, 1984).

31. See Richard Freeman, Douglas Kruse, and Joseph Blasi, "Worker Responses to Shirking under Shared Capitalism," in Kruse, Freeman, and Blasi, *Shared Capitalism at Work*, 77–104.

32. For the preceding sections see Joseph Blasi, Richard Freeman, Christopher Mackin, and Douglas Kruse, "Creating a Bigger Pie? The Effects of Employee Ownership, Profit Sharing and Stock Options on Workplace Performance," in Kruse, Freeman, and Blasi, *Shared Capitalism at Work*, 139–166.

33. Douglas Kruse, Joseph Blasi, and Richard Freeman, *Does Shared Capitalism Help the Best Firms Do Even Better?* (Cambridge, MA: National Bureau of Economic Research, 2011, Working Paper 7745).

34. Managers appear to be either increasingly concluding that the better company culture is optimal or learning from each other as they compare one company to another. For this evidence see Douglas Kruse, Joseph Blasi, and Rhokeun Park, "Shared Capitalism in the U.S. Economy," in Kruse, Freeman, and Blasi, *Shared Capitalism at Work*, 61 (table 1.6).

CHAPTER 6. THE ROAD TO INCREASING THE CITIZEN'S SHARE

1. See George W. Carey, *The Federalist Papers* (Champaign: University of Illinois Press, 1994), No. 62.

2. Pope John Paul II endorsed employee ownership in the encyclical *Laborem Exercens* with these words: "In the light of the above, the many proposals put forward by experts in Catholic social teaching and by the highest Magisterium of the Church take on special significance: proposals for joint ownership of the means of work, sharing by the workers in the management and/or profits of businesses, so-called shareholding by labour, etc. Whether these various proposals can or cannot be applied concretely, it is clear that recognition of the proper position of labour and the worker in the production process demands various adaptations in the sphere of the right to ownership of the means of production." See John Paul II, *Laborem Exercens* (Vatican City: The Vatican, September 14, 1981), Part 14 (Work and Ownership). Available at: http://www.vatican .va/holy_father/john_paul_ii/encyclicals/documents/hf_jp-ii_enc _14091981_laborem-exercens_en.html. See the expanded notes for additional information.

3. In 2010, President Obama set up the National Commission on Fiscal Responsibility and Reform, cochaired by Alan Simpson and Erskine Bowles, with direction to find ways to improve the fiscal situation in the medium term and fiscal sustainability in the long run. While the commission did not reach unanimity in its deliberations, it brought the

problems of long-run fiscal deficit to the center of national discourse and provided much valuable information on the nature of the problems facing the country.

4. Graeme Nuttall, *Sharing Success: The Nuttall Review of Employee Ownership* (London: Government of the United Kingdom, 2012). In October 2012, Chancellor George Osborne, announced a scheme that would require employees to give up employment rights, such as the right to redundancy pay and the right to ask for flexible working, in exchange for between £2,000 and £50,000 worth of shares in the company they work for. The House of Lords voted down this proposal in March 2013. This is the sort of property oppressing liberty policy that Madison warned about. See Jason Beattie, "George Osborne's Scheme for Workers to Give Up Rights in Return for Shares Blocked by House of Lords," *Mirror News* at: http://www.mirror.co.uk/news/uk-news/george-osbornes-plan -workers-give-1850280?tabPane=Comments. See also a recent report by a Washington think-tank addressing the United States: David Madland and Karla Walter, *Growing the Wealth: How Government Encourages Broad-Based Inclusive Capitalism* (Washington, DC: Center for American Progress, 2013).

5. The President George W. Bush White House Office of Faith-Based Initiatives is a precedent that was continued by President Obama.

6. See Ben Rattray, "Victory over Debit Fee Is a Sign of Power," CNN, November 4, 2011, http://www.cnn.com/2011/11/04/opinion/rattray -consumers-fight-back/index.html, and "Molly Katchpole, Who Battled Bank of America, Is in the Running for Time's 'Top 100,'" HuffPost DC, March 26, 2003, http://www.huffingtonpost.com/2012/03/29/molly -katchpole-time-magazine_n_1387997.html.

7. MassMutual and the Kennesaw State University Family Firm Institute, *American Family Business Survey* (Boston: MassMutual Financial Group, 2010), 4.

8. The four hundred taxpayers cited do not comprise the upper 1 percent or the upper 0.1 percent or 0.001 percent. It is 400 out of 140,494,127 returns, which is the upper 0.00028 percent. See also http://www.irs.gov /pub/irs-soi/09intop400.pdf, table 1.

9. For example, the capital gains taxes through 2012 range from 25 to 35 percent for most income brackets for short-term capital gains. For a good review of the history of capital gains in the United States see the entry by Gerald Auten, "Capital Gains Taxation," in *The Encyclopedia of Taxation and Tax Policy*, 2nd edition, ed. Joseph J. Cordes, Robert D. Ebel, and Jane G. Gravelle (Washington, DC: Urban Institute Press, 2005). For the 1999

entry see http://www.urban.org/publications/1000519.html (accessed June 29, 2012).

10. On the Romney tax plan see http://www.marketwatch.com/story /romney-vs-obama-how-theyd-tax-your-portfolio-2012-11-01.

11. Polly Curtis, "Osborne's £6.25bn Savings Plan Hits Baby Bonds and Students," *Guardian*, May 24, 2010, http://www.guardian.co.uk/politics /2010/may/24/george-osborne-spending-cuts-6bn, and "George Osborne Outlines Detail of £6.2bn Spending Cuts," BBC News, May 24, 2010, http://news.bbc.co.uk/2/hi/uk_news/politics/8699522.stm. See also Julia Weerdigier and Landon Thomas Jr., "British Budget Adheres to Austerity While It Cuts the Top Tax Rate," *New York Times*, March 21, 2012, http://www.nytimes.com/2012/03/22/business/global/britain -sticks-to-austerity-in-new-budget-plan.html?_r=0.

12. Thomas Paine, *Agrarian Justice* (Rockville, MD: Wildside Press, 2010; and http://www.socialsecurity.gov/history/tpaine.html). See the State of Alaska Permanent Fund Dividend Division at http://www .pfd.state.ak.us/. For an earlier Alaskan proposal based on Louis Kelso's ideas through U.S. Congressional enabling legislation on (the now expired) Subchapter U of the Internal Revenue Code, see Jerry N. Gauche, "General Stock Ownership Corporations: Another Step in Broadening Capital Ownership," *American University Law Review*, Volume 30: 731–764.

13. On Individual Development Accounts see http://cfed.org/assets/pdfs/IDA _Fact_Sheet_2009_12_12.pdf.

14. Here is an example of one possible baby bond proposal. Groups of accounts would be managed by financial services firms. Each newborn's account would receive a $2,500 loan from retail bonds that could be sold to the population to fund starting the accounts. Children's accounts would receive an additional $2,500 loan upon the child completing elementary school and high school. The account would be invested in diversified mutual funds to be high-dividend paying, preferably with less risky preferred stock and other bonds. Some of these mutual funds could possibly invest in corporations with broad-based profit sharing, employee stock ownership, or combinations of these. Government guidelines would set ground rules for the fees to be charged, the diversification, and a modest-costing insurance program to insure accounts against fraud. Any private citizen could contribute any amount to any individual child's account, and there could potentially be a modest tax incentive for such contributions. After twenty-one years of age, a child could elect to receive the dividend income in cash from the account. The financial

services firm would repay the principal at an annual interest rate. Because of the long investment horizon, the original loan could be repaid and capital income available for young people and adults. Under strict guidelines, the government might allow certain financial services firms to borrow funds at the discount window of the Federal Reserve Bank to increase the capital of these accounts if the capital was invested in less risky preferred stock issues of corporations with high dividends and a strong likelihood of repayment. We would like to acknowledge the advice and counsel of Luis Granados, a lawyer at McDermott Will and Emery in Washington, DC, who worked on an original early version of this idea for the United States and graciously discussed his proposal with us. Cornell Law Professor Robert C. Hockett has explored a range of other broad ownership financing proposals. For example, see Robert C. Hockett, "A Jeffersonian Republic by Hamiltonian Means: Values, Constraints & Finance in an Authentic American Ownership Society," Southern California Law Review, Volume 79 (2005): 45–164. See the expanded notes for further references.

15. For the detailed policy proposal see Richard Freeman, Joseph Blasi, and Douglas Kruse, *Inclusive Capitalism for the American Workforce* (Washington, DC: Center for American Progress, March 2011), 24, and the expanded notes.

16. There are several approaches to trying to get an accurate estimate of the cost of these deductions to the taxpayer. For a Treasury study focusing only on stock options see Scott Jaquette, Matthew Knittel, and Karl Russo, *Recent Trends in Stock Options* (Washington, DC: U.S. Department of the Treasury, Office of Tax Analysis, Working Paper 2003), 14 and table 1, and 28. For more detail see the expanded notes.

17. The independent Tax Foundation estimates the special ESOP tax expenditures amount to less than 1 percent of the almost $700 billion in special corporate tax incentives from 2010 to 2016. See the President's Economic Reform Advisory Board—the White House, *The Report of Tax Reform*, 77, table 9, "Special Tax Provisions Substantially Narrow the Tax Base," line 7 from the U.S. Department of the Treasury Office of Tax Analysis. See also an independent private-sector corroborating source: Scott A. Hodge, *Who Benefits from Corporate Loopholes?* Tax Foundation Fiscal Fact Sheet no. 260 (Washington, DC: Tax Foundation, March 2, 2011), table 1, "Tax Expenditures That Benefit Corporations, Fiscal Years 2010–2016," at http://taxfoundation.org/article/who-benefits-corporate -loopholes (accessed July 20, 2012).

18. See Freeman, Blasi, and Kruse, 2011.

19. See Government Accountability Office, *Private Pensions: Top-Heavy Rules for Owner-Dominated Plans* (Washington, DC: Government Accountability Office, GAO-HEHS-00-141, 2000). The GAO here cites the Revenue Act of 1942, P.L. 77-753 (162) in footnote 4 on 6. The letter from Secretary Summers's Treasury Department is on 43.

20. The exact estimates are listed in Special Privilege Tax Expenditures for Corporations: Revenue Lost to the Citizens of the United States from Major Business Tax Provisions, 2008–2014.

Accelerated Depreciation/Expensing Provision	$662. Billion

WHAT IT IS: When determining their taxes, businesses can deduct from their income the cost of new plant or equipment but they are allowed to do it at a faster rate. This reduces corporate taxes by the amount shown and citizens foot the bill.

Deduction for U.S. Production/Manufacturing Activities	$258. Billion

WHAT IT IS: When determining their taxes, businesses can deduct from their income part of their earnings on products that they create in the U.S. but "products" include fast food hamburgers and even software. This reduces corporate taxes by the amount shown and citizens pay for it.

Research and Experimentation (R&E) Tax Credit	$133. Billion

WHAT IT IS: When determining their taxes, businesses receive a tax credit for the cost of research and development of new and improved goods or services. This costs the other taxpayers the amount shown and citizens make up the lost revenue to the Treasury.

Total	$1.053 Trillion

See the President's Economic Reform Advisory Board—The White House, *The Report of Tax Reform*, 77, table 9, Special Tax Provisions Substantially Narrow the Tax Base, line 7 from the U.S. Department of the Treasury Office of Tax Analysis. See also an independent private sector corroborating source: Scott A. Hodge, *Who Benefits from Corporate Loopholes*? at: http://taxfoundation.org/article/who-benefits-corporate-loopholes (accessed July 20, 2012). See the expanded notes.

21. For a copy of the Iowa legislation, see https://www.legis.iowa.gov/DOCS /NOBA/84_HF2284_HFA.pdf. On the governor's goals for ESOPs, see https://governor.iowa.gov/2012/05/governor-branstad's-statement-on -close-of-the-2012-legislative-session/. The Iowa legislation was nonpartisan and passed the legislature by a vote of 92–3 with action soon expected in the Senate. On the Workforce Investment Act, see http:// dept.kent.edu/oeoc/buyoutassistance/preliminaryfeasibility.htm with a related initiative by the state of Michigan. The New Jersey Legislation was introduced in December 2012 by Assemblyman Upendra Chivuluka, the Deputy Speaker of the Assembly and is A3626. The Cleveland initiative is sponsored by the Democracy Collaborative at http:// democracycollaborative.org/. A related book discusses the role of cooperatives and ESOPs in economic democracy. See Gar Alperovitz, *What Then Must We Do?* (White River Junction, VT.: Chelsea Green Publishing, 2013), 25–50, 55, 63–64. The worker cooperative employment estimate was made in May of 2013 by Brent Hueth of the Wisconsin Center as an update to table 2.2 of the recent census of worker cooperatives. Note that some worker cooperatives report customers or part-time workers as "members," so the relevant estimate is the number of actual full-time employee equivalents. See Steven Deller, Ann Hoyt, Brent Hueth, and Reka Sundaram-Stukel, *Research on the Economic Impact of Cooperatives* (Madison: University of Wisconsin Center for Cooperatives, revised June 19, 2009), 11 (table 2.2). Available at: http://reic.uwcc .wisc.edu/downloads/. We acknowledge the generous assistance of Brent Hueth and Steve Deller. On the steelworkers initiative see http://www. usw.org/our_union/co-ops. For examples, see a 2000 worker cooperative home health care firm at http://www.chcany.org/, http://arizmendi. coop/resources, and http://www.usworker.coop/system/files /Intro-American-Worker-Cooperatives-with-case-studies.pdf. For technical assistance groups see http://www.praxiscg.com/, http:// ica-group.org/, and http://www.ncba.coop/ncba/about-co-ops/co-op -types/worker-cooperatives.

22. The Deficit Reduction Act of 1984 created the incentive allowing financial lenders (including sponsors of corporate bonds that financed ESOPs) to deduct 50 percent of their interest income on the loans from their taxable income resulting in these lenders offering loans to finance public company ESOPs at a lower interest rate than loans not creating broad-based employee stock ownership. For the law and documentation of the transactions during this period, see Blasi and Kruse, *The New Owners*, 33–87, especially, 46, 73–77. For example, in the 1980s Procter & Gamble sought to raise a billion dollars with bonds to buy stock for an

ESOP, and the bond issue was greatly oversubscribed, as were many others financing employee ownership. Bonds can be issued to finance the purchase of large stakes by public companies or to raise funds to finance worker buyouts. Financial firms could also create a publicly traded retail bond that helps a diversified basket of public companies finance employee ownership stakes that could be sold to mutual funds and pension funds and 401(k) plans or develop mutual funds covering corporations that are leaders in broad-based profit sharing and employee ownership. The former CEO of ADT, Ray Carey, has suggested that 401(k) plans invest in bonds to finance rebuilding the nation's infrastructure. See Keslerand Rossiter, 317 (*Federalist* No. 62).

23. Mass Mutual Financial Group/Kennesaw State University Cole College of Business/Family Firm Institute, *American Family Business Survey*, 3, 4. On the "transfer failures" of small businesses see Nuttall, *Sharing Success*, 38.

24. This tax benefit is Section 1042 of the Internal Revenue Code. Members of the House of Representatives and the Senate have introduced the "Promotion and Expansion of Private Employee Ownership Act of 2011" to expand the availability of Employee Stock Ownership Plans to owners of S corporation stock. For more detail see the expanded notes.

25. For example, one way to do this is to allow estates that sell to an ESOP or worker cooperative or similar broad plan to pay the estate tax on only half the proceeds of the sale.

26. Extensive research shows that, when given the opportunity, workers will sometimes overinvest their savings in company stock in 401(k) plans. The research of Daniel Kahneman has looked at the decision processes whereby workers underdiversify and overemphasize the impact of the past performance of their company on future performance and tend to invest too much of their portfolio into their own company stock in 401(k) plans. See, Daniel Kahneman, *Thinking Fast and Slow* (New York: Farrar, Strauss and Giroux, 2011). For an analysis of 401(k) plans, see James M. Poterba, "Lessons from Enron: Employer Stock and 401(k) Plans," *American Economic Review* 93, no. 2 (May 2003): 398–404; Shlomo Benartzi, "Excessive Extrapolation and the Allocation of 401k Accounts to Company Stock," *Journal of Finance*, 56, no. 5 (2001): 1747–1764; and Shlomo Benartzi and Richard Thaler, "Naïve Diversification Strategies in Defined Contribution Plans," *American Economic Review*, 91, no. 1 (2001): 79–98. For the proportion of workers who actually did overinvest in their 401(k) plans in the NBER surveys of the Shared Capitalism Research Project, see Kruse, Freeman, and Blasi, eds., *Shared Capitalism at Work*, 121.

27. The research of Harry Markowitz observes that about 10–15 percent of
an investment portfolio under the proper conditions and an otherwise
diversified portfolio may be a prudent amount of an employee's overall
total investment portfolio in company stock. See Harry Markowitz,
Joseph Blasi, and Douglas Kruse, "Employee Stock Ownership and
Diversification," *Annals of Operations Research* 176, no. 1 (2010): 95–107.
On worker attitudes and risk in these plans, see Joseph R. Blasi, Douglas L.
Kruse, and Harry M. Markowitz, "Risk and Lack of Diversification
under Employee Ownership and Shared Capitalism," in Kruse, Free-
man, and Blasi, eds., *Shared Capitalism at Work*, 105–138 and 121–128 for
Markowitz's estimates. Recently, work by Danny Yagan, who is at the
Center for Equitable Growth at the University of California at Berkeley,
observes that alternative ways of structuring diversification in a
worker's portfolio might permit an employee to have a larger allocation
in company stock without increasing portfolio risk. See Danny Yagan,
"Why Do Individual Investors Chase Stock Market Returns? Belief in
Long-Run Market Momentum and Consequences for Employee
Portfolio Allocations" (Berkeley: University of California at Berkeley,
December 2012), 11–12.

28. See Bill Clinton and Al Gore, *Putting People First: How We Can All Change
America* (New York: Three Rivers Press, Random House, 1992). For an
analysis of this policy, see Richard Freeman, Joseph Blasi, and Douglas
Kruse, *Inclusive Capitalism for the American Workforce*.

29. For a history of this policy, see Blasi and Kruse, *The New Owners*, 33–62,
115–119, and 71–77 for a discussion of national employee ownership
capital markets for publicly traded corporations, and table 1.2 on 78 for a
tally of the major employee stock ownership transactions and the volume
of transactions by major investment banks. See also Elizabeth Wehr,
"Effort to Alter ESOP Rules Stirs Strong Reactions," *Congressional Quarterly
Weekly Report* 47, no. 27 (July 8, 1989): 1682–1686 and James Brockhardt
and Robert Reilly, "Employee Stock Ownership Plans after the 1989 Tax
Law," *Compensation and Benefits Review* (September 1, 1990), 29.

30. For the Financial Accounting Standards Board point of view, see Kris
Hudson, "FASB Chairman Tackles Tough Task of Accounting Reform,"
Denver Post, April 8, 2003, n.p.. For the point person in the Senate's point
of view, see Richard A. Oppel Jr., "Senator Urges Change in How Stock
Options Are Handled," *New York Times*, July 13, 2002, 1. For the high-
technology industry's point of view, see Andrew S. Grove and Reed E.
Hundt, "Stock Options Work," *Washington Post*, October 8, 2008, A29. For
a group of academics opposing the reform, see Kip Hagopian, "Point of
View: Expensing Employee Stock Options Is Improper Accounting,"

California Management Review 48, no. 4 (Summer 2006): 136–156. For the study of the effect of stock option expensing on the incidence of broad-based stock options and employee stock ownership, see Joseph R. Blasi and Douglas L. Kruse, *Measurement of the Incidence of Stock Options and Employee Stock Ownership before and after Expensing* (New Brunswick, NJ: Rutgers University School of Management and Labor Relations, October 16, 2007). For an examination of the entire debate, see Jonathan Weil and Jeanne Cummings, "The Stock Option Showdown—Accountants May Finally Win, Force Payments to Be Expensed; Tech Companies Are Livid," *Wall Street Journal*, March 9, 2004, C1.

EPILOGUE

1. The term "property-owning democracy" was used by philosopher John Rawls. See John Rawls, *A Theory of Justice: Original Edition* (Cambridge, MA: Harvard University Press, 2005), 140, 258. For a perspective on economic democracy, see David Ellerman, *Property and Contract in Economics: The Case for Economic Democracy* (Cambridge, MA: Blackwell, 1992) available at www.ellerman.org and David Ellerman, "Inalienable Rights: A Litmus Test for Liberal Theories of Justice," *Law and Philosophy* 29, no. 5 (September 2010): 571–599.

2. Peter D. Hart Associates did a 1975 poll examining the support for the idea of broad-based employee ownership and profit sharing across the political spectrum. There was evidence of broad nonpartisan support. For example, the national poll found substantial support for broad-based employee stock ownership in corporations by independents, conservatives, and liberals alike, with a majority of Americans willing to support a candidate for president who presented such a vision for America. The share idea was the only national economic policy idea that most Americans believed would do more good than harm. Citizens believed that a national model where companies shared profits would improve the condition of the economy. Other national polls find that almost three-quarters of citizens believe people in companies with significant employee stock ownership pay more attention to the quality of their work, work harder, and pay more attention to the company's financial performance, and that the share idea offers greater access to wealth without redistribution or an expansion of the size of government. See Douglas Kruse and Joseph Blasi, "Public Opinion Polls on Employee Ownership and Profit Sharing," *Journal of Employee Ownership Law and Finance* 11, no. 3 (Summer 1999): 3–26. The article reviews all national polling on the subject using the database of the Roper Center for Public Opinion Research at the University of Connecticut.

3. As the book goes to press, the increase in inequality and the stagnation of the earnings of citizens outside of the superrich has shown no signs of abating under Democratic or Republican administrations. For 2011, the most recent U.S. Census data found that median family income dropped for the middle class over the last two years by 9 percent compared to 1999. From 2009 to 2011 the income of the richest 1 percent grew by 11 percent, while incomes of everyone else went down. The top 10 percent received 46.5 percent of all income in 2011, the largest percentage since 1917. See Annie Lowrey, "Incomes Flat in Recovery, But Not for the 1%," *New York Times*, February 15, 2013, 1. For a separate analysis of the Census data, see Richard Fry and Paul Taylor, *An Uneven Recovery, 2009–2011: A Rise in Wealth for the Wealthy; Declines for the Lower 93%* (Washington, DC: Pew Research Center, April 23, 2013) available at: http://www.pewsocialtrends.org/2013/04/23/a-rise-in-wealth-for-the-wealthydeclines-for-the-lower-93/.

ACKNOWLEDGMENTS

We are grateful to the Russell Sage Foundation and the Rockefeller Foundation for grants to the National Bureau of Economic Research Shared Capitalism Research Project to support the empirical economic studies in this book. Kate McFate, the president and CEO of the Center for Effective Government, worked with us when she was deputy director at the Rockefeller Foundation. Eric Wanner, the former president of Russell Sage, made valuable comments during the research and writing of the book. We wish to thank dean Susan J. Schurman, associate dean Dave Lepak, former dean David L. Finegold, and former associate dean Steven Director, all of the School of Management and Labor Relations at Rutgers University, for their support and encouragement. We thank the National Bureau of Economic Research in Cambridge, Massachusetts, and Professor Martin Feldstein of Harvard, who was president of NBER during much of the work, and the current NBER president, Professor James Poterba of MIT, for hosting the NBER Shared Capitalism Research Project; and we thank the Foundation of Enterprise Development and the Beyster Family, especially founder J. Robert Beyster and president Mary Ann

Beyster, for the Beyster Endowment that supports the J. Robert Beyster Professorship at Rutgers held by Blasi and that provided summer support for Blasi and Kruse and conference support for Freeman. Joseph Blasi is grateful to the School of Historical Studies and its faculty at the Institute for Advanced Study in Princeton, New Jersey, where much of the historical work was done when he was a member from 2007 to 2008; the School of Social Science and its faculty, also at the institute, where he was a member and where he has participated in weekly seminars; former institute director Peter Goddard; Princeton University's Center for the Study of Social Organization and its director Paul DiMaggio, who arranged for Blasi's courtesy appointment as a visiting scholar from 2010 to 2011; and Professor Viviana Zelizer of the Princeton Department of Sociology, who arranged for a courtesy appointment in the department that allowed access to historical databases and archives and libraries that were critical for the study. The staff and resources of the following libraries and archives were particularly helpful for access to primary sources: the Archives and Manuscript Collection at Columbia University, the Smith College Archives, and the College Archives at Middlebury College (for the John Bates Clark Papers); the Carey Library at the School of Management and Labor Relations at Rutgers University (especially Donna Schulman and Eugene McElroy); the Department of Rare Books and Special Collections at Princeton University's Firestone Library (for the Lyman H. Atwater Papers); the Ferdinand Hamburger University Archives at Johns Hopkins University (on the nineteenth-century Hopkins studies); the Firestone Library at Princeton University; the George Eastman Archive and Study Center at George Eastman House in Rochester (and Elizabeth Brayer, the Eastman biographer); the George Washington Presidential Library at Mount Vernon (for access to the digital edition of Washington's papers); the Historical Collections Department of Harvard Business School's Baker Library (for the Peace Dale Archives, the Henry S. Dennison Papers, and the Waltham Watch Collections); the Historical Studies–Social Science Library at the Institute for Advanced Study in Princeton, New Jersey (especially director Marcia Tucker) for extensive help with historical databases and microfilms; the Industrial Relations Section collections at Princeton University Library's Social Science Reference Center; the Library of Congress and its Newspaper and Current Periodical Reading Room (for access to the Cincinnati newspaper collection to study William Cooper Procter); the Kelso Institute (and Patricia Hetter Kelso); the Maryland State Archives in Annapolis and the Maryland Historical Society in Baltimore (for the Lord Baltimore collections on colonial land tenure); the Leclaire (Illinois) National Historic District archives (on Nelson O. Nelson); the National Archives in College Park, Maryland (for Alexander Hamilton's Treasury Department records on the cod fishery); the New Bedford (Massachusetts) Whaling Museum (on the fisheries); the Pillsbury Archives at General Mills (especially the help of Tess Abel Hohman, Suzy Goodsell, and Kendra Malinowski to study Charles A. Pillsbury and George S. Pillsbury); the Procter & Gamble corporate archives (especially archivist Ed Rider and the entire staff) in Cincinnati; the Profit Sharing Research Foundation (and former president David Wray); Rotunda, the online edition of the University of Virginia's American Founding Era Collection (for access to the Adams, Hamilton, Jefferson, Madison, and Washington papers' digital editions); the Rutgers University Libraries (for access to online historical collections);

the Seeley G. Mudd Manuscript Library and its director Dan Linke at Princeton University (for the William Cooper Procter records); the University of Rochester Rush Rhees Library; THOMAS (the online legislative service) of the Library of Congress; the University of Vermont Bailey/Howe Library; and the Widener Library at Harvard University. J. Robert Beyster, Gerald Greenwald, the late George S. Pillsbury, and Arthur Rock generously agreed to interviews regarding the contemporary history of these subjects.

We express our appreciation to the National Opinion Research Center (NORC) at the University of Chicago (its director Tom Smith, its co-principal investigator Peter Marsden of Harvard, and research associate Jibum Kim) for carrying out and preparing the data for the 2002, 2006, and 2010 U.S. national General Social Surveys of equity and profit sharing, for which the Employee Ownership Foundation, along with the Foundation for Enterprise Development, the National Center for Employee Ownership, and the Profit Sharing/401(k) Council of America, provided supplemental funding; the Great Place to Work Institute, in particular co-founder and CEO Robert Levering and co-founder Amy Lyman, for collaborating with our "best companies" research, as well as the Alfred P. Sloan Foundation (and vice president Gail Pesyna) for grants making the "best companies" empirical analysis possible; the Russell Sage Foundation's director of publications Suzanne Nichols; David Madland and Karla Walter of the Center for American Progress and congressman Dana Rohrabacher (R-California) and his legislative assistant Jeff Vanderslice, who helped us in moving our thinking from the research to the policy agenda; Ellen Weber and Elena Orama at Rutgers, Marian Zelazny and Terrie Bramley at the Institute for Advanced Study, and freelance research assistants Caroline Macirowski and Joseph Macirowski (who helped Blasi) and Shital Asarpota (who helped Blasi and Kruse); a group of anonymous reviewers selected by Yale University Press for their critical comments; and many readers from several disciplines and professions who generously read the manuscript at various stages. Blasi also thanks Adam Blumenthal, Caroline Walker Bynum, Ray Carey, Maurie Cohen, Nicola Di Cosmo, Freeman Dyson, Charles Fay, Yosef Kaplan, the family of William Cooper Procter, Whitney MacMillan, Jonathan Ree, Corey Rosen, Jonathan Smith, Pat Sullivan, Michael Walzer, Philip Warburg, and Malon Wilkus for their support and for many helpful discussions. Freeman also thanks Alex Bryson and Martin Conyon, who collaborated on work on shared capitalism in the United Kingdom, Jennifer Amodeo-Holl for reading and clarifying his contributions to the manuscript, and most of all, he thanks the citizens of the older and younger generation, his mother Sylvia Freeman, and his children Morgan Terence Freeman and Rhyana Beckett Freeman.

During the time the book was written we learned a lot from discussions with more than seventy-five fellows, PhD students, and scholars, at the annual Mid-Year Fellows Workshop in honor of Louis O. Kelso, the annual summer Beyster Symposium that is part of the Fellowship Program supporting young and emerging scholars in this area at Rutgers University's School of Management and Labor Relations, and the New York conference sponsored by the Russell Sage Foundation and the Rockefeller Foundation. The meetings included Harry M. Markowitz of the University of California at San Diego (at the summer Beyster Symposia) and Daniel Kahneman of Princeton University and Eric Maskin of Harvard University (at the New York conference), whose feedback and ideas we appreciate.

The book simply would not have been possible without the hard work and advice of our agent Susan Rabiner of the Susan Rabiner Literary Agency, who believed in this book when she first read it, shaped its substance enormously, and shepherded it at every stage. We do not know what we would have done without her by our side. Our editor at Yale University Press, William Frucht, has continually enriched the book since it came into his hands and pushed us hard to expand and improve it. Working with him is an absolute pleasure. The Yale group, especially Jaya Aninda Chatterjee and Mary Pasti, together with Chris Basso, Michael Haggett, and Glen Novak of Westchester Book Services have been the demanding and patient perfectionists that we needed at that stage.

Most important of all, without the support of our families we could never have attempted this work, and we certainly would never have finished it. For their great patience and constant encouragement, Joseph Blasi would like to thank his wife, Nancy Bonus, and his son Theodore Bonus Blasi (who also served as his father's research assistant at the Institute for Advanced Study and several historical archives) for putting up with this very long project, along with his parents, Angelo and Jean, and his sister Tina Blasi, and Dwight Wooster. Doug Kruse thanks his wife and colleague, Lisa Schur, for their rich life together, his parents, Lowen and Ruth Kruse, his sister and her family, Jorika, Barry, Lauren, and Kiera Stockwell, and family members Janet Schur and Michelle and Madison Link. Many others helped us along the way, and we are grateful to them.

J.R.B., R.F., D.K.

July 11, 2013

INDEX

Brin, Sergei, 59–60, 61, 62–63

broad-based capitalism: critics of, 225–226; economic reform potential, 122; free-rider objection, 182–183; locus of, 118–119, 122; public support for, 226, 273n2; skeptical views of, 124–125. *See also* NBER Shared Capitalism study

broad-based capitalism, corporate leaders role in developing: 1880s–1920s industrialists, 136–142; combining forces, 146–153; industry organizations, 157–159

broad-based capitalism, development of: academic institutions and, 153–156; beginnings, 125–126; benefits espoused, 147, 149–150, 155; educational and research programs, 157–158; industrial homestead legislation, 159–166; the railroads, 126–129; tax regulation and benefits, 156–159; unions and, 131, 133, 135, 147–148, 150, 153, 156–159; welfare capitalism movement, 153

broad-based capitalism, economic case for: fast-food franchise field experiment of profit sharing, 173–174, 194; meta-analysis, 170–172; NBER Shared Capitalism study, 177–188; research studies, 192–194

broad-based capitalism, employee participation in: combination of shares, 113; co-monitoring behaviors, 167–168, 182–188; by company, industry, occupation, 117; critics of, 148, 181; in different parts of the economy, 117; economic benefits, 114–117, 121; ESOPs, 164; General Social Survey, 109–110; historically, 3–7; income levels and, 120–121; private-sector/full-time wage and salary workers, 112–113; profit- /gain-sharing vs. stock options/ownership, 113; risk to workers, 152, 155, 160, 162–163, 214–217; statistics, 112–113, 117, 151, 222–223

broad-based capitalist firms: entrepreneurial successes, 94, 97–101; failures, 101–108; small and medium businesses, 89–94; on the stock exchanges, 82; success, predicting, 167–170. *See also* specific companies

broad-based stock options, 221–223

Bryson, Alex, 173

Buchanan, James, 38

Burns & McDonnell, 95

Bush, (G. H. W.) administration, 219, 220–221

Bush, (G. W.) administration, 9, 212, 221

Cabot, George, 4

capital gains tax, 157, 205–206, 213

capital income, 9–15; concentra-
tion of capital income, 14,
232n26, 233n29
The Capitalist Manifesto (Kelso &
Adler), 159
Carey, Ray, 158, 271.
Cargill, 83, 84
Carnegie, Andrew, 140–141,
255n18
Carnegie Steel Homestead Strike,
132, 140
Carter, Jimmy, 217
CH2M Hill Companies, 86
Chart Rehabilitation, 95
Chevron, 75
Chivukula, Upendra, 270n21
Child Trust Fund (baby bonds),
206–207, 267n14
Christianity and the Social Crisis
(Rauschenbusch), 132–133
Cisco Systems, 77–78
citizenship, property requirement
for, 40
citizen's share: benefits of increasing, 226–227; radical case,
225–226; traditional case,
224–225
citizens' share, policy mistakes:
exclusive equity and profit-
sharing plans, subsidizing,
217–219; financing employee
ownership with wages, 214–
217; public company ESOP
tax incentives eliminated,
219–221; stock option plans
eliminating middle-class
workers, 221–223

citizens' share, policy suggestions
to increase: academic discussion and research, 199; baby
bonds, 206–207, 267n14;
B corporations, 211; benchmarks to qualify for assistance,
203; capital gains tax reforms,
205–206; corporate tax reforms,
210; estate tax for sales of
family firms to ESOPs, 213–214;
executive incentive pay tax,
207–209; incentivize financial
institutions to invest, 212–213;
information sharing at all
levels, 202–203; national level,
commit to and prioritize,
197–199; overview, 201–202;
procurement policies revised,
209–210; SBA programs, 203;
state level, 211–212; tax
expenditures for business
disallowed, 210; worker
cooperatives capital funding,
211–212
Civil Rights Act (1866), 40
Clark, John Bates, 133–134,
243n13
Clinton, Bill administration, 9,
208, 212, 217, 219, 220–221
Clinton, Hillary, 207
Coca-Cola, 77
cod industry, 2–9, 11–12, 134
The Commonwealth of Oceana
(Harrington), 28
ComSonics Corporation, 89–94
Concentration of wealth, 9–15,
232n26, 233n29, 274n3

employee participation in, 164; estates selling to, tax breaks for, 163–164, 213–214; examples around the U.S., 95–97; Fortune 100, 75, 76, 77, 78 , 80; financing, 70, 93; General Accounting Office study, 172, 173, 193; government role, 160–165; higher pay and benefits, 181–182, 263–264; Hundred Best Companies to Work For, 93, 190; grants of stock, 111, 116; Iowa legislation, 212, 270; largest private companies, 82–88; law on diversification of holdings, 164; law on mandatory voting rights, 165; majority and one hundred percent employee-owned, 164, 248n25; market value, present-day, 93, 164; New Jersey legislation, 212, 270; nonexecutive members of the board of directors, 165; number of companies and total employees, 93, 119, 164; policies to expand employee ownership, 195–214; S corporations, 163, 213, 271; searchable database and map, 249; size of stakes, 115–116, 120–121; small and medium-size businesses, 89–94,119,191; statistics, 93, 164, 248n25, 259n 30; stock market companies, 82–88, 163–164; stock matches for 401(k) plan contributions, 82, 111, 216, 219; support of

Senator Hubert Humphrey, 160; support of President Ronald Reagan, 161; support of John D. Rockefeller 3rd, 161; survival study, 193–194, 261n11; tax expenditures, 209, 268; tax incentive for banks to loan to ESOPs, 212–213, 219–221; tax incentive for deducting ESOP dividends, 219–221; tax incentive for small businesses to sell to an ESOP, 163–164; tax regulation and benefits, 161–166, 219–221

Employer and Employed (AAPPS newsletter), 136

Enron, 102–105

Enron:The Smartest Guys in the Room (book and film), 103

Entertainment Partners, 95

The Entrepreneurial Group (Ruef), 97

entrepreneurial start-ups, 94, 97–101; . *See also specific companies*

entrepreneurship, Jefferson, 3

ESOP Association, 97, 164, 248n23, 248n24, 248n25; peer awards, 248n26

estates selling to ESOPs, tax breaks for, 163–164, 213–214

Evergreen Cooperatives of Cleveland, 94, 211

Exxon Mobil, 75

family businesses selling to ESOPs, tax breaks for, 163–164, 204, 213–214

National Center for Employee
Ownership, 87, 97; employee
ownership and winners of
the 100 Best Company to
Work For competition, 93,
247n22; Employee Own-
ership One Hundred, Largest
Majority-Employee-Owned
Corporations,87n1; ESOPs
as retirement benefits study,
264n29; searchable ESOP map,
249n27; statistical profile of
employee ownership, 93, 248n5,
249n27; 259n30
National Civic Federation,
148–150, 170
National Industrial Conference
Board, 150–152, 154, 157
National Opinion Research Center
(NORC), 109–110, 278
National Reform Association,
38–39
National Science Foundation, 110
NBER Shared Capitalism study:
introduction, 175–177; methodology, 176–177; 100 Best Companies to Work for in America
competition data, 189–191;
summary, 191–192; Trust Index©
scores, 191
NBER Shared Capitalism study
results: attitudes, positive, 180;
benefits, higher levels of,
181–182; co-monitoring
behaviors, 182–188; increased
suggestions, 179–180; innovation supported, 180; loyalty and

pride increased, 178–179;
turnover reductions, 177–178;
wages, higher levels of,
181–182; willingness to work,
179; work conditions, improved,
182–183
Nelson, Nelson O., 138–139, 151
New Belgium Brewing, 96
"New Ideals in American Busi-
ness" (Tarbell), 69
The New Owners: The Mass Emer-
gence of Employee Ownership
in Public Companies (Blasi and
Kruse), 263n28, 272n29
Night Calls (television), 90
Nixon, Richard, 161
Nobles, Bill, 73, 247
Northern Pacific Railroad, 129
Northwest Ordinance of 1787, 30,
36
Notes on the State of Virginia
(Jefferson), 30
Noyce, Robert, 57

100 Best Companies to Work for
in America competition, 189

Owen, Robert, 131; and James
Madison, 131

David Packard, 246
Padilla Speer Beardsley, 96
Page, Larry, 59–60, 61, 62–63
Paine, Thomas, 24, 207
Panic of 1873, 129
Parsons, 94
pay at risk, 181

Rabble Machine Company, 96

railroads, 40, 126–129, 147

Rauschenbusch, Walter, 132–133

Reagan, Ronald, 160–161, 212

Report on Manufactures (Hamilton), 5–6

Report on the American Fisheries, 2, 3, 4

Republican Party, 38, 53–54, 56

Revenue Act, 157, 166

Revolutionary War debt, 31

Rock, Arthur, 57, 245

Rockefeller, John D., 75, 140

Rockefeller, John D., Jr., 152–155

Rockefeller, John D., 3rd, 160–162

Rockefeller Colorado Fuel & Iron Company, 152

Rockefeller Foundation, 154–155, 275

Rodgers, Loren, 97

Rohrabacher, Dana, 278

Romney, Mitt, 205–206

Roosevelt, Theodore (Teddy), 143, 144, 147

Rosen, Corey, 279

Ruef, Martin, 97

Russell Sage Foundation, 275–276, 278–279

S&C Electric, 96

SAIC, 83

Sandlin, Miles, 92

Schmidt, Eric, 62

S. C. Johnson & Sons, 84–85

Scot Forge, 96

Sears, 158

Section 162(m), 208, 217–219

share-based capitalism, 151

Shared Capitalism at Work (Kruse, Freeman, and Blasi), 175; online, 262n14

Sheetz, 86

Sherman, William Tecumseh, 40

Sixteenth Amendment, 157

slavery, 8–9, 31, 238n32

Sloan Foundation, Alfred P., 278

Small Business Administration (SBA), 203

small businesses, public views on, 10

Smilie, John, 23

Smith, Adam, 18, 175

Smith, Tom, 278

Social Gospel movement, 132–133

Soltow, Lee, 13

Southern Homestead Act, 40

Southwest Airlines, 71–74

The Southwest Airlines Way (Gittell), 74

Special Conference Committee, 152–153, 154, 170

Staley, Paul, 73

Standard Oil of New Jersey, 154–156

state centers of employee ownership, 203

Stembridge, Deborah, 72

stock option expensing, 221–223

stock options, 111–112, 114–117; effect of stock option expensing on broad-based stock options, 221–223. *See also* broad-based capitalism

Sun Automation, 96
Sylvis, William H., 131

Tarbell, Ida Minerva, 68–70
taxes: capital gains, 157, 205–206, 213; incentives, 3–7, 141; legalization, 157
tax reform: capital gains, 205–206; corporate tax incentives for ESOPs, 162–166; ESOP regulation and benefits, 162–166, 219–221; estates selling to ESOPs, tax breaks for, 163–164, 213–214; executive incentive pay, 207–209, 217–219; tax breaks conditional on citizen shares, 5–6; tax expenditures for business disallowed, 210
Teapot Dome scandal, 146
technology sector, public views on, 10
transparency, corporate, 149
Thaler, Richard, 271n26
Trust Index© (Great Place to Work Institute), 189–191
trusts, formation of, 129

unionized companies, 71, 107, 131
Union Pacific Railroad, 128
unions, broad-based capitalism's development and, 131, 133, 135, 147–148, 150, 153, 156–159
United Airlines, 105–108
United Kingdom: economic power of the aristocracy, 12; Treasury-sponsored study of British firms, 172–173, 192–193
United Parcel Service, 77

wage slaves vs. craftspeople, 125–126
Wagner Act, 156
Walker, Francis Amasa, 134–135, 136, 164
Waltham Watch Company, 130
Wanner, Eric, 275
Washington, George, 1–2, 5, 16, 25, 37, 229n1, 230n6, 230n13,233n1
Wawa, 85
wealth gap, 7–9, 12–15, 18, 20–26, 131, 205–206, 274n3
The Wealth of Nations (Smith), 18
the wealthy elite: founding fathers on, 31, 34–35, 45–46; power and influence of, 12, 18, 20–26, 42, 126
Wegmans Food Markets, 85
welfare capitalism movement, 153
Weltman, Dan, 181, 261n11, 262n25
We the Owners (film), 166
Wharton School, 153–156
Whitehill, Robert, 23, 25
White House Office of Broad-based Capitalism, 198
Will-Burt Company, 96–97
Willing, Thomas, 25
Wilson, Woodrow, 143, 144–145, 147
WinCo Foods, 86
W.L. Gore & Associates, 96
Wojcicki, Susan, 61